Computerized Accounting
using QuickBooks Pro 2020
Sixth Edition

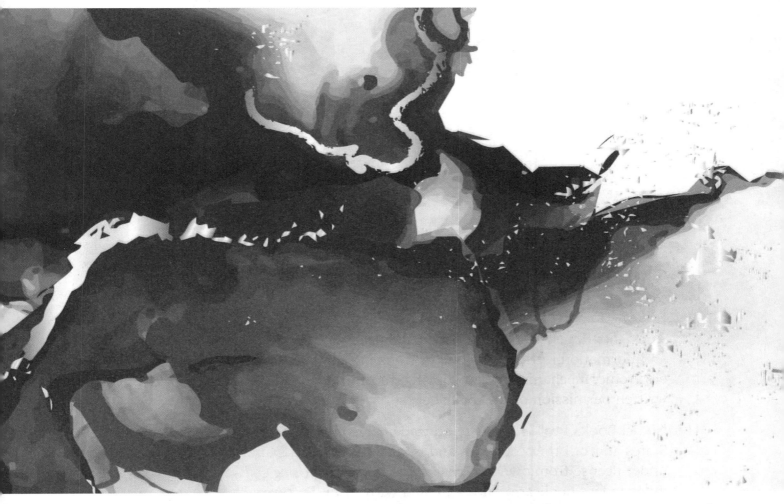

Alvin A. Arens ~ D. Dewey Ward ~ Carol Borsum Sohn
Instructions ~ Book 1 of 2

© 2020

Copyright by Armond Dalton Publishers, Inc.

Okemos, Michigan

ISBN 978-0-912503-79-0

Printed in the United States of America

— ATTENTION —

Access Your E-Materials

Armond Dalton Publishers provides you with step-by-step instructions to register on the Armond Dalton Resources website, access the proprietary data sets, register with Intuit, and download the Quickbooks software.

▶ *Go to www.armonddaltonresources.com and click on E-Materials.*

▶ *Use the E-Materials drop-down menu and select QuickBooks Pro 2020, 6th edition.*

▶ *Select the E-Materials that best suit your situation, Personal Computer or Lab Computer.*

▶ *Follow the E-Material instructions without skipping any steps.*

– This process will take about an hour. –

TABLE OF CONTENTS

(continued on the following page)

Overview of Maintenance, Processing Information, and Internal Controls

3

Obtaining Information from *Quickbooks*, Including Reports

4

Practice — Maintenance Activities 5

Practice — Purchases and Cash Disbursements Cycle Activities 6

(continued on the following page)

Practice — Purchases and Cash Disbursements Cycle Activities *(continued)* — 6

Practice — Sales and Cash Receipts Cycle Activities — 7

(continued on the following page)

Practice — Sales and Cash Receipts Cycle Activities *(continued)*

Practice — Payroll Cycle and Other Activities

Recording Transactions, Performing Month-end Procedures, Recording Year-end Adjusting Entries, and Printing Reports

9

New Company Setup

Acknowledgments

Greatly prized are the exceptional efforts of Regina Rexrode for word processing in preparation of the manuscript, Patricia Naretta for extraordinary proofreading and other assistance, and Erica Borsum for her valuable comments in testing the entire project.

Finally, the encouragement and continuing support of family, friends, and associates have contributed in large measure to the completion of this book.

This page is intentionally blank.

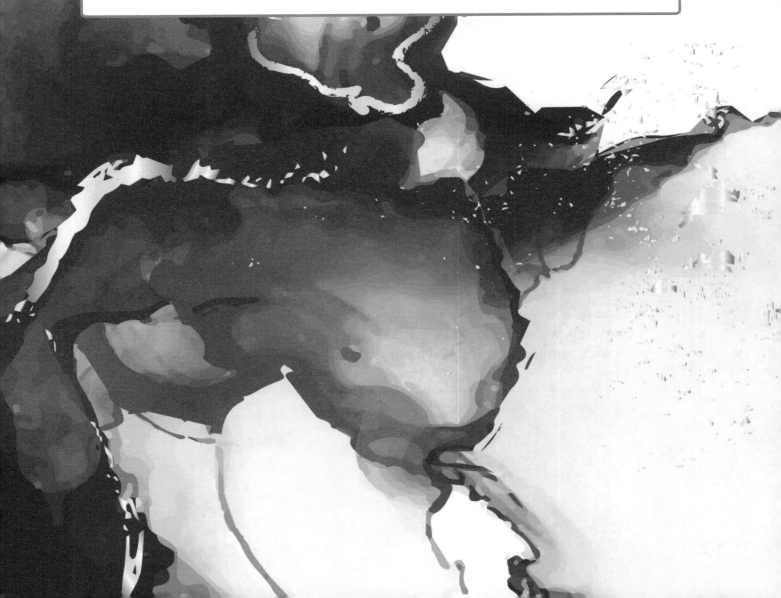

1
Chapter

INTRODUCTION

Introduction

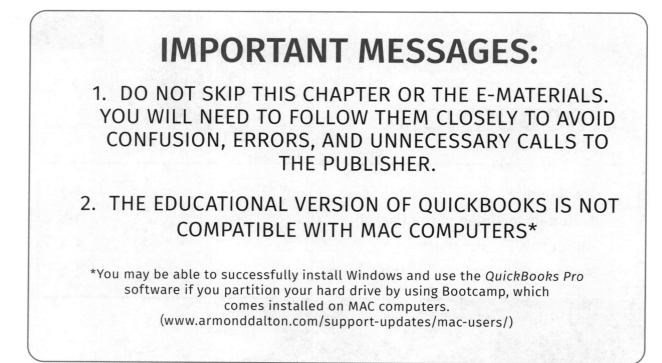

IMPORTANT MESSAGES:

1. DO NOT SKIP THIS CHAPTER OR THE E-MATERIALS. YOU WILL NEED TO FOLLOW THEM CLOSELY TO AVOID CONFUSION, ERRORS, AND UNNECESSARY CALLS TO THE PUBLISHER.

2. THE EDUCATIONAL VERSION OF QUICKBOOKS IS NOT COMPATIBLE WITH MAC COMPUTERS*

*You may be able to successfully install Windows and use the *QuickBooks Pro* software if you partition your hard drive by using Bootcamp, which comes installed on MAC computers. (www.armonddalton.com/support-updates/mac-users/)

Welcome to learning *QuickBooks Pro® 2020*. You will be using these materials to learn how to use an accounting package by following a carefully designed approach.

For the entire project, the following symbol is used to indicate that you are to perform a step using your computer:

Whenever you see this symbol in the left margin, you should complete the related step, which is shown in italics. You should not begin doing an activity with your computer until the symbol is shown.

Materials Included in the Package

The materials that you have purchased are made up of three items:

1. **Code to provide access to the company data files and homework you will need for this project.** The sticker in the lower-left corner of the Instructions book cover includes the one-time-use code you will need to access the company datasets and homework used in this project. The code is hidden by a scratch-off coating in the middle of the sticker. *Gently* scratch off the coating using a coin or something similar. **Do not apply too much pressure when scratching the coating or you might also damage the code.**

2. **Instructions book**—This book is the starting point for all assignments. It will guide you through *QuickBooks*. Unless your course instructor informs you otherwise, **you should start with Chapter 1 and proceed through the materials without skipping any parts.**

   The software is an education version of the *QuickBooks Pro 2020* program. The education version of the software is similar to the software used commercially by thousands of companies, except that the software is a 160-day trial version.

> The software that you will download contains several educational versions of the *QuickBooks* software: *QuickBooks Pro* (the software that is the subject of this book), *QuickBooks Accountant*, and several different industry editions of *QuickBooks Premier*. The way the software is designed, the user can toggle back and forth between editions after installation. However, the default edition that opens each time the software is opened is *QuickBooks Accountant*, which is virtually the same as *QuickBooks Pro*. Rather than have you toggle to *QuickBooks Pro* each time you open the software, which becomes tedious after several times, you should just leave the screen at *QuickBooks Accountant*. For simplicity, we will refer to the software as *QuickBooks* throughout the remainder of the project.

3. **Reference book**—The Reference book provides instructions for using each of the windows discussed in these materials. You will be referring to the Reference book frequently in later chapters. You will be instructed when to use the Reference book as you go through the Instructions book.

About this Project

By doing this project you will learn about *QuickBooks,* accounting software which is commercially available and widely used by many small and medium-sized companies throughout the world. More importantly, you will learn what this type of system offers companies to more effectively operate their businesses. Some of the things you will learn include the following:

- How to process economic events with *QuickBooks.*
- The effects of processing transactions on a wide variety of data files in the system that help companies operate their businesses more effectively.
- How a company enters information such as its general ledger, vendor, and customer accounts into the system.
- How to make inquiries of the data files as a part of managing a business.
- Ways to analyze data to improve business decisions.
- The nature of the internal controls included in the system to prevent and detect errors.
- Ways the system helps a company process data and prepare reports efficiently and quickly.

An important distinction between a paper system and computerized system such as *QuickBooks* is the lack of visibility in much of what takes place in a computerized system because it is electronic. The challenge with this lack of visibility is the difficulty understanding what is happening in the system. This lack of understanding in turn causes many users to either use the system improperly or fail to take advantage of all of its capabilities.

This project is intended to help you bridge the gap between what you know about a paper-based and a computer-based accounting information system. The benefit to you is an enhanced ability to contribute immediately to a business in a computer environment as an accountant, auditor, or user of information generated by such a system.

As you go through the different learning steps, you will be asked to identify where and how data are processed, perform inquiries into the system to analyze the data, make customized changes to the system, establish and test controls, and prepare reports to support business decision-making. You will learn these tasks by following the guidance provided as you proceed through the materials.

Three important characteristics of accounting software are (1) its ability to generate multiple-use information without entering information more than once, (2) the incorporation of shortcut methods to enter data, and (3) the embedding of internal controls in the software to detect and prevent errors. There are hundreds of examples of all three characteristics in most accounting software. An example of the first is the automatic update of other records when a sales invoice is prepared, such as the sales journal, general ledger, and accounts receivable master files. An example of the second is the automatic inclusion of a customer's name and address when the customer's identification number is entered in the system. An example of the third is the rejection of an accounting transaction where relevant information, such as the customer's name, is not entered for a transaction.

There is a wide variety of accounting software available for companies to purchase and modify for their company's needs. Examples of accounting software for medium-size and larger-size companies are *Microsoft Dynamics® GP* and *NetSuite*. The software used in this project, *QuickBooks*, is widely used by small businesses and is commercially available from Intuit. The reason for selecting *QuickBooks* for this project is that, although the software is relatively easy to use, it also includes several internal controls that can be implemented to improve controls over accessing and processing accounting information.

Key Activities Included in the Project

Accountants perform several types of activities when they use accounting software such as *QuickBooks* to keep accounting records for companies. You will do many of these activities during the project. These activities are introduced in the E-Materials and Chapter 2 and are dealt with more extensively in later assignments. Following are key activities you will be doing in the project:

- **Install the *QuickBooks* software and back up data.** You will learn this in the E-Materials (*QuickBooks* E-Materials) that you download from the Armond Dalton Resources website. *Note:* **Installing the *QuickBooks* software is not applicable to students doing the project in a computer laboratory where the software is already installed on the individual machines in the lab or on a network.**

- **Open the *QuickBooks* program and open a company.** You must be able to access *QuickBooks* and the company for which you will be performing activities.

- **Perform maintenance.** An important characteristic of accounting software is the automatic performance of many mechanical activities by the computer. To permit the computer to do these activities, maintenance is done to provide an adequate database of information. For example, *QuickBooks* permits a user to enter a customer's identification number and the software automatically includes the customer's name and address on a sales invoice.

- **Process transactions, including all information needed for record keeping.** Accountants spend most of their time processing transactions. This is a major emphasis of the project. An example of processing transactions is entering data to bill customers for shipped goods, preparing the sales invoice, and recording the sale and related accounts receivable, including updating subsidiary records for accounts receivable and inventory.

- **Inquire about and analyze recorded information.** Management, employees, and outside users frequently need information about data in the system. For example, if a customer calls about an apparent incorrect billing, it is important to respond quickly. *QuickBooks* provides access to data in a variety of ways to permit many different types of inquiries.

- **Review and print reports.** Users of accounting information need reports in a proper format with an adequate level of detail for their decision making. Examples include an aged trial balance for accounts receivable, an income statement, and a report of sales by sales person or product. *QuickBooks* permits many different reports to be prepared and printed and allows tailoring to meet users' needs.

2
Chapter

FAMILIARIZATION

Introduction

This chapter illustrates *QuickBooks* features and provides practice using the program so that you are able to complete assignments for the project. Do not skip this chapter.

The discussion assumes that you have a working knowledge of Windows. If you need additional guidance for using Windows, consult your Windows user manual.

There are five primary activities in *QuickBooks*, all introduced in this chapter and dealt with extensively in later chapters. In most cases there is more than one way to access each of these activities, also covered in this chapter.

1. Open the *QuickBooks* Program and Open a Company—Used as is implied by the title.
2. Maintenance—Used to add, change, or delete information about such things as customers, vendors, employees, and general ledger accounts (chart of accounts).
3. Processing Information Tasks—Used to perform the tasks needed to process and record transactions such as processing a sales transaction or weekly payroll.
4. Obtaining Information—Used to obtain information already included in *QuickBooks* about such things as a customer address or a recorded sales transaction.
5. Reports—Used to view and print a wide variety of reports, such as an aged trial balance and a comparative income statement.

Open the *Quickbooks* Program and Open a Company

Starting now, you will use the computer to perform tasks with *QuickBooks*. In this chapter, the instructions are reasonably detailed to make certain that you understand how to use *QuickBooks* correctly and efficiently.

Depending on which version of Windows you are using, certain window functions and the appearance of the windows may differ slightly. However, the *QuickBooks* elements and functions are identical between different versions of the Windows operating system.

Do not be concerned about making mistakes while performing familiarization activities in this chapter. It is important that you practice each activity and learn by doing.

Depending on whether or not this is the first time you've installed *QuickBooks*, various windows may or may not open. None of them are critical to the installation process, so the windows are not illustrated here. Following are brief descriptions of these windows, as well as the steps you should follow if they open.

> *If you receive a message at any time that tells you there is a product update available, make sure you have Internet access and then follow the instructions for installing the product update.*

> *If the "How QuickBooks uses your Internet Connection" window opens, click OK to close it.*

> *If the "QuickBooks Setup" window opens that says "Let's get your business set up quickly," click Other Options → Open Existing File to open the Open or Restore Company window. Then close the Open or Restore Company window.*

> *If at any time the Accountant Center window opens, remove the checkbox in the lower-left corner next to "Show Accountant Center when opening a company file" and close the window.*

> *If the QuickBooks Usage Study window opens, click No to close the window.*

If, at any time, you decide that you want to start the chapter again, you may do so by restoring the Rock Castle Construction and Larry's Landscaping & Garden Supply datasets following the instructions in the E-Materials. You may want to do so if you believe that you do not understand the material in the chapter.

To begin using *QuickBooks*, complete the following steps.

> *If you already have the QuickBooks software open and see the No Company Open window shown at the top of page 2-4, skip to the top of page 2-4.*

> *If you already have the QuickBooks software open to one of the five companies you restored using the E-Materials instructions, click File → Close Company and then skip to the top of page 2-4.*

> *Click the "QuickBooks Premier–Accountant Edition 2020" icon on your desktop. It may take a couple of minutes to load.*

> *If you do not have the program icon on your desktop, click Start → QuickBooks → QuickBooks Premier–Accountant Edition 2020 to get the opening QuickBooks screen.*

Eventually, the No Company Open window will appear on your screen.

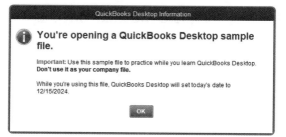

No Company Open
Select a company that you've previously opened and click Open

COMPANY NAME	LAST MODIFIED	FILE SIZE
Waren Sports Supply.QBW	05/15/2020, 03:03 PM	20.68 MB
Super OFP.qbw	05/15/2020, 03:02 PM	17.43 MB
sample_product-based business.qbw	05/15/2020, 03:01 PM	47.23 MB
sample_service-based business.qbw	05/15/2020, 03:01 PM	36.70 MB

Open
Edit List

LOCATION C:\Users\Public\Documents\Intuit\QuickBooks\Sample Company Files\QuickBooks 2020\

Create a new company   Open or restore an existing company   Open a sample file   Find a company file

As shown in the previous window, you should see all five companies that you restored earlier using the instructions in the E-Materials. If you do not see those companies in this window, return to the E-Materials (available for download on armonddaltonresources.com) and restore all five companies before continuing with this chapter.

▶ *Locate "sample_product-based business.qbw" file from the list of company files shown in the window and either double-click on it or highlight it and then click Open.*

A window may open that says that it needs to update your company file.

▶ *Click Yes.*

Next, a window opens that informs you that the file is for practice only and that the date is set to 12/15/2024 for this sample company.

QuickBooks Desktop Information

ⓘ **You're opening a QuickBooks Desktop sample file.**

Important: Use this sample file to practice while you learn QuickBooks Desktop. **Don't use it as your company file.**

While you're using this file, QuickBooks Desktop will set today's date to 12/15/2024.

OK

▶ *Click OK to open Rock Castle Construction, a product-based company that you will use extensively in later chapters. If the Accountant Center window opens, uncheck the "Show Accountant Center when opening a company file" checkbox.*

When Rock Castle Construction opens, the bar at the top of the window includes the company name.

▶ It is common in *QuickBooks* for the Live Community and Help window to open automatically on the screen. We suggest that you close that window. You can get help by using Help on the Menu Bar any time you want it.

▶ After the software is installed and during subsequent sessions using the software, various messages may appear from Intuit. Examples include windows that ask you to participate in a survey or whether or not you want to purchase Intuit's forms and documents. Whenever these types of windows open while you are using the software, check the box that says "Do not display this screen again" (if it is available) and then close the window. These materials do not list all of the possible pop-up windows that may appear. Follow the preceding instructions for each pop-up window so that it does not open again.

▶ *Click File → Close Company to close the Rock Castle Construction window.* *QuickBooks* will again display the No Company Open window indicating that no company is open.

▶ *Open Rock Castle Construction again.*

Open Another Company

Whenever you open *QuickBooks*, you can open a previously opened company from the list in the No Company Open window. If you wish to open a different company, close that company and select a different company from the list.

You can also open a previously opened company without closing the existing company.

▶ *Select File to open a drop-down list shown at the top of the following page.* (Only the top few items are shown here.) Next to Open Previous Company there is a small arrow. It is called an expansion arrow, which indicates the availability of an additional list. *Note:* Depending on the work you have already done on this project, your window might show fewer or more previous companies open.

▶ *Hold the cursor over Open Previous Company to show an expansion list, which includes the names of companies that are available in QuickBooks software, listed in the order they were last opened.* You can now open any company in the expansion list by clicking on the company name.

▶ *Move up one menu option and select Open or Restore Company to open the Open or Restore Company window. Then click the Next button.*

▶ *Select sample_service-based business to open Sample Larry's Landscaping & Garden Supply.*

▶ *Practice opening and closing QuickBooks and opening and closing companies until you feel comfortable doing so.*

Quickbooks Navigation Overview

▶ *Open Rock Castle Construction.* The window that is first displayed when you open a company is usually the Home Page, which is shown below.

▶ *If the Home Page isn't displayed, click the Home icon shown near the top-left portion of the window.*

Menu bar

Name of the Open Company

Icon bar

Home Page

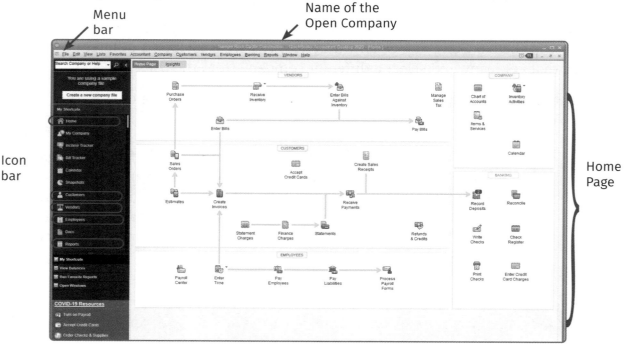

QuickBooks Window

Following is a description of key parts of the *QuickBooks* window with the Home Page open.

> Name of the Open Company—In this case, it is Rock Castle Construction.

> Menu Bar—The Menu Bar is organized like most Microsoft Windows applications, but adapted to *QuickBooks*. With a few exceptions discussed later these materials use only the File menu. You used the File menu in the previous section.

> Icon Bar—The Icon Bar is located on the left side of the Home Page. The first icon is the Home Page icon. The other Menu Bar icons that you will use are Customers, Vendors, Employees, and Reports, all circled in the preceding illustration. *Note:* You may need to expand the icon list area if you cannot see it.

> Home Page—The Home Page is the main part of the window and includes all information below the Menu Bar. The Home Page is critical for these materials because it is the primary way you will access all maintenance and processing activities.

The middle section of the Home Page includes three buttons that correspond to Centers on the Icon Bar. The three icons are for vendors, customers, and employees.

> ▶ *Click the Customers button in the Home Page shown below.*

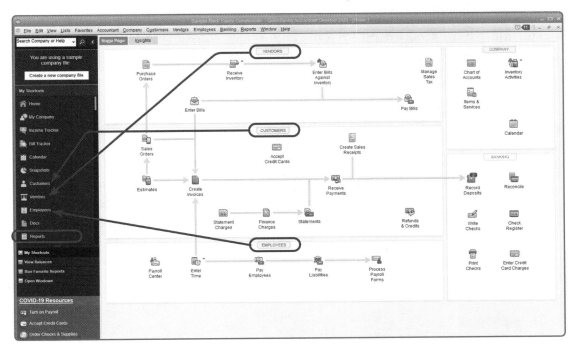

> ▶ *Observe the window and close.*

▶ *Click the Customers icon (* 🧑 Customers *) on the Icon Bar. It opens the same window. Either of these approaches to open the Customer Center is acceptable, depending on your preference. The same is true for the Vendor Center and the Employee Center, but there is no button on the Home Page for the Report Center so you will use the Icon Bar to access that center.*

▶ *Return to the Home Page by clicking the Home icon (* 🏠 Home *) or closing the Customer Center window.*

▶ *Practice opening and closing centers using the center buttons on the Home Page and the Icon Bar icons including the Reports icon (* 📊 Reports *) until you feel comfortable doing so. Close all windows except the Home Page.*

> Use care in closing windows to avoid closing the *QuickBooks* main window. In most cases, the open window has a close icon identical to the main window.

Maintenance

As stated earlier in the chapter introduction, maintenance is used to add, change, or delete information about such things as customers, vendors, and general ledger accounts (chart of accounts). Maintenance is critical to computerized accounting systems and is discussed in detail later.

It is useful to think of maintenance as developing and providing information for master files in an accounting system. One major master file is for customers, which includes information about each customer such as the name and address, credit limits, and key customer contact.

The five key master files in *QuickBooks* are customers, vendors, employees, inventory (Items & Services), and chart of accounts.

▶ *Click the Vendors button (* VENDORS *) in the top middle of the Home Page to open the Vendor Center window, the top portion which is shown on the following page. One tab and one icon on the window deal with maintenance. (Both are circled in the following example.)*

▶ *Click the Vendor's tab if it is not already highlighted. A list of vendors is included on the left side of the screen. These vendors were previously added during maintenance.*

▶ *Scroll down the Name column and double-click on Hamlin Metal to access the Edit Vendor window shown below. If a New Feature window opens, select "Do not display this message in the future" click OK, then close the window. The Address Info tab is open and includes information about the company.*

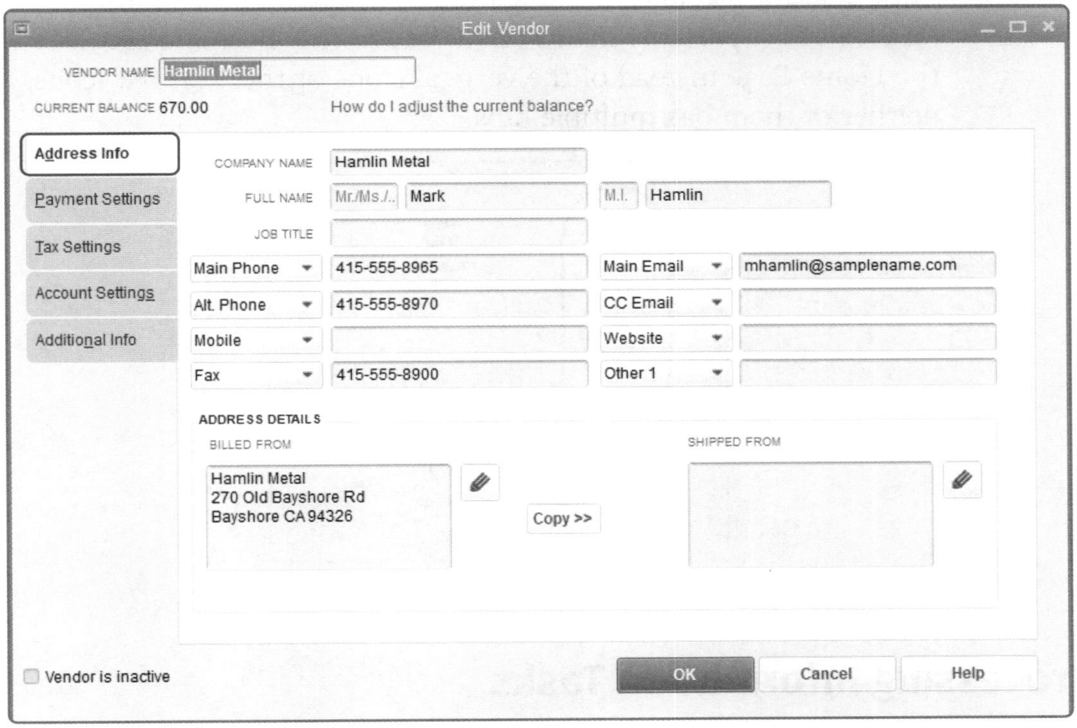

- ▶ *Click the Additional Info tab to see additional information entered during maintenance.*

- ▶ *Click OK to return to the Vendor Center.*

- ▶ *Click the New Vendor icon (* New Vendor... ▾ *) at the top of the window and select New Vendor to open the New Vendor window.* It looks exactly like the previous window except that it is blank in the headings and other boxes. The only exception is the 12/15/2024 in the date box, which is the default date for Rock Castle Construction. For a new vendor, the *QuickBooks* operator will complete this window for all three tabs.

- ▶ *Return to the Home Page and practice opening and closing maintenance tabs for existing and new customers, employees, and vendors, including opening the Edit windows until you feel comfortable doing so.*

- ▶ *Close all windows except for the Home Page.*

- ▶ *Click Chart of Accounts, then the Items & Services icons on the right portion of the Home Page partially shown below for practice.* Both are accessed through the Home Page instead of the vertical icons or the Icon Bar icons, and neither of them has multiple tabs.

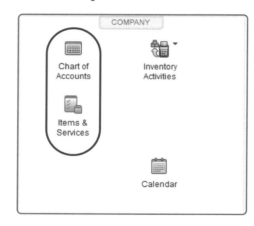

Processing Information Tasks

As stated in the introduction, processing information tasks is used for processing and recording transactions. It is the primary activity in computerized accounting systems and the main focus of Chapters 5 through 8.

There are three primary information processing categories in *QuickBooks* that are consistent with the three most common cycles in accounting systems as follows:

1. Sales and cash receipts (Customers in *QuickBooks*)
2. Purchases and cash disbursements (Vendors in *QuickBooks*)
3. Payroll (Employees in *QuickBooks*)

▶ *Open the Home Page for Rock Castle Construction if it is not already open.* The tasks to process and record transactions are indicated by icons connected by arrows in the Vendors, Customers, and Employees portion of the Home Page as shown on each circled portion of the Home Page window below.

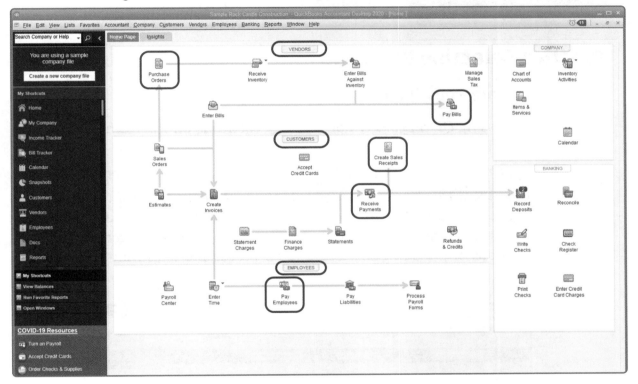

▶ *Move and hold your cursor over each icon in the Vendors portion of the Home Page without clicking on it. Doing so allows you to read what is accomplished when the activity indicated by the icon is completed.* The connecting lines show the direction of flows for processing information for the purchase process. The Vendors portion of the window flows from Purchase Orders through Receive Inventory to Enter Bills to Pay Bills. The Customers and Employees portions of the Home Page are similar to the one for Vendors, but obviously the activities are different.

▶ *Move your cursor over each icon in the Customers portion of the Home Page without clicking on it to learn what activity each icon is used to accomplish.*

Again, the icons include connecting lines showing the direction of flow of the sales process. The process starts with Estimates (if used), Create Invoices, and continues through Finance Charges to Receive Payments and Record Deposits.

▶ *Move your cursor over each icon in the Employees portion of the Home Page in the same way you did for vendors and customers.*

Review the flow of tasks for each of the three sections on the Home Page. Each starts with the beginning of an accounting process and continues through to the end of that process. As you will see later, the processes include the automatic recording of transactions and updating a variety of records. Completing the assignments in later chapters will help you better understand these processes.

Practice Selecting Windows

Using the Home Page Icons

To practice accessing *QuickBooks* windows using the icons on the Home Page complete the following.

▶ *Return to the Home Page for Rock Castle Construction if it is not already open.*

▶ *Click the Create Invoices icon (Create Invoices) in the Customers portion of the Home Page to open the Create Invoices window shown below.* The window is in the format of a sales invoice and is used for billing customers for shipments of goods or providing services, and for processing sales transactions in *QuickBooks*.

▷ *Close the Create Invoices window and then click the Purchase Orders icon (📄 Purchase Orders) in the Vendors portion of the Home Page to open the Create Purchase Orders window shown below.*

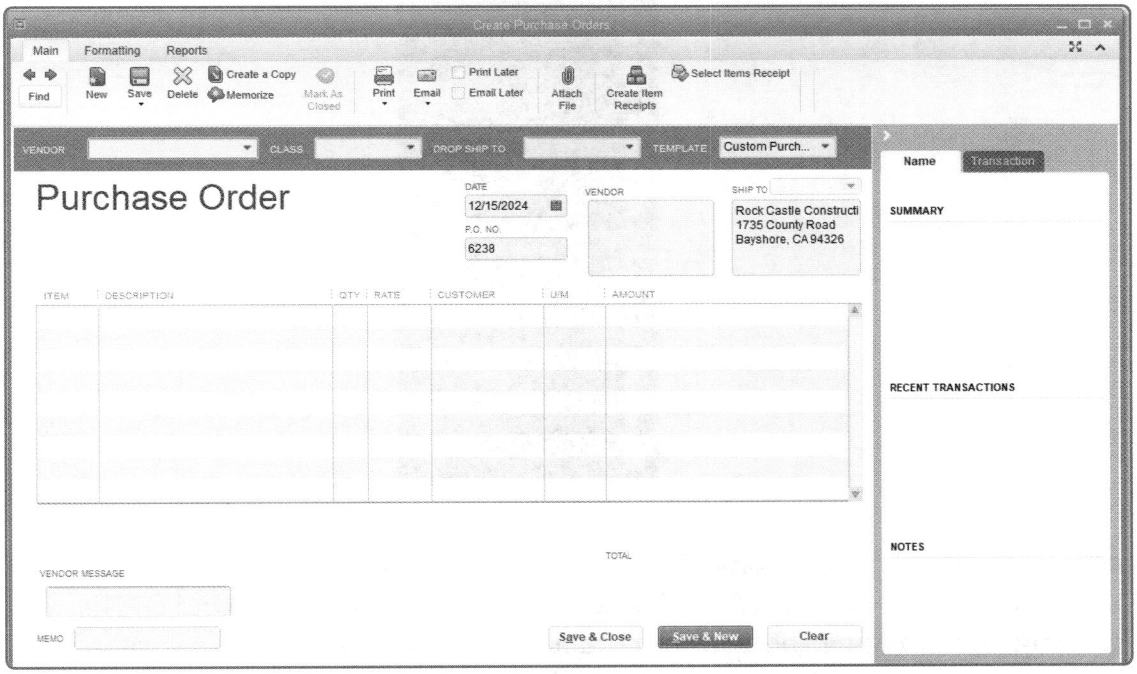

The document in the window is different, but the concept is the same as for the Create Invoices window you opened previously.

▷ *Practice clicking icons in each of the Vendors, Customers, and Employees portion of the Home Page until you feel comfortable doing so.*

▷ *Close all windows except the Home Page.* If there is a message asking if you want to record any transaction now, click No.

> The remainder of this book and the Reference book include instructions for recording transactions and performing maintenance and other tasks using *QuickBooks*. To limit repetition in the project, the materials do not instruct you to close each window when you have finished recording a transaction or completing maintenance or other tasks. When you are done with each window, close the window.

You will now practice opening windows using three different approaches that accomplish the same thing you just did.

Using the Centers on the Icon Bar

An alternative to using Home Page icons is to use the Icon Bar shown above. **Note:** If you cannot see all of the Icon bar icons, you may need to expand the list by clicking and dragging the bottom border to expand it. The three relevant Icon bar icons are Customers, Vendors, and Employees.

▶ *Click the Customers icon on the Icon Bar to show the Customer Center window partially shown below.*

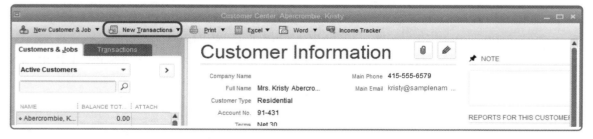

▶ *Click the New Transactions icon (* New Transactions ▼ *), circled in the preceding window) to drop down the list shown at the top of the next page.* The list includes almost the same names as the ones on the icons in the Customers portion of the Home Page.

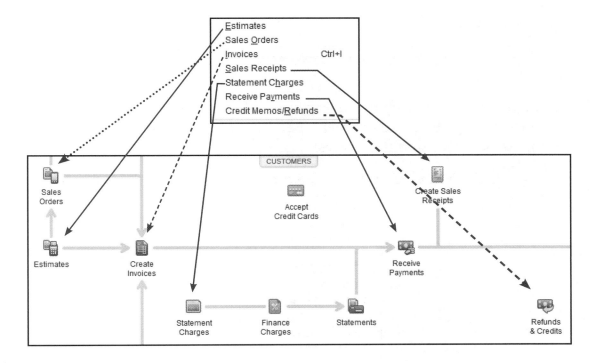

▶ *Click Invoices to open the same Create Invoices window that you opened using the Create Invoices icon on the Home Page.*

▶ *Return to the Home Page and click the Vendors icon (* 🔲 Vendors *) on the Icon Bar → click on New Transactions → Purchase Orders to open the same blank Create Purchase Orders window that you opened using the Purchase Orders icon on the Home Page.*

Using the Center Buttons on the Home Page [CUSTOMERS] [VENDORS] [EMPLOYEES]

Another alternative to using Home Page icons or Icon Bar icons is to use the center buttons on the Home Page. The three relevant buttons are Customers, Vendors, and Employees.

▶ *Return to the Home Page and click the Customers button on the Home Page to open the Customer Center, which is identical to the one you opened using the Customers icon in the Icon Bar.*

▶ *Practice using the center Home Page buttons for Customers, Vendors, and Employees until you feel comfortable opening a variety of windows.*

Using the Menu Bar

File Edit View Lists Favorites Accountant Company Customers Vendors Employees Banking Reports Window Help

A third alternative to using Home Page icons, Icon Bar icons, or center buttons on the Home Page is to use the Menu Bar. The three relevant Menu Bar items are Customers, Vendors, and Employees.

▶ *Click Customers on the Menu Bar to open the drop-down list shown below.*

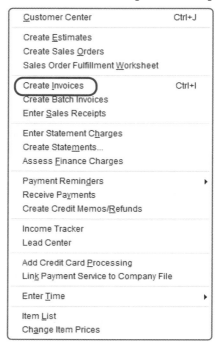

▶ *Click Create Invoices (circled in the previous list) to open the same Create Invoices window that you have now opened several times.*

▶ *Practice using the Menu Bar drop-down lists for Customers, Vendors, and Employees until you feel comfortable opening a variety of windows.*

These materials typically use the Home Page icons to open *QuickBooks* windows for processing and maintenance tasks, not the other alternatives discussed. The reason is to help you better understand the processes followed in maintaining, processing, and recording transactions. When you use the icons on the Home Page you can visualize the activities that have taken place before the item you are dealing with and what will take place next to complete all activities in a cycle.

You will use the Reports icon on the Icon Bar because reports are not included as icons on the Home Page. You will also use the Menu Bar for other activities that are not included on the Home Page, such as making general journal entries and preparing bank reconciliations.

A Typical *QuickBooks* Window

You will now explore a typical *QuickBooks* window and practice using some common features of the software.

> ▶ *Open Rock Castle Construction if it is not already open.*
> ▶ *Click the Home Page icon → Create Invoices to open the Create Invoices window, if it is not already open.* The window is now blank except for information in three boxes. The Date and Due Date boxes include 12/15/2024 and the Invoice # box includes 1100. This data is referred to as default information.

Default Information

Default settings are established through original company setup or subsequent maintenance activities. The availability of this default information reduces the time needed to enter repetitive transaction information and the likelihood of mistakes. Default settings are one of the most important benefits of computerized accounting software. The Create Invoices window on your screen includes only a few items of default information. As you proceed, additional default information is automatically added.

The Create Invoices window on your screen should look like the one on page 2-21, except it will not include the circled letters. This window is an example of a typical window for processing transactions using *QuickBooks*. You will use this window to practice using common *QuickBooks* features. The window includes many description fields, entry boxes that are completed with default information, empty entry boxes, and various buttons.

To begin you will select a customer using a drop-down list.

▶ *Click the Customer: Job drop-down list arrow.* A listing of all customers for Rock Castle Construction is shown.

▶ *Locate the up/down scrolling arrows on the right side of the Customer: Job list. Use the down arrow to examine the listing.* Observe that almost every customer includes a name and subheading under the name. The subheading is the name of a job for that customer. For example, for the customer Ecker Designs there are two jobs, Office Expansion and Office Repairs.

> Some companies in this project include both customers and jobs, while others have only customers. A common example of a company that uses jobs is a construction company that has one or more projects for the same customer. Sample Rock Construction is a construction company. Retail and wholesale companies have customers but do not typically use jobs.

▶ *Select the job Utility Shed for customer Johnson, Gordon as shown below.*

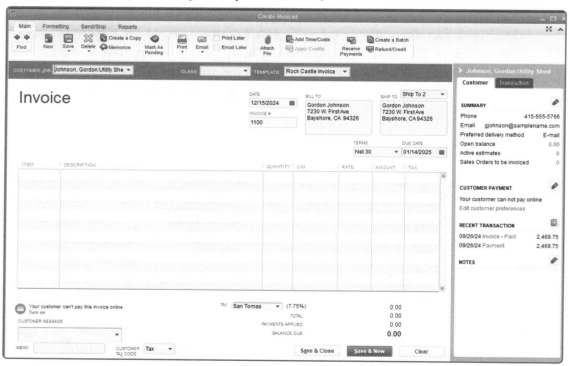

Description Fields

Description fields include labels that describe the information that must be typed, selected, or accepted to complete the window. For example, Customer: Job, Bill To, Date, and Invoice # are all description field labels in the Create Invoices window on your screen (shown on page 2-21). Each description field corresponds to an entry box where information exists or is to be entered.

Entry Boxes

Entry boxes are typically located directly below or to the right of the description fields but are sometimes located to the left or elsewhere. For simplicity, the term "box" is used throughout the remainder of the project, instead of "entry box."

In the Create Invoices window, many of the boxes now include considerably more default information than existed when you first opened the window. By selecting a customer, *QuickBooks* added additional information that has already been established during maintenance for this customer.

The [Tab] key on your keyboard is used to move to the next box in a window, to skip through boxes that you want to leave blank, to accept default data, or to move to the next box after you have entered data. You may also use your touchpad or mouse to skip around anywhere on the entry screen that you like. These project materials assume you are using the [Tab] key to move consecutively through the entry boxes.

To move the cursor backward through the boxes that already include information, use the mouse to move the cursor to a previous box or press [Shift] [Tab].

For now, you are only practicing/learning the use of [Tab] in *QuickBooks*, without concern for the contents of the boxes.

> ▶ *Make sure the cursor is on Johnson, Gordon: Utility Shed in the Customer: Job box. Press [Tab] three or four times and watch the cursor on the screen as it moves from one box to another.* When the cursor goes through a box that already includes information, that information is being accepted without change.

> ▶ *Next, use the touchpad or mouse to go back to the Customer: Job box.*

▷ *Press [Enter] once.* The following message appears.

Note: You should not use [Enter] to advance to the next box.

▷ *Click OK.*

▷ *Click the drop-down list arrow next to Customer: Job and change the customer to Smith, Lee: Patio.* The default information changes for the different customer, which is what you expect.

▷ *Change customers again to any one you choose.* There is now new information in the default boxes for the customer you selected.

In most *QuickBooks* windows used in this project, there are boxes in which you do not need to enter information. Either the default information is correct or the information is not applicable to the transaction. The Reference book instructions for recording each type of transaction in *QuickBooks* focus on boxes in which you need to perform some type of activity, such as typing information or selecting an option from a list of available choices. If a box is not discussed, you should not do anything with that box. For example, if the document number box is not mentioned in the instructions for a specific *QuickBooks* window, the default entry is correct and you can therefore press the [Tab] key to go to the next box.

Entering Information Into Boxes

There are different ways to enter information into the boxes of a window or show that information. The circled letters **A** through **D** in the Create Invoices window shown below correspond with the discussion in the following sections.

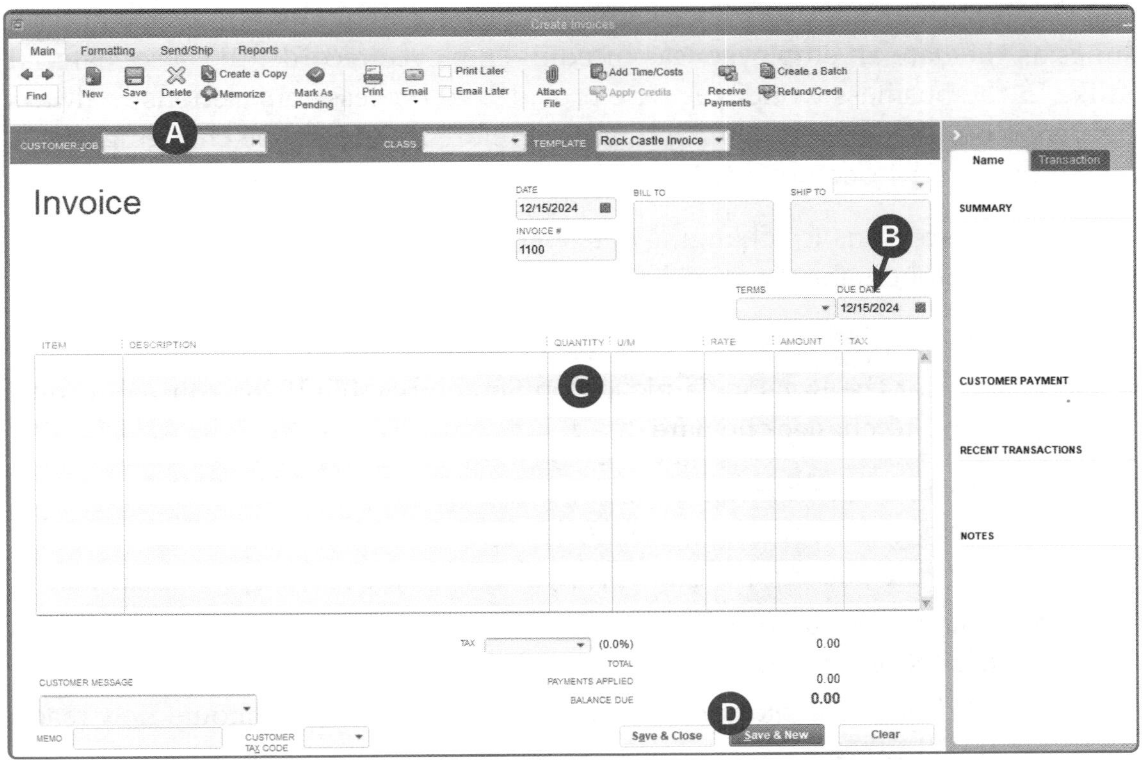

A Drop-Down List Arrow ▾

Drop-down list arrows are identifiable by an adjacent down pointing arrow. You have already used drop-down list arrows several times. Clicking a drop-down list arrow allows users to see a list of available choices on the drop-down list. An example of a drop-down list arrow in the Create Invoices window is to the right of the Customer: Job box. Clicking on it drops down the complete list of company customers. You can then scroll up or down that list and select the customer you want by clicking on that line, then selecting it as you did earlier for Smith, Lee: Patio.

> ▶ *Open a brand new Create Invoices window by clicking the Clear button in the bottom-right corner of the Create Invoices window. Then click in the Item box until the drop-down list arrow appears → click the arrow → select Wood Door: Exterior.* Observe that the following boxes are automatically updated: Description, Rate, Amount, and Tax. This is another example of a default entry.

B   Date Box

Many *QuickBooks* windows include date boxes for entering the date of transactions or other date information such as the invoice date in the Create Invoices window. In many cases for windows where data is being processed, the default entry in the date box is the current date. That is not the case for maintenance windows for such things as the date an employee was hired in employee records. In these materials, unlike in the business world, the date provided to process transactions is always different from the current date. You will therefore frequently be changing the default date to the one provided.

There are two options for changing dates: (1) Use the calendar button, or (2) type the date as numbers for the month, day, and year.

Calendar Button (▦). Assume that Rock Castle Construction made a sale to Robson, Darci for the Robson Clinic job on September 16, 2024. You will use the calendar button to change the date.

▶   *Open the Create Invoices window if it is not already open* → *select Robson, Darci: Robson Clinic in the Customer: Job box.*

▶   *Click the calendar button to the right of the Date box to open the calendar.*

▶   *Change the month and year to September 2024 by clicking on the left arrow until September - 2024 is shown at the top of the calendar.*

▶   *Click day 16 in the calendar.* The date in the Date box should now read 09/16/2024.

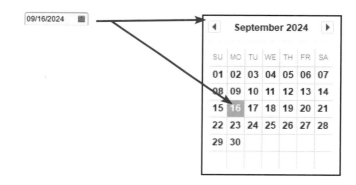

▶   *Delete the transaction by clicking the Clear button in the bottom-right portion of the window.*

▶ *Click on Customer: Job box → select Robson, Darci: Robson Clinic again.*

▶ *Highlight the entire date in the DATE box.*

▶ *Type the date using one or two numbers for the month, two for the day, and two or four for the year. Type 09/16/2024 → [Tab] to enter the same date that you entered above.*

There are other options to enter the same date. These include the following:

■ 9/16/24
■ 9.16.24
■ 9-16-24
■ 091624
■ 09162024

You can also highlight any one or two numbers and change just those. You should use whichever method you prefer.

▶ *Practice entering dates using the calendar button or typing the date using different options until you feel comfortable doing so.*

 C   Text Boxes

Text boxes are boxes in which you enter information by typing. *QuickBooks* has several text boxes in most windows. One example in the Create Invoices window is Quantity for the quantity billed.

▶ *Open the Create Invoices window if it is not already open → select Duncan, Dave for the Customer: Job box → [Tab] to the Item box.*

▶ *Enter 9/20/24 in the Date box.*

▶ *Select Wood Door Exterior → [Tab], [Tab], then type 3 in the Quantity box for the shipment of the three exterior doors → [Tab]. Observe that QuickBooks automatically extends the unit selling price of $120 times the quantity and adds the 7.75% tax when you typed the quantity in the Quantity box. Your window should show a total of $387.90 for the invoice.*

Now assume that customer Dave Duncan decided to have the doors shipped to 1445 Forest St. (same city and state).

▶ *Use the mouse to enter the second line of the Ship To box.*

▶ *Type the new address in the Ship To address box. Your window should now look like the one that follows at the top of the next page.*

▶ *Click the Save & Close button at the bottom of the window to save the transaction.* The following window appears.

▶ *Click the Yes button.* That will change the address on Duncan's customer maintenance record.

▶ *Click on the Save & Close button if the window does not close automatically.*

D Buttons

Save & Close   Save & New   Clear

You have already used buttons several times. There are dozens of them in *QuickBooks*. You will practice selecting three buttons.

▶ *Open the Create Invoices window again.* The three buttons on the bottom of the window are common to all transaction windows.

▶ *Select Balak, Mike in the Customer: Job box.*

▶ *Click the Save & Close button.* A warning window opens indicating that you cannot record a blank transaction.

▶ *Click the OK button to return to the Create Invoices window.*

▶ *Click the Clear button.*

Radio Button (○   ⊙). A radio button is used where there are two or more options available, but only one option can be selected. *QuickBooks* has only a few radio button options. To practice using the radio button, complete the following:

▶ *Return to the Home Page and click the Pay Bills icon ( ) in the Vendors potion of the Home Page to open the Pay Bills window.* There are two sets of radio buttons on the window.

▶ *Click the Assign check number radio button at the bottom of the window to fill that radio button.* Observe that the To be printed radio button is now unmarked.

▶ *Click the To be printed radio button to change it back to the original setting.*

Tabs

Three of the five maintenance activities and some other windows use tabs to allow an easy way to include information while keeping the amount of information in each window manageable. You have already used tabs for the Vendors Center.

▶ *Return to the Home Page and click the center Customers button on the Home Page to open the Customer Center, partially shown at the top of the following page.* There are two tabs in the Customer Center: Customers & Jobs and Transactions. The Customers & Jobs tab is now open, indicated by the bold and highlighted text of the tab. A listing of all customers is included below the tab.

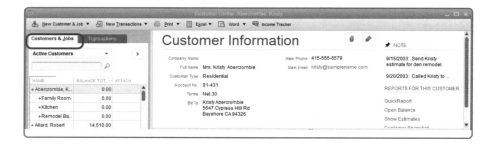

▶ *Click once on the name Allard, Robert on the list.* Observe that the left portion of the partial window shown below now includes the heading Customer Information.

▶ *Click the Edit Customer button on the top-right portion the window (✎) to open the Edit Customer window shown next. If the window on your screen is not the same as that shown here, it may be maximized. If so, click the Restore Down button (⬚) on the menu row (File, Edit, View, etc.), but not the entire QuickBooks window.* The Address Info tab is open for the window and includes information that was entered through maintenance. Almost all boxes include information.

Edit Customer

CUSTOMER NAME Allard, Robert

CURRENT BALANCE 14,510.00 How do I adjust the current balance?

Address Info

Payment Settings

Sales Tax Settings

Additional Info

COMPANY NAME

FULL NAME Mrs. Amanda M.I. Roberts

JOB TITLE

Main Phone ▼ 650-555-3422   Main Email ▼ rallard@myemail.com

Alt. Phone ▼ 650-555-8349   CC Email ▼

Mobile ▼   Website ▼

Fax ▼ 650-555-9804   Other 1 ▼

ADDRESS DETAILS

INVOICE/BILL TO   SHIP TO Ship To 1 ▼

Robert Allard   Robert Allard
92834 Chandler St.   92834 Chandler St.
Millbrae, CA 94030   Millbrae, CA 94030

Copy >>

☑ Default shipping address

☐ Customer is inactive   OK   Cancel   Help

▶ *Click the Payment Settings tab.* Two boxes in this window have default information (Payment Terms and Preferred Delivery Method).

▶ *Click the Sales Tax Settings tab.* The Tax Code and Tax Item boxes contain default information.

▶ *Click the Additional Info tab.* The boxes are empty except for the Customer Type box.

▶ *Click the Cancel button to return to the Customer Center.*

Print and Export to Excel

Print 🖶 Print ▾

A wide variety of information in *QuickBooks* can be printed. Only one example is shown.

▶ *Close the Customer Center. From the Home Page, select the Vendor Center. Make sure the Vendors tab is open. You may have to click the Restore Down button if the top part of your screen does not look like the one shown next. The top of the window is shown below with two icons circled.*

▶ *Click the Print icon (🖶 Print ▾) drop-down list arrow to show three items → click Vendor List to open a small List Reports window → click OK to open the Print Reports window shown below. If the List Reports window opens, select "Do not display this message in the future" and then click OK.* **Note:** *You may have different selections showing in this window, depending on what printer(s) you have available for your computer.*

Print Reports

Settings Margins

Print to:
- ● Printer: Adobe PDF on Documents*.pdf ▾   Options...
- ○ File: ASCII text file ▾

Note: To install additional printers or to change port assignments, use the Windows Control Panel.

ORIENTATION:
- ○ Portrait
- ● Landscape

PAGE RANGE:
- ● All
- ○ Pages:
  From: 1   To: 9999

PAGE BREAKS:
- ☑ Smart page breaks (widow/orphan control)

Number of copies: 1
☑ Collate

☐ Fit report to 1 page(s) wide
☐ Fit report to 1 page(s) high

☐ Print in color (color printers only)

[Print] [Cancel] [Help] [Preview]

▶ *Click the Preview button (* Preview *) to show the Vendors List that will be printed if you print the list. Click Next page to see the rest of the list.* It is always desirable to preview the printing to avoid printing information that you do not want to print or prefer to be in a different format.

▶ *Click the Close button to return to the Print Reports window and then close the Print Reports window to return to the Vendor Center.*

Export To Excel Excel ▼

It is often useful to export information from *QuickBooks*, especially when the data available includes more information than the user wants. For example if the user wants a list of vendor payables in excess of $1,000 that information can be provided by first exporting to Excel.

▶ *Make sure the Vendor Center is open → click once on Bayshore Water on the Vendors tab list.* **Note:** Do not click twice because that will open the Edit Vendor window.

▶ *Click the Excel icon (* Excel ▼ *) drop-down list arrow → click Export Transactions to open the Export window shown below.*

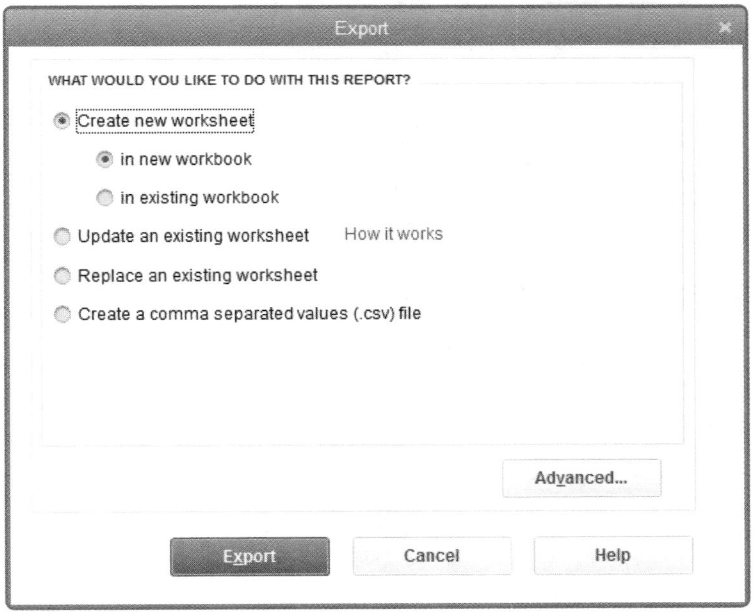

▶ *Click the Export button (* Export *) to export to Excel the Excel worksheet with a list of transactions for Bayshore Water.* You can now change the Excel worksheet, including formats to meet your needs.

▶ *Close the Excel worksheet without saving it.*

▶ *Return to the Home Page and click the Reports icon to open the Report Center with the Standard tab open to Company & Financial. Double-click on the report named "Profit & Loss Standard" to open the report.*

The report on your screen may contain slightly different numbers depending on what you have done in the project so far. Do not be concerned about the content of the report. Below is a partial image of the report.

	Dec 1 - 15, 24
▼ Ordinary Income/Expense	
▼ Income	
▼ 40100 · Construction Income	
40110 · Design Income	3,000.00
40130 · Labor Income	20,378.00
40140 · Materials Income	12,401.91
40150 · Subcontracted Labor Income	15,461.25
Total 40100 · Construction Income	51,241.16
▼ 40500 · Reimbursement Income	
40520 · Permit Reimbursement Income	0.00
Total 40500 · Reimbursement Income	0.00
Total Income	51,241.16
▼ Cost of Goods Sold	
50100 · Cost of Goods Sold	2,894.18
▼ 54000 · Job Expenses	
54200 · Equipment Rental	1,550.00
54300 · Job Materials	9,045.86
54400 · Permits and Licenses	-175.00
54500 · Subcontractors	5,837.00
54520 · Freight & Delivery	69.60
Total 54000 · Job Expenses	16,677.46
Total COGS	19,571.64
Gross Profit	31,669.52
▼ Expense	
▼ 60100 · Automobile	
60110 · Fuel	81.62
Total 60100 · Automobile	81.62
▼ 62100 · Insurance	
62130 · Work Comp	1,214.31

QuickBooks Help Menu

QuickBooks has an extensive Help menu that you can use if you need further information to complete activities in the project. Because the Help menu is easy to use and is likely similar to other Help menus you have used, detailed instructions are not included here.

The Help menu includes a QuickBooks Desktop Help option.

▶ *Click Help → QuickBooks Desktop Help option to open the following window.*

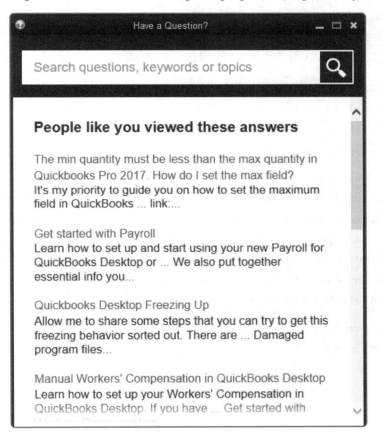

You can type terms, phrases, or entire questions in the search box to find additional guidance for specific topics. *QuickBooks* even provides step-by-step guidance in several areas.

▶ *Close all Help menus to return to the Home Page.*

Chapter Summary

After completing Chapter 2, you have now learned:

- ✔ how to open and close companies.
- ✔ how to work with various Centers (Customer, Vendor, Employee, Report).
- ✔ how to work with the features that are available on the Home Page, Menu bar, and Icon bar.
- ✔ an overview of maintenance and processing information tasks.
- ✔ how to print information and export to Excel.
- ✔ how to access features in the Help menu.

You should now save your work by making periodic backups of Rock Castle Construction and Larry's Landscaping & Garden Supply using the instructions in the E-Materials you downloaded from the Armond Dalton Resources website. Be sure to use descriptive file names, such as "Rock Castle after Ch 2" or something similar.

Before starting the homework for Chapter 2, you should restore both Rock Castle Construction and Larry's Landscaping & Garden Supply using the initial backups you downloaded from the Armond Dalton Resources website. Restore both companies before proceeding to the Chapter 2 homework assigned by your instructor, which is available on the Armond Dalton Resources website at www.armonddaltonresources.com.

If you cannot recall how to make a periodic backup or restore a backup, refer to the E-Materials located at www.armonddaltonresources.com.

3

Chapter

OVERVIEW OF MAINTENANCE, PROCESSING INFORMATION, AND INTERNAL CONTROLS

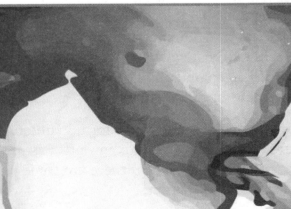

Introduction

This chapter provides an overview of maintenance, processing information, and internal controls in *QuickBooks*. You need to understand each of these because they are used extensively in the remainder of these materials.

As discussed in Chapter 2, there are four related types of information or activities included in *QuickBooks*. The first two included below are discussed in this chapter and the last two in the next chapter. In addition, this chapter includes processing controls over processing information.

1. **Maintenance**—Used to add, change, and delete information about such things as customers, vendors, and general ledger accounts. Maintenance is critical to computerized accounting systems. It was introduced in the last chapter and is discussed in detail next.
2. **Processing Information Tasks**—Used to perform the tasks needed to process and record transactions. It is the primary activity in computerized accounting systems and was also introduced in the last chapter.
3. **Obtaining Information**—Used to obtain a wide variety of information in *QuickBooks* that has already been entered through maintenance and processing information. Examples include a list of all customers and a list of all sales transactions for a month. *QuickBooks* permits using alternative methods to access this information.
4. **Reports**—Used to view and print a wide variety of reports such as an aged trial balance and a comparative income statement.

Maintenance

Maintenance means establishing the information in the system that permits the automatic and convenient processing of transactions and preparing reports. Examples include setting up general ledger accounts, customer accounts, and employee payroll information. After such information databases are set up in maintenance, *QuickBooks* automatically completes many parts of data entry in the processing windows, such as completing the customer address, terms, and the general ledger sales account for processing sales to a customer.

You will use five maintenance windows to perform maintenance for the five areas introduced in Chapter 2: customers, vendors, inventory items, employees, and chart of accounts. For each maintenance window there are three possible maintenance tasks: add, change, or delete information.

The maintenance part for setting up a new company in *QuickBooks* is time consuming. You will do maintenance to set up a simple company in a later chapter. For now, you are introduced to maintenance to understand what has already been entered into the system.

An important internal control in maintenance is the inability to add, change, or delete any transaction data by doing any type of maintenance task. For example, it is impossible to add, change, or delete sales transactions by doing customer maintenance.

Examine Existing Maintenance

You will now view customer maintenance that has already been done for Rock Castle Construction.

▶ *Open Rock Castle Construction.*

▶ *Click on Home Page → Customers → Customers & Jobs tab, if not already open, to access the list partially shown below.*

Customer Center Window → Customers Jobs Tab

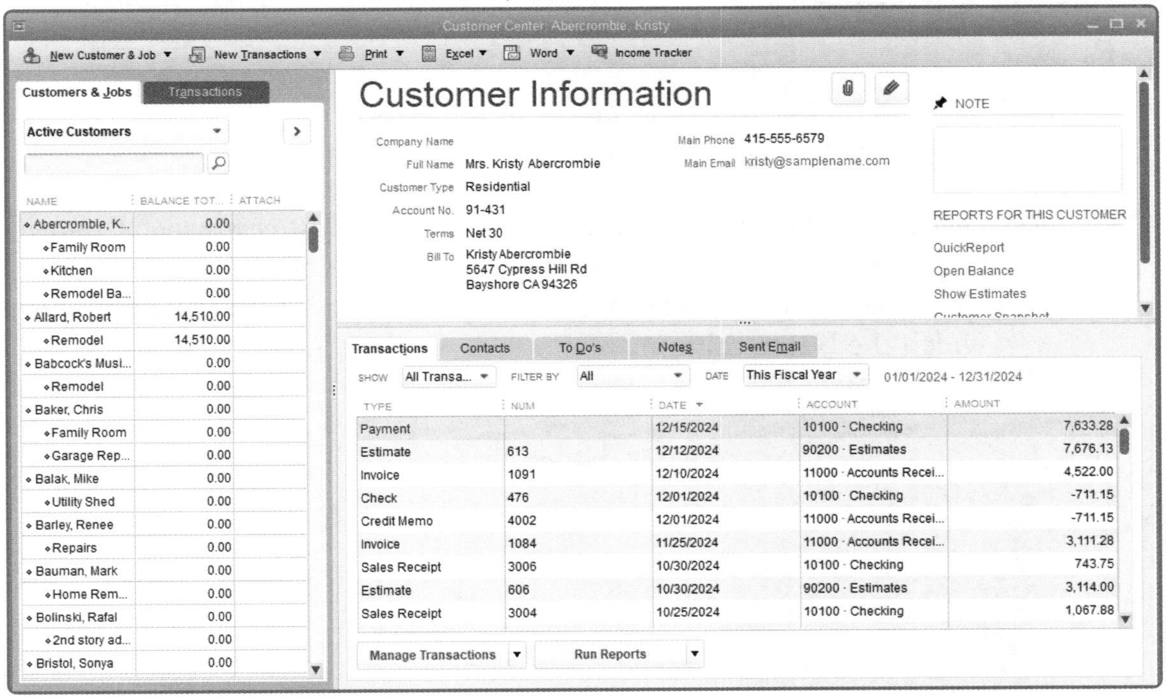

▷ *Click the arrow in the drop-down list box that is below the "Customers & Jobs" tab description, select Customers with Open Balances, then scroll and click once on Campbell, Heather. This shows only those accounts with open balances, partially shown below. The window shows all customers with open balances on the left side and shows Heather Campbell's information on the right side. Do not be concerned if the balances on your screen are shown in a different sort order.*

Customer Center Window → Customers & Jobs—Customers with Open Balances

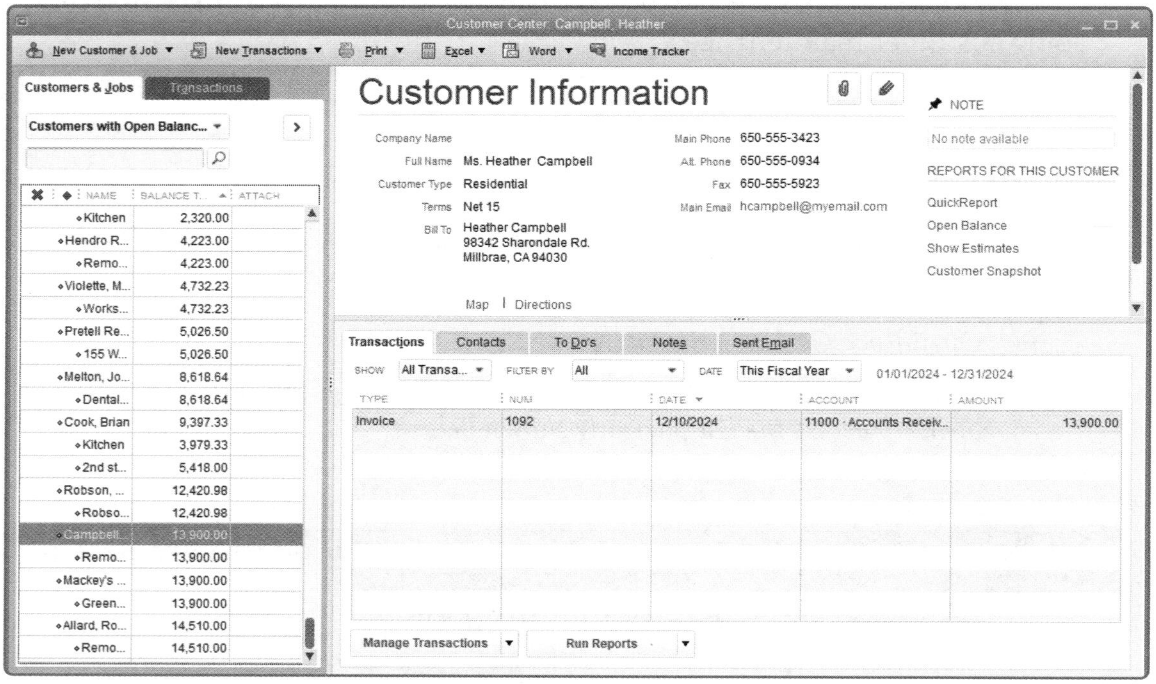

▷ *Double-click Campbell, Heather to open the Edit Customer window shown at the top of the following page.* If you cannot see her full name in the Customers & Jobs tab section of the previous window, you may have to widen the Name column.

Edit Customer Window—Address Info Tab

All of the information in the Edit Customer window was previously entered through maintenance. The top part of the window includes the customer name and the current balance. The Address Info tab is already open. Notice that the Company Name is blank for Campbell, Heather. It is common to have empty boxes in a window for the information that is not relevant to that customer. The information completed includes the customer name, invoice/bill to and ship to addresses, and several boxes for contact information.

▶ *Click the Additional Info tab.* Tabs are common in maintenance windows to permit including a considerable amount of information. The same window is edited, but the information in each tab differs (see top of next page). Notice how several boxes are complete in this tab but just as many are blank.

Edit Customer Window—Additional Info Tab

- ► *Click the drop-down list arrow next to the Customer Type box.* The customer in this case can be residential or commercial.
- ► *Click the drop-down list arrow next to the blank Rep box.* The only thing shown is <Add New>.
- ► *Click <Add New> to open the New Sales Rep window.* This permits the *QuickBooks* operator to add a sales representative at any time. Most drop-down list arrows in maintenance permit adding a new first item or another item to an existing list by including <Add New>.

New Sales Rep Window

- ► *Close the New Sales Rep window and click the Payment Settings tab.* See top of next page for any default information for Heather Campbell.

Edit Customer Window—Payment Settings Tab

- *Close the Edit Customer window for Campbell, Heather and reopen it. Observe that the default open tab is Address Info even though it was not the last open tab.*
- *Close the Edit Customer window for Campbell, Heather.*
- *Close the Customer Center window to return to the Home Page.*

Based on this discussion you should reach two conclusions:

1. A large amount of information can be entered into each type of maintenance window.
2. The information in the maintenance windows was originally entered through setup maintenance unless it was changed during editing.

Performing Maintenance For a New Account

Next, you will practice adding a new record, which is one of the three types of maintenance tasks listed earlier. For now you will only add a new customer record. You will do additional maintenance in Chapter 5.

When a company obtains a new customer, a new record must be created in *QuickBooks*. Sufficient information must be included when the new customer information is added to permit effective and efficient transaction processing and useful information for management. For example, if management wants to know the sales territory and sales rep for a given sale at some future time, that information needs to be entered during maintenance.

During this part of practice, you will add a new customer record for Rock Castle Construction, using the New Customer window.

▶ *Open Rock Castle Construction if it is not already open.*

▶ *Open the Customer Center.*

▶ *Add a new customer record for Wooden Nursery using the information in the box that follows and the instructions listed after the box, but do not save the new record until you are told to at the end of this section.* Not all boxes in the New Customer window and related tabs are applicable to Wooden Nursery.

■	**Customer Name:**	Wooden Nursery
■	**Opening Balance:**	0
■	**As of:**	8/16/2024

Address Info Tab

■	**Company Name:**	Wooden Nursery
■	**Main Phone:**	650-701-1000
■	**Main E-mail:**	wooden@woodennursery.com
■	**Website:**	www.woodennursery.com
■	**Fax:**	650-701-7254
■	**Invoice/Bill To:**	Wooden Nursery
		Fred Wooden
		561 Lancaster
		Holland, CA 94036
■	**Ship To:**	Same Address (Note: click on Copy → OK)

Payment Settings Tab

■	**Credit Limit:**	30,000.00
■	**Payment Terms:**	2% 10, Net 30
■	**Price Level:**	Commercial

Sales Tax Settings Tab

■	**Tax Code:**	Tax (Taxable Sales)
■	**Tax item:**	E. Bayshore/County (not East Bayshore option)

Additional Info Tab

■	**Customer Type:**	Commercial

▶ *Click the Home Page → Customers button.* The Customer Center displays the list of customers under the Customers & Jobs tab.

▶ *Click on the arrow next to the New Customer & Job button on the top of the window. Click New Customer to open the New Customer window.*

▶ *Complete all relevant boxes for the heading and the four tabs using the preceding information. Some boxes may not be applicable to the new customer.*

▶ *Review the contents of the New Customer window for completeness and accuracy.*

The diagram below and those on the following two pages show the completed New Customer windows, including the four tabs you completed for Wooden Nursery.

Completed New Customer Window—Address Info Tab

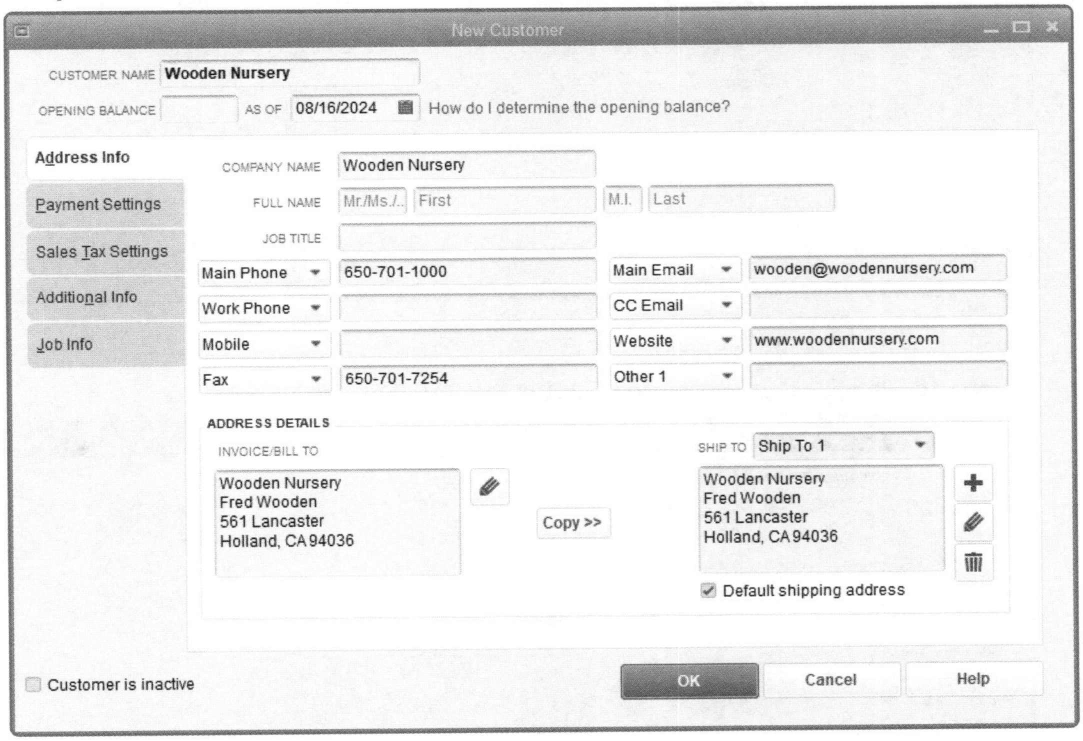

Completed New Customer Window—Payment Settings Tab

Completed New Customer Window—Sales Tax Settings Tab

Completed New Customer Window—Additional Info Tab

> ▶ *If your data entry windows are consistent with the preceding diagrams, click the OK button in the New Customer window to save the information. If there are errors, correct them before saving the record.*

Performing Maintenance To Delete an Account

When you delete any account in maintenance, the account is eliminated from *QuickBooks* permanently. You must therefore delete only accounts that are not likely to be used in the future.

Fortunately, *QuickBooks* has built-in controls to prevent users from deleting accounts that include financial data. For example, it would cause considerable difficulties if a customer with an account receivable balance was eliminated from the records. In that case, the customer would not be billed for the amount owed and the accounts receivable trial balance would not agree to the general ledger.

> ▶ *Click the Customers & Jobs tab in the Customer Center to display the list of customers, if they are not already displayed.* Observe that customer Ecker Designs on the list has a balance of $1,468.30. You may need to scroll to find Ecker Designs.

▶ *Right-click Office Repairs for Ecker Designs on the list of customers → Delete Customer: Job on the list of options provided to open the QuickBooks Message window below. QuickBooks identifies both the problem and a solution. Read that information.*

▶ *Click the Cancel button and the customer will not be deleted.* That is the approach that is followed in this project.

▶ *Select "All Customers" in the first drop-down list of the Customers & Jobs tab if not already selected.* Observe that Carr's Pie Shop on the list of customers has a zero balance outstanding.

▶ *Right-click the Remodel job under Carr's Pie Shop on the list of customers → Delete Customer: Job on the list of options provided to open the same QuickBooks Message as the preceding one.* Even though the balance is zero, *QuickBooks* will not permit the account to be deleted because it is used in at least one transaction this accounting period.

▶ *Click the Cancel button and the customer will not be deleted.* The account can be deleted at the beginning of the next year after the current year's accounts are closed.

▶ *Right-click Wooden Nursery on the list of customers → Delete Customer:Job on the list of options provided to open the Delete Customer:Job window.*

▶ *Click OK to delete the account.* Because you just created this customer record and there are no transactions for this customer, *QuickBooks* allows you to delete the customer record.

▶ *Examine the list of customers and attempt to locate Wooden Nursery.* It should no longer be on the list.

▶ *Close all windows and return to the Home Page.*

Processing Information Tasks

After an accountant is satisfied with maintenance for all five windows, information processing activities can begin. Additional maintenance, such as adding a new customer, can be and often is done during these activities.

Information processing activities are the most time-consuming part of any accounting system. For most companies, there are both a wide variety and a large volume of processing activities, usually done every day, but certainly every week and month. Although these activities are technically processing activities, it is easier to think of them as processing accounting transactions. For example, getting a customer order is not a sales transaction, but the purpose is to sell goods, which is a sales transaction. For the remainder of the book we refer to these activities as processing transactions.

Turn to the table of contents for Chapters 6 through 8 and observe that most of the topics involve processing transactions. You will begin processing transactions in this chapter, and then learn and practice all types of transactions included in this book in Chapters 6 through 8.

As an introduction to transaction processing, complete the following steps to process a sales transaction.

 ▶ *Open Rock Castle Construction if it is not already open.*
 ▶ *Click the Home Page → Create Invoices icon to open the Create Invoices window.*
 ▶ *Close the Create Invoices window.*

To learn an alternative method of opening the Create Invoices window, complete the following steps.

 ▶ *Click on the Customers button in the middle of the Home Page to open the Customer Center window → click on the drop-down list arrow next to New Transactions near the top of this window → select Invoices to open the same Create Invoices window as the preceding one. Note that the default customer for this invoice is the first customer in the list: Kristy Abercrombie.*
 ▶ *Delete Kristy Abercrombie from the Customer:Job box and then close the Create Invoices window.*

To learn a third method of opening the Create Invoices window, complete the following steps.

 ▶ *Click the Customers button on the Menu Bar to open a drop-down list → select Create Invoices to open the same Create Invoices window as the one shown previously.*

All three methods are equally acceptable and are applicable for opening most windows in *QuickBooks*. We will use the first method whenever a window can be accessed using an icon on the Home Page.

The Create Invoices window is now used to help you understand processing a sales transaction.

▶ *Select the Customers button from the middle of the Home Page → click the Customers & Jobs tab if not already open → click once on Remodel under Babcock's Music Shop to highlight that line → click the drop-down button next to New Transactions and select Invoices.*

▶ *Press [Tab] and observe that the cursor goes to Class.* Observe the large amount of information that has already been included as default information for Babcock's Music Shop. Assume you have no interest in Class or Print Preview and you are satisfied with the Rock Castle Invoice format in the next box.

▶ *Press [Tab] until you are in the DATE box → Change the date to 12/20/2024, using the Date button.* Observe that the TERMS are Net 15 and the DUE DATE was automatically changed to 01/04/2025.

▶ *Press [Tab] to reach the SHIP TO box and use the drop-down list to select Ship To 1.*

▶ *Press [Tab] until you enter the TERMS box and observe that the default terms are Net 15 and the DUE Date is now 15 days later than the invoice date you just entered. Change TERMS to Net 30.* Observe the automatic change in the DUE DATE.

▶ *Press [Tab] until your cursor is in the blank box under the ITEM heading. Select Light Pine under the Cabinets heading.* Observe that the unit cost of $1,799.00 is included in the RATE column and the total amount of $1,799.00 is included in the AMOUNT column. The San Tomas tax jurisdiction is included along with the tax rate of 7.75% and the tax amount. The total amount due is also included.

▶ *Press [Tab] until you enter the QUANTITY column, and type 4 for the quantity invoiced and press [Tab].* Observe that the amount changed as well as the tax and total.

▶ *Press [Tab] until the cursor is on the second row under the Item heading. Select Framing (Framing labor) from the drop-down list and type 8 to represent 8 hours in the Quantity box. In the Rate box select the commercial rate of $49.50.* Observe that much of the information in the window resulted from you having to make only a small number of data entries. The sources of most of the other default information are maintenance and the retrieval and calculation abilities of *QuickBooks*.

What is the increase in accounts receivable from Babcock's Music Shop for this transaction? It is $8,149.69, which is shown as the Balance Due at the bottom of the window. What is the accounting entry for the transaction? It includes a debit to accounts receivable of $8,149.69, a credit to sales tax payable of $557.69, and a credit to sales revenue for the difference. It also includes a debit to cost of goods sold and a credit to inventory for the cost of the four light pine kitchen cabinets. You will learn to access that information in the next chapter.

Do not save this transaction yet, but you can see by examining the buttons at the bottom of the window that it is easy to do so when you are ready to record the transaction.

Correcting a Transaction Before It Is Recorded

Transaction entry errors can be corrected by clicking the box containing the error and reentering the correct information.

▶ *Change the date to December 15, 2024.*

▶ *Change the first Item to Wood Door: Interior.*

▶ *Change the Quantity for the first item in the invoice window to 5.*

▶ *Change the Rate category in the second line to Industrial, with a rate of $46.75. The total amount of the sale at the bottom of the screen should now be $761.90.*

▶ *Click the Save & Close button to record the sales invoice and return to the Home Page and click Yes when asked if you want to change the default credit terms for this customer.*

Now you will determine if the transaction was included in the *QuickBooks* records.

▶ *Click the Customers button on the Home Page to go to the Customer Center. Click the Transactions tab, which is the tab next to the Customers & Jobs tab. If Invoices is not the highlighted item, make it so now. The top of the window now shows Customer Center: Invoices. Is the preceding sales transaction included? Yes, unless you made an error.*
Close the Customer Center: Invoices window.

Deleting or Voiding a Transaction

There is a difference between deleting and voiding transactions even though they have the same effect on all totals, including those on the financial statements. When you delete a transaction, all evidence of the transaction is eliminated from the records. When you void a transaction, *QuickBooks* retains the transaction information in the system, but records the amount as zero.

A *QuickBooks* user should void a transaction if it is impractical to prepare the same document again. This is common when a company uses pre-numbered documents and discovers an error after the document was printed, or if the document was mutilated or destroyed during the printing process. Good internal controls require that the sequence of all pre-numbered documents be accounted for in the relevant transactions journal. This is the reason for including the voided items as part of the audit trail. For example, assume the company prepared and printed pre-numbered payroll Check No. 864 to an employee but the recorded number of hours worked was incorrect or the printer jammed and destroyed the check in the printing process. In either case a new check will have to be prepared. The *QuickBooks* payroll preparer will void the original check, preserving the audit trail, and prepare a new one.

A *QuickBooks* user should delete a transaction if there is no need to preserve an audit trail. For example, if the transaction errors can be corrected before printing pre-numbered documents or if the documents are not pre-numbered, then the user can simply delete the current attempt and reenter the transaction. In the previous example, assume that internal controls require an independent review of the payroll preparation before the checks have been printed. Errors discovered during this process can be corrected using *QuickBooks*, and printed afterward. In the preceding example, if the error was caught before Check No. 864 was printed, the preparer can delete the transaction and prepare a new transaction for Check No. 864. Even in this case, it is equally acceptable to void the transaction and prepare a new one instead of deleting the transaction.

You will now practice both deleting and voiding transactions for Rock Castle Construction.

▶ *Open the Customer Center.* It should open to Customer Center: Invoices window. The Transactions tab and Invoices on the drop-down list will have been already selected because that was the setting when you last closed the Customer Center above.

▶ *Double-click Invoice No. 1093 for the Lew Plumbing sale on 12/12/2024 to open the Create Invoices for that transaction.*

▶ *Click the arrow beneath the Delete button to reveal two choices: Delete and Void → click Void.*

▶ *Click the Save & Close button at the bottom of the window, and click Yes when asked if you want to save your changes.*

▶ *Return to the Customer Center: Invoices and examine the line for Invoice No. 1093.* The customer name is still there, but it now has a zero invoice total.

▶ *Double-click the invoice number to open the invoice.* Observe that the invoice is now marked "Void" in the Memo box in the bottom-left corner of the window. This is the method used by *QuickBooks* to deal with voided transactions.

▶ *Close the Create Invoices window, returning to the Invoices List. Double-click Invoice No. 1089 for the Mike Violette sale on 12/05/2024 to open the Create Invoices window for that transaction.*

▶ *Click the arrow beneath the Delete button to reveal two choices: Delete and Void → click Delete.*

▶ *Click OK when the Delete Transaction window appears. Also click OK if a second window appears.*

▶ *Return to the Customer Center: Invoices and examine the line for Invoice No. 1089. The transaction is no longer there.* This is the method used by *QuickBooks* to deal with deleted transactions.

▶ *Close all windows to return to the Home Page.*

▶ *Click the Reports icon from the Icon Bar → Accountant & Taxes in the left column → double-click on the Voided/Deleted Transactions Summary report under Account Activity to open the report.* You can also use the Run button (green arrow) beneath the report to open it. Observe that both the Deleted and Voided transactions you just completed are included. This is a useful internal control.

▶ *Return to the Report Center → select Sales in the left column → double-click on the Sales by Customer Detail report (or click the Run button beneath the report) to open the report. Scroll down to Lew Plumbing and observe that the transaction is still included, but now with a zero invoice amount. Now scroll down the report and observe that invoice No. 1089 to Mike Violette is not included.* Again, you can see the difference between a voided and deleted transaction.

▶ *Close all windows to return to the Home Page.*

Quick Add

Assume the *QuickBooks* user is processing sales transactions for a day and one of them is a credit sale to a new customer. When the company expects additional transactions with the customer in the future, it is appropriate to follow the maintenance process that was shown earlier. The maintenance is likely to be done as a part of the transaction recording process. This is often called "maintenance on the fly."

If the company does not expect additional transactions with that customer, which is reasonably common, it is appropriate to include less information when doing the maintenance procedures than is normally followed. This is referred to as Quick Add, which is shown next. Assume that a one-time new customer, Abbot Nursery, is purchasing inventory for cash.

▶ *Click on Create Sales Receipts icon under Customers on the Home Page to open the Enter Sales Receipts window.* You will enter only the minimum information that permits you to practice Quick Add. Observe in the window before you enter anything that the only default information included is for the DATE, SALES NO., and Tax.

▶ *Type Abbot Nursery in the Customer: Job box → press [Tab] once to open the following window:*

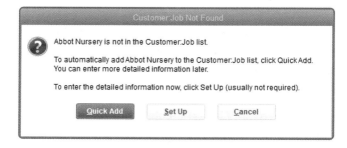

▶ *Click the Quick Add button. Now observe that the only additional information that was added was the name in SOLD TO.*

▶ *Change the date to 12/13/2024 → click the Check button → Type 16214 in the CHECK NO. box → press [Tab] until the ITEM box becomes highlighted.*

▶ *Select Wood Door: Exterior for the ITEM → Type 3 for the QTY.*

▶ *Using the Tax drop-down list arrow at the bottom of the window, select E. Bayshore/County (not the East Bayshore option). The Invoice Total should be $388.98.*

▶ *Click the Print button. The Information Changed window below appears.*

▶ *Click Yes.* Do not print the document, but return to the Enter Sales Receipts window and click Save & Close.

- *Click the Customers button on the Home Page → Customers & Jobs tab.* Is Abbot Nursery included on the list? Yes, and the customer information section of the window shows the cash sale of $388.98.
- *Click the Reports icon from the Icon Bar → select Sales → select Sales by Customer Detail.* Observe that the cash sale to Abbot Nursery was recorded.
- *Close the report, return to the Customers & Jobs tab of the Customer Center and double-click Abbot Nursery to open the Edit Customer window.* Observe that there is no information included other than the name. It is easy to add additional information to the record later if the customer becomes a repeat customer.

Maintenance on the fly is commonly done for all five of the categories of maintenance discussed in the first part of the chapter, but Quick Add usually applies only to customers and vendors. Why? Answer: It is common to encounter new customers, vendors, employees, inventory, and general ledger accounts while processing transactions, therefore Maintenance on the fly applies to all five categories. Information about all new employees, inventory items, and general ledger accounts is normally needed for at least the rest of the current accounting period. For one-time sales to customers and one-time purchases from vendors there is no need for continuing information; therefore, Quick Add only generally applies to these two.

Internal Controls

There are many internal controls included in the *QuickBooks* software to minimize the likelihood of errors and fraud. In this chapter, a few controls are introduced to help understand these internal controls.

Two important categories of controls are those applicable for processing transactions and those that restrict access to the software. The next section discusses controls applicable to processing transactions.

Controls Over Processing Transactions

QuickBooks includes many controls to minimize errors and reduce the time it takes to enter data. To keep the amount of time needed to complete the chapter reasonable, only a sample of processing controls is included. The controls discussed include: automatic entry controls, automatic calculation and posting controls, complete data controls, valid data controls, and exceeded limits controls.

Automatic Entry Controls

Automatic entry controls automatically enter information after receiving a cue from the person entering the data. These controls reduce data entry time and reduce the likelihood of data entry errors.

▶ *Open Rock Castle Construction if it is not already open. Open the Home Page and then open the Create Invoices window.*

▶ *Click the drop-down list arrow for Customer: Job and select Family Room for Chris Baker. Then in the ITEM box select Wood Door: Interior using the drop-down list arrow. Some information is automatically entered as a result of these two entries. The window below shows these.* Note that you may have a different document number on your window, depending on what you have done in the project so far. Ignore the document number.

Completed Create Invoices Window

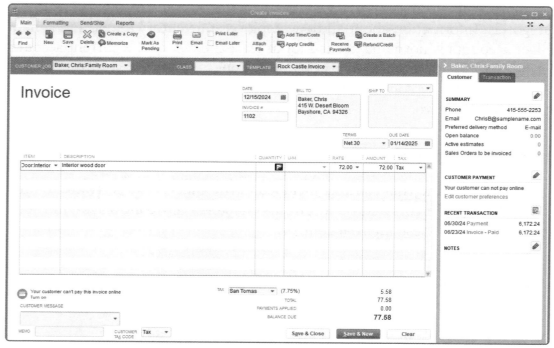

Almost every window in *QuickBooks* includes automatic entry controls. Keep the current window open.

Automatic Calculation and Posting Controls

Automatic calculation and posting controls automatically calculate or post information after the person entering data has entered other information or clicked certain buttons, usually Print or Save. These controls reduce the time required to process and record transactions, as well as decrease the likelihood of errors. An example of an automatic calculation control is the calculation of sales invoice information.

▶ *Using the Create Invoices for Family Room for Chris Baker in the previous steps, type 4 in the Quantity box and press [Tab].* Observe that several calculations are automatically made in the Create Invoices window. These are shown in the window that follows.

Create Invoices Window

▶ *Close the window and do not save the transaction.*

In addition to the calculations made in a transaction processing window, *QuickBooks* also automatically updates considerable other information when the transaction is saved. For example, for a sales transaction like the preceding one, the information updated includes the following: various sales listings, customer balance listing, aged receivables, general ledger trial balance, income statement, and balance sheet.

Automatic posting controls are used throughout *QuickBooks*. Transaction information is automatically posted to subsidiary records, the general ledger, and other records through the use of the Print and Save buttons in various windows after transaction information is entered. Internal controls are among the most important reasons companies use accounting software.

Complete Data Controls

Complete data controls inform the person entering data into the system that information needed to process the transaction has been omitted. When these controls are not met, the software provides an error message in the window informing the user that certain information is missing.

▶ *Click Create Invoices on the Home Page to open the Create Invoices window.*

▶ *Select Wood Door: Interior in the ITEM box using the drop-down list arrow, but leave the Customer: Job box blank. Type 4 in the Quantity box → click Save & Close. The following window appears. This is an example of complete data control.*

▶ *Click OK → close the Create Invoices window and do not save the transaction.*

Valid Data Controls

Valid data controls minimize the likelihood of entering incorrect data into the system. Similar to complete data controls, *QuickBooks* provides an error message or does not recognize the data when invalid data is entered into a window.

▶ *Click Create Invoices on the Home Page to open the Create Invoices window.*

▶ *Click the drop-down list arrow for Customer: Job and select Family Room for Chris Baker. Then in the ITEM box select Wood Door: Interior using the drop-down list arrow → type the letter h in the Quantity box → press [Tab]. The following window appears.*

This field is numeric and will not accept alphanumeric data.

▶ *Click OK and change the h to 3.*

▶ *While still in the Create Invoices window, change the date in the DATE box to 12/35/2024 → press [Tab]. The following window appears.*

> ▶ *Click OK* → *close the Create Invoices window and do not save the transaction.*

These are just two examples of valid data controls in *QuickBooks*.

Exceeded Limits Controls

Exceeded limits controls inform the person entering data that the transaction is not authorized due to such things as a sale exceeding a customer's credit limit or a sale when there is insufficient inventory on hand to fill the order. The following is an example of this control.

> ▶ *Click Create Invoices on the Home Page to open the Create Invoices window.*
>
> ▶ *Click the drop-down list arrow for Customer: Job and select Family Room for Chris Baker. Then in the ITEM box select Door Frame using the drop-down list arrow* → *type 30 under QUANT* → *press [Tab].* The following window appears.

<table>
<tr><td colspan="2">Not Enough Quantity</td></tr>
<tr><td colspan="2">You don't have sufficient quantity available to sell 30.00 of the item Door Frame</td></tr>
<tr><td>Quantity on hand</td><td>21</td></tr>
<tr><td>Quantity on other Sales Orders</td><td>0</td></tr>
<tr><td>Quantity Reserved for Assemblies</td><td>15</td></tr>
<tr><td>Quantity available</td><td>6</td></tr>
<tr><td colspan="2">OK</td></tr>
</table>

You will therefore need to reduce the units in the Quantity box to be equal to or less than the quantity on hand.

▶ *Click OK → close the Create Invoices window and do not save the transaction.*

Password Control

An important internal control in computer systems is limiting who has access to the software. Restricting access reduces the likelihood of both errors and fraud. *QuickBooks* permits restricting access to the software by the use of a password. After a password is initially set up in *QuickBooks*, the software can be accessed only by entering the password whenever *QuickBooks* is opened.

Chapter Summary

After completing Chapter 3, you have now learned:

- ✔ an overview of maintenance activities.
- ✔ how to process data and correct data entry.
- ✔ some of the internal control features available in the software.

You should now save your work by making periodic backups of Rock Castle Construction and Larry's Landscaping & Garden Supply using the instructions in the E-Materials you downloaded from the Armond Dalton Resources website. Be sure to use descriptive file names, such as "Rock Castle after Ch 3" or something similar.

Before starting the homework for Chapter 3, you should restore both Rock Castle Construction and Larry's Landscaping & Garden Supply using the initial backups you downloaded from the Armond Dalton Resources website. Restore both companies before proceeding to the Chapter 3 homework assigned by your instructor, which is available on the Armond Dalton Resources website at www.armonddaltonresources.com.

If you cannot recall how to make a periodic backup or restore a backup, refer to the E-Materials located at www.armonddaltonresources.com.

OBTAINING INFORMATION FROM *QUICKBOOKS*, INCLUDING REPORTS

4
Chapter

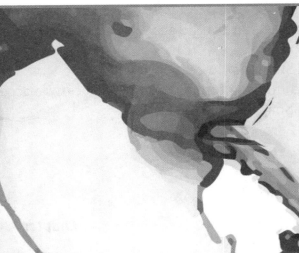

Introduction

The maintenance and processing information tasks that were discussed in Chapters 2 and 3 are the inputs into *QuickBooks* that create several outputs. These include such things as sales invoices, checks, updated master files, and lists of transactions. A considerable amount of these outputs are relevant and needed by management and other users to make business decisions. This chapter provides an overview of ways this information can be obtained from *QuickBooks*, including how to access transactions and other data to correct errors or make changes in the data. Following is a repetition of Chapter 3 of the two categories of obtaining information:

1. **Obtaining Information**—Used to obtain a wide variety of information in *QuickBooks* that has already been entered through maintenance and processing information. Examples are a list of all customers and all sales transactions for a month. *QuickBooks* permits using alternative methods to access this information.
2. **Reports**—Used to view and print a wide variety of reports such as an aged trial balance and a comparative income statement.

Obtaining Information

A typical company's accounting information in *QuickBooks* includes a wide variety of data that can be easily accessed. There are several alternative ways to access the information, depending on personal preference and the type of information you want to access. The four main ways are:

1. **Maintenance**—Accessed starting from the Home Page, then through the various centers such as the Vendor Center. Maintenance is used primarily to obtain information about master files including customers, vendors, employees, inventory, and the chart of accounts. You were introduced to using maintenance to obtain information about customers earlier in Chapter 3. This will be covered in greater detail in Chapter 5.
2. **Lists**—Accessed through Lists in the Menu Bar. Lists includes several category titles that can be accessed to obtain a wide variety of information.
3. **Company Snapshot Accessed through the Icon Bar**—A wide variety of detailed information and summaries can be accessed through the Company Snapshot button.

4. **Drill Down**—Accessed by double-clicking on lines in a large number of lists and other records. Users can access detailed information about transactions and other records by using the drill-down feature.

You have already practiced obtaining information using Maintenance in Chapter 3. The other three methods are covered in this chapter.

Lists

Customers, vendors, employees, and management often want information about recorded transactions or balances and need to determine whether information has been recorded correctly. Lists, such as a list of customers, are one way to get that information. These lists for vendors, customers, and employees and their related transactions are accessed through Centers. Because chart of accounts and inventory items do not have related transactions lists, they are accessed directly from the Home Page. First we deal with Centers.

Centers can be accessed either from the buttons in the center of the Home Page or from the Icon Bar.

▶ *Open Rock Castle Construction if it is not already open.*

▶ *Click the Vendors icon on the Icon Bar to open the Vendor Center.*

▶ *If it is not already the default tab, click the Vendors tab to open a list of Rock Castle's vendors, including account balances. Your screen should look similar to the following illustration.*

Vendor Center: A Cheung Limited

New Vendor... ▼ | New Transactions ▼ | Print ▼ | Excel ▼ | Word ▼ | Bill Tracker

Vendors | Transactions

Active Vendors

NAME	BALANCE TOT	ATTACH
A Cheung Limited	0.00	
Bank of Anycity	0.00	
Bayshore CalOil ...	0.00	
Bayshore Water	0.00	
Bruce's Office Ma...	0.00	
C.U. Electric	750.00	
Cal Gas & Electric	122.68	
Cal Telephone	91.94	
CalOil Company	0.00	
City of Bayshore	0.00	
City of East Bays...	1.37	
City of Middlefield	0.00	
Custom Kitchen...	0.00	
Daigle Lighting	1,591.00	
Davis Business ...	0.00	
Dianne's Auto Sh...	0.00	
East Bayshore A...	0.00	
East Bayshore T...	0.00	
Employment Dev...	0.00	
Express Delivery ...	0.00	
Fay, Maureen Lyn...	0.00	
Federal Treasury	0.00	
Funds Transfer	0.00	
Gallion Masonry	0.00	
Great Statewide ...	0.00	

Vendor Information

Company Name: A Cheung Limited
Full Name: Ms. Angela Cheung
Billed From: A Cheung Limited
Angela Cheung
3818 Bear Rd. West
Berkeley, CA 94688

Map | Directions

Main Phone: 510 555 5723
Fax: 510 555 5733
Main Email: AC@CheungLimited.com

NOTE

REPORTS FOR THIS VENDOR
QuickReport
Open Balance

Order 1099 Forms
Order Checks

Transactions | Contacts | To Do's | Notes | Sent Email

SHOW: All Transactions | FILTER BY: All | DATE: This Fiscal Year | 01/01/2024 - 12/31/2024

TYPE	NUM	DATE	ACCOUNT	AMOUNT
Purchase Order	6237	12/15/2024	90100 · Purchase Orders	-3,500.00
Bill Pmt -Check	267	02/28/2024	10100 · Checking	-2,000.00
Bill		01/31/2024	20000 · Accounts Payable	-2,000.00
Bill Pmt -Check	248	01/31/2024	10100 · Checking	-3,500.00
Bill		01/20/2024	20000 · Accounts Payable	-2,000.00
Bill		01/02/2024	20000 · Accounts Payable	-1,500.00

Manage Transactions ▼ | Run Reports ▼

▶ *Click the Transactions tab to open a list of options shown in the following window.*

Vendor Center: Purchase Orders

New Vendor... | New Transactions ▼ | Print | View Vendor Info | Export...

Vendors | Transactions

- Purchase Orders
- Item Receipts
- Bills
- Bill Payments
- Checks
- Credit Card Activities
- Sales Tax Payments

FILTER BY: All Purchase Orders | DATE: All

VENDOR	NUM	DATE	DELIVERY DATE	AMOUNT
A Cheung Limited	6237	12/15/2024	12/15/2024	3,500.00
Custom Kitchens of Bayshore	6201	01/04/2024	01/04/2024	435.00
Daigle Lighting	6236	12/15/2024	12/15/2024	65.00
Daigle Lighting	6229	12/01/2024	12/01/2024	571.32
Daigle Lighting	6232	12/07/2024	12/07/2024	163.25
Larson Flooring	6213	10/06/2024	10/06/2024	6,400.00
Larson Flooring	6231	12/03/2024	12/03/2024	4,750.00
Larson Flooring	6230	12/01/2024	12/01/2024	341.20
Lew Plumbing	6235	12/12/2024	12/12/2024	403.40
McClain Appliances	6210	10/01/2024	10/01/2024	2,100.00
McClain Appliances	6211	10/01/2024	10/01/2024	1,780.00
McClain Appliances	6208	08/11/2024	08/11/2024	380.50
McClain Appliances	6205	07/14/2024	07/14/2024	3,690.00
McClain Appliances	6216	10/17/2024	10/17/2024	3,065.00
Patton Hardware Supplies	6228	11/30/2024	11/30/2024	3,459.20
Patton Hardware Supplies	6207	07/23/2024	07/23/2024	754.50
Patton Hardware Supplies	6225	11/26/2024	11/26/2024	13,695.00
Perry Windows & Doors	6212	10/05/2024	10/05/2024	1,800.00
Perry Windows & Doors	6220	10/24/2024	10/24/2024	810.00
Perry Windows & Doors	6221	11/18/2024	11/18/2024	7,820.00
Perry Windows & Doors	6222	11/18/2024	11/18/2024	2,325.00
Perry Windows & Doors	6223	11/26/2024	11/26/2024	50.00
Perry Windows & Doors	6219	10/22/2024	10/22/2024	3,530.00
Perry Windows & Doors	6100	07/15/2023	07/15/2023	144.75
Perry Windows & Doors	6218	10/17/2024	10/17/2024	180.75
Perry Windows & Doors	6227	11/28/2024	11/28/2024	2,400.00

Manage Transactions ▼ | Run Reports ▼

▶ *Close all windows to return to the Home Page.*

▶ *Click the Vendors button on the Home Page to open the Vendor Center → click the Vendors tab to open a list of all vendors, including account balances.*

▶ *Click the Transactions tab to open a list of options that are identical to the preceding window.* These few steps show that either approach works. The same is true for customers and employees. The chapters in this book typically start with the Home Page, but either approach for accessing the Center is acceptable.

▶ *Click Bills in the list of options shown in the Transactions tab. Observe that the top of the window now includes Vendor Center: Bills.* This same type of information is provided for all options for the three centers.

The vendor bills listing to the right of the options includes all recorded purchase transactions for a selected period. The information can be shown in a variety of ways.

It is often useful to reorder the information in a window to make it easier to view and analyze. Any list can be sorted on any column heading, reordering it either alphabetically, numerically, or by date. It is done by clicking the column heading for the column you want sorted. *QuickBooks* sorts the list on the column you click without changing the details of any record. It is similar to the Sort command in Excel, except that it is done automatically by *QuickBooks* after you click the column heading. Clicking the column heading a second time reverses the ascending or descending order of the sort that was just done.

▶ *Click the Open Balance heading at the top of the Open Balance column.* Observe how the Bills List is sorted by the amount of the account balance with the order of the list changing to ascending order from the smallest amount due to the largest amount due. (You may need to scroll the list to see this.)

▶ *Click the Open Balance heading again.* Observe how the order of the list reverses to descending order from the largest amount due to the smallest amount due.

▶ *Click once and then again on each of the other column headings and observe the change in the order of the list for that column.*

▶ *Click the drop-down list arrow in the Filter By box near the top of the Vendor Center: Bills window → click Open Bills to list only the vendors that are still owed money. Then click All Bills on the drop-down list and observe that there are more items listed.* Similar information is also available for customer transactions and employee transactions.

▶ *Click the drop-down list arrow in the Date box near the top of the Vendor Center: Bills window.* Observe that there are many date options available for users to select.

▶ *Click successively on two or three of the options and observe how the lists change.* These date options are also available for both customer and employee transactions.

Hiding Information From View

Lists windows contain considerable information that can be hidden from view. This is done to avoid excessive information being displayed in the window. Deleting a column has no effect on the *QuickBooks* data and any column in the window can be added back to the list at any time.

▶ *Return to the Home Page and open the Customer Center: Invoices list, using the method you just learned for opening Vendor Center: Invoices.*

▶ *Click View in the Menu Bar → select Customize Transaction List Columns on the drop-down list of options to show the following Customize Columns window.*

The Chosen Columns box includes the columns currently included in the Customer Center: Invoices window in the order they are in the window, from left to right. The Available Columns box list includes all other columns that can be added to the window.

▶ *Click Terms in the Available Columns box list to highlight that item and then click the Add button (Add >) in the center of the window to add it to the bottom of the Chosen Columns box.* Note that you can also double-click on an item to add it to the Chosen Columns list.

▶ *Click Aging in the Chosen Columns list to highlight that item and then click the Remove button (< Remove) in the center of the window. Click OK to accept and* *save the two changes you made.* Doing so closes the Customize Columns window. The Customer Center: Invoices window now includes the changes that you made.

> You can change the width of columns in the window in the same way that you do in Excel. Move the cursor to the line next to column name until it turns into a cross and move the column to the width you want. Double-clicking on the line adjusts the size automatically.

▶ *Click View in the Menu Bar → select Customize Transaction List Columns on the drop-down list again → click Default and click OK.* The two changes you just made are removed and the settings are now returned to the default settings.

▶ *Open the Customize Columns list window again (View → Customize Transaction List Columns) and then click any item in Chosen Columns. Click Remove repeatedly.* When you try deleting the last item, you should get the following message:

> "This column can't be removed because it's currently the only column displayed."

▶ *Click OK, and then click the Default button to return the columns to the original settings.*

It is also possible to change the order of the columns in a Lists window by using the Move Up (Move Up) and Move Down (Move Down) buttons.

▶ *In the Customize Columns window, select Customer under Chosen Columns. Click the Move Down button five times to move Customer to the next to the last item. Select Amount and then click the Move Up button four times to move it to the top of the list.*

▶ *To practice using Customize Columns, add, remove, and reorder items until you have only the following items included in the Chosen Columns list, from top to bottom: Customer, Type, Terms, Amount, and Open Balance.*

▶ *Click OK to see the resulting Customer Center: Invoices list. Are they in the correct order?* If not, return to the Customize Columns window and make the necessary changes.

▶ *Open the Customize Columns window again → click Default and click OK.* The settings are now returned to the default settings.

Lists are equally useful for both Chart of Accounts and Items & Services (Inventory), but these two are opened directly from the Home Page with one available list for each.

▶ *Return to the Home Page and click the Items & Services icon in the Company section of the Home Page to open the Item List.*

▶ *Click View on the Menu Bar → click Customize Columns → scroll down the Available Columns list and observe the large number of options that are available for inventory items for customization.*

To summarize, the List function is one of the most valuable sources of information in *QuickBooks*. You have already seen the large number of lists available and how there are different ways to access lists. You have also seen how you can change the order of the data in a list by clicking on a column heading. One characteristic of the List function is the ability to add and delete columns from lists. It is the only source of information in *QuickBooks* that includes this feature.

Exporting to Excel

You have already learned in the last section dealing with Lists that you can sort information in Lists windows to provide the information in different formats. You also learned that you can add, delete, or change the order of columns in a Lists window. *QuickBooks*, however, does not permit removing from view individual or certain types of transactions, such as say those under $50.

Exporting to Excel is useful to further analyze, delete, or rearrange information and to prepare reports of the revised information. Exporting information is easy and can be done with almost all *QuickBooks* data, including data in Reports, Maintenance, and Lists. You will now learn how to export to Excel.

▶ *If not open already, reopen the Customer Center: Invoices window for Rock Castle Construction (click Customers → Transactions tab → Invoices).*

▶ *Use the Customize Columns window to include only the following columns in the order listed: Amount, Customer, and Date.*

▶ *Select All Invoices in the Filter By box and then select This Fiscal Year-to-date in the Date box.*

▶ *Click the Export icon (Export...) at the top of the Customer Center: Invoices window to open the Export window shown on the following page.*

> *The default selection is typically "Create new worksheet." If the default is not as shown in the preceding window, make sure that the "Create new worksheet" radio button is selected.*

> *Click Export. All data in the Customer Center: Invoices window is sent to an Excel worksheet, which will be displayed on your computer screen. If it is not displayed, click the Excel icon on the bottom of your screen.*

> *Change the data on the Excel worksheet in the following ways:*
>   - *Arrange the amounts in descending order.*
>   - *Delete all accounts with a balance of less than $7,000.00.*
>   - *Type a new header including the following three lines: Rock Castle Construction, Customer Invoice List, and 10/01/24 to 12/15/24.*
>   - *Bold the new header and all column headings.*
>   - *Total the amount column.*

The report on your screen should look similar to the following report. Note that the illustration includes just the bottom portion of the spreadsheet. Do not be concerned if your report has slightly different balances.

> *Close Excel without saving the file.*

Rock Castle Construction		
Customer Invoice List		
10/01/24 to 12/15/24		
Amount	**Customer**	**Date**
15,435.00	Pretell Real Estate:155 Wilks Blvd.	11/20/2024
14,085.30	Cook, Brian:2nd story addition	10/30/2024
13,900.00	Mackey's Nursery and Garden Supply:Greenho	10/20/2024
13,900.00	Campbell, Heather:Remodel	12/10/2024
12,754.14	Melton, Johnny:Dental office	11/20/2024
12,420.98	Robson, Darci:Robson Clinic	12/15/2024
8,656.25	Natiello, Ernesto:Kitchen	12/14/2024
8,305.95	Teschner, Anton:Sun Room	11/28/2024
7,764.78	Teichman, Tim:Kitchen	10/15/2024
107,222.40		

Company Snapshot

Company Snapshot provides access to much of the same information that is available in the various centers.

> ▶ *Open Rock Castle Construction to the Home Page. Click Company from the Menu Bar and then click Company Snapshot to access the following window. Do not be concerned if your window contents differ slightly.*

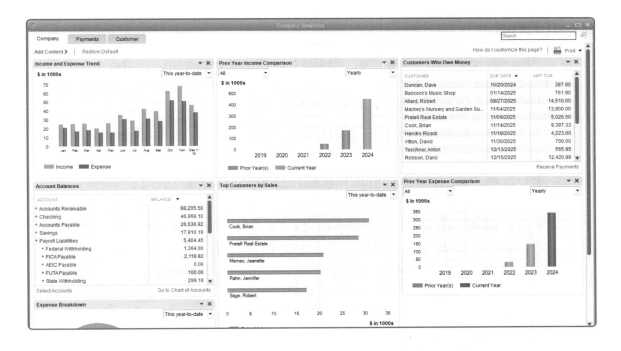

Observe on the Company Snapshot window that there are many sections of data. You may have to maximize the window and scroll down to see all of the available areas. This same information is available elsewhere by accessing information from the Home Page, for example:

- **Account Balances** — Available using the Chart of Accounts icon.
- **Customers Who Owe Money** — Available using the Customer Center: Invoices window (Customers icon → Transactions tab → Invoices).

The Income and Expense Trend graph and the remaining portion of the window are helpful to some users but are not used in these materials. As a result, the Company Snapshot window is not essential and is therefore not used in these materials.

▶ *Click View in the Menu Bar – Customize Icon Bar → select Snapshots on the list under the Icon Bar Content → click Delete and click OK to remove the Snapshots icon from the Icon Bar.* Assuming you deleted the icon, it should now be gone.

▶ *Close the Company Snapshot window.*

> It is acceptable to leave any icon on the Icon Bar or remove it if it is not used. The default settings on the Icon Bar are established by *QuickBooks* and are set for each company. Therefore, if you want one or more icons removed from the Icon Bar for all companies, you must do so separately for each company.

Drill Down

The drill-down feature is used to obtain additional information about a transaction, account, or other data in a list or report. Following are just a few of many possible examples of the *QuickBooks'* drill-down feature.

  ▶ *Open the Home Page for Rock Castle Construction if it is not already open.*

  ▶ *Open the Customer Center: Invoices list window if it is not already open.*

  ▶ *If the layout of the window is not the default layout, use the View → Customize Transaction List Columns method to restore the default settings.*

  ▶ *Click the Customer heading at the top of the Customer column to put them in alphabetical order if they are not already in that order.*

  ▶ *Click once on Invoice No. 1069 for customer Jacobsen, Doug:Kitchen.* You may need to expand the number column to find that invoice.

Observe that the entire row of data for the transaction is now highlighted.

  ▶ *Click once on other rows under any of the column headings and observe that it doesn't matter where you click the row, the entire row becomes highlighted.*

  ▶ *Double-click the line for Invoice No. 1069 for Jacobsen, Doug:Kitchen, opening the Create Invoices window.* The window shown is the invoice that was prepared when the customer was billed October 23, 2024.

If Jacobsen or management wants information about the invoice, it is easy for the accountant at Rock Castle Construction to provide the information by starting with the Customer Center: Invoices and drilling down to the sales invoice of interest.

▶ *Close the Create Invoices window and the Customer Center: Invoices window to return to the Home Page.*

▶ *Click the Items & Services icon to open the Item List window.*

▶ *Double-click Cabinets: Light Pine (Light pine kitchen cabinet wall unit in the Description column) to open the Edit Item window for that inventory item. Like for sales transactions, QuickBooks can provide useful information for management or outsiders. This same drill-down approach is applicable to all QuickBooks lists.*

▶ *Close all windows except the Home Page.*

▶ *Click the Reports icon and then click the Sales selection to open the Report Center window shown on the following page.*

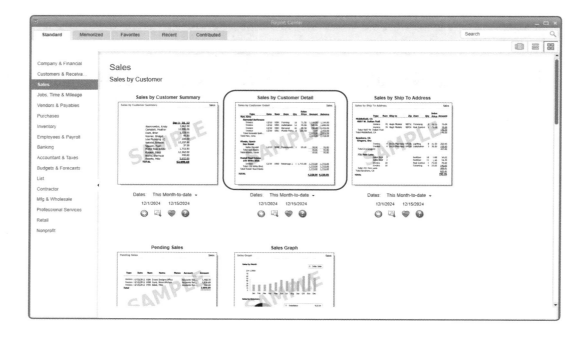

▶ *Double-click Sales by Customer Detail (circled) to open the Sales by Customer Detail window. Select This Fiscal Year-to-date in the Dates' drop-down list. Do not be concerned if your report contains slightly different amounts.*

Type	Date	Num	Memo	Name	Item	Qty	U/M	Sales Price	Amount	Balance
Abbot Nursery										
Sales Receipt	12/13/2024	3009	Exterior woo...	Abbot Nursery	Wood D...	3		120.00	360.00	360.00
Total Abbot Nursery						3			360.00	360.00
Abercrombie, Kristy										
Family Room										
Invoice	06/07/2024	1043	Exterior woo...	Abercrombie, Kris...	Wood D...	6		119.96667	719.80	719.80
Invoice	06/07/2024	1043	Enter a Desc...	Abercrombie, Kris...	Deposit	1		517.20	517.20	1,237.00
Invoice	06/07/2024	1044	Exterior woo...	Abercrombie, Kris...	Wood D...	4		120.00	480.00	1,717.00
Invoice	06/07/2024	1044	Deposit App...	Abercrombie, Kris...	Deposit	1		-517.20	-517.20	1,199.80
Sales Receipt	10/25/2024	3004	Removal lab...	Abercrombie, Kris...	Remova...	6.5		35.00	227.50	1,427.30
Sales Receipt	10/25/2024	3004	Installation la...	Abercrombie, Kris...	Installati...	4		35.00	140.00	1,567.30
Sales Receipt	10/25/2024	3004	Decking lum...	Abercrombie, Kris...	Lumber:...	1		650.00	650.00	2,217.30
Sales Receipt	10/30/2024	3006	Removal labor	Abercrombie, Kris...	Remova...	4.75		35.00	166.25	2,383.55
Sales Receipt	10/30/2024	3006	Repair work	Abercrombie, Kris...	Repairs...	16.5		35.00	577.50	2,961.05
Total Family Room						44.75			2,961.05	2,961.05
Kitchen										
Invoice	02/01/2024	1024	Removal labor	Abercrombie, Kris...	Remova...	16		35.00	560.00	560.00
Invoice	02/01/2024	1024	Electrical wo...	Abercrombie, Kris...	Subs:Ele...	4		57.75	231.00	791.00
Invoice	02/01/2024	1024	Plumbing	Abercrombie, Kris...	Subs:Plu...	8		52.50	420.00	1,211.00
Invoice	02/01/2024	1024	Install tile or ...	Abercrombie, Kris...	Subs:Til...	12		42.00	504.00	1,715.00
Invoice	02/01/2024	1024	Painting	Abercrombie, Kris...	Subs:Pa...	4		36.75	147.00	1,862.00
Invoice	02/01/2024	1024	Dishwasher	Abercrombie, Kris...	Appliance	1		430.00	430.00	2,292.00

- ▶ *Scroll down to Jacobsen, Doug:Kitchen and observe that there are several lines with the number 1069. Move your cursor over any portion of any of the invoices. Observe that a magnifying glass with a Z in the center appears. This has the same effect as the highlight you used above.*

- ▶ *Double-click any line on the Jacobsen, Doug:Kitchen entries to open the same Create Invoices window that you opened earlier.*

- ▶ *Close the Create Invoices and the Sales by Customer Detail window to return to the Report Center window.*

- ▶ *Click Accountant & Taxes on the left column → double-click General Ledger to open the General Ledger window → select This Fiscal Year-to-date in the Dates drop-down list → scroll to account 40130, Labor Income, and double-click Num 1069. You will open sales invoice 1069 for Jacobsen, Doug:Kitchen.*

- ▶ *Close all windows to return to the Home Page.*

- ▶ *Return to the Customer Center and open the Received Payments list in the Transactions tab.*

- ▶ *Double-click Check No. 9384 from Aaron Davies to open the Receive Payments window shown below.*

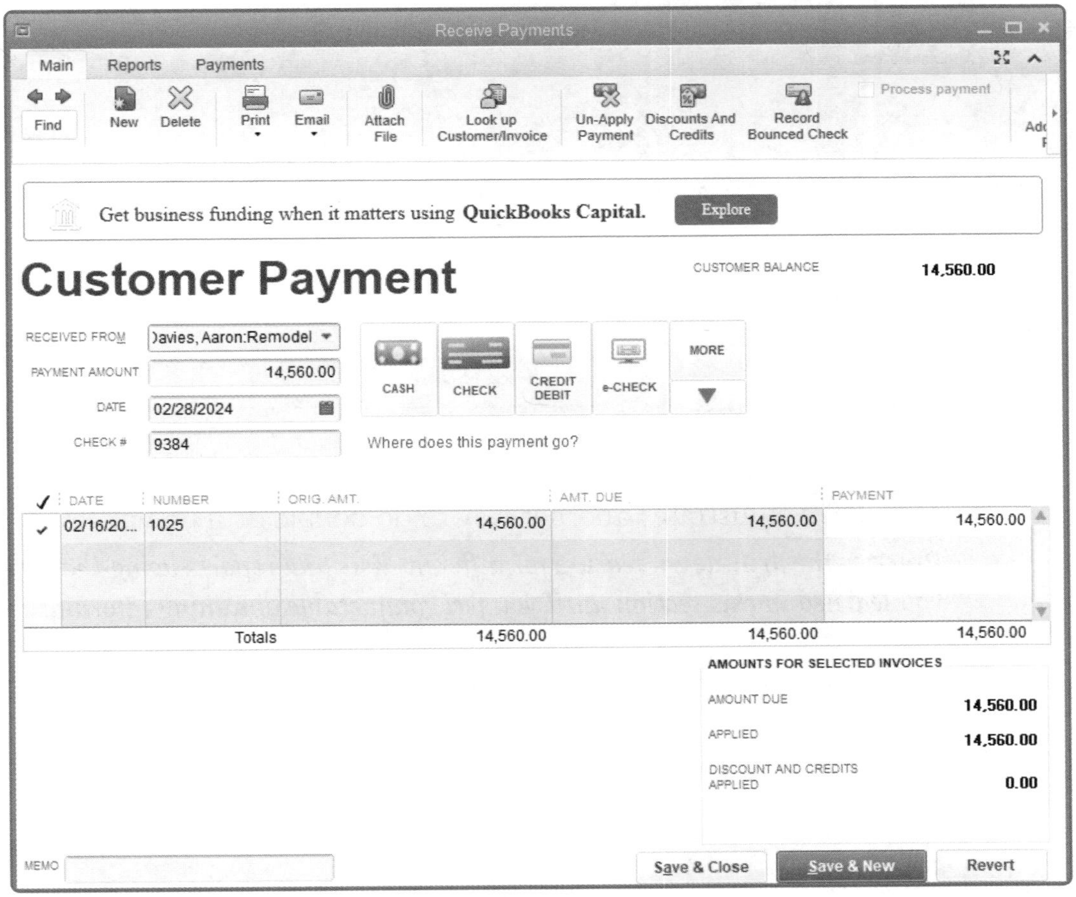

▶ *Double-click anywhere on the line that includes the amount of the payment. This opens the customer invoice that resulted in the payment on Check No. 9384. This an example of a double drill down, a highly useful feature in QuickBooks.*

▶ *Close all windows to return to the Home Page.*

▶ *Click the Employees button to open the Employee Center window → select the Transactions tab and select Paychecks from the list.*

▶ *Double-click Check No. 10073 to Dan T. Miller to open the Paycheck – Checking window shown below.*

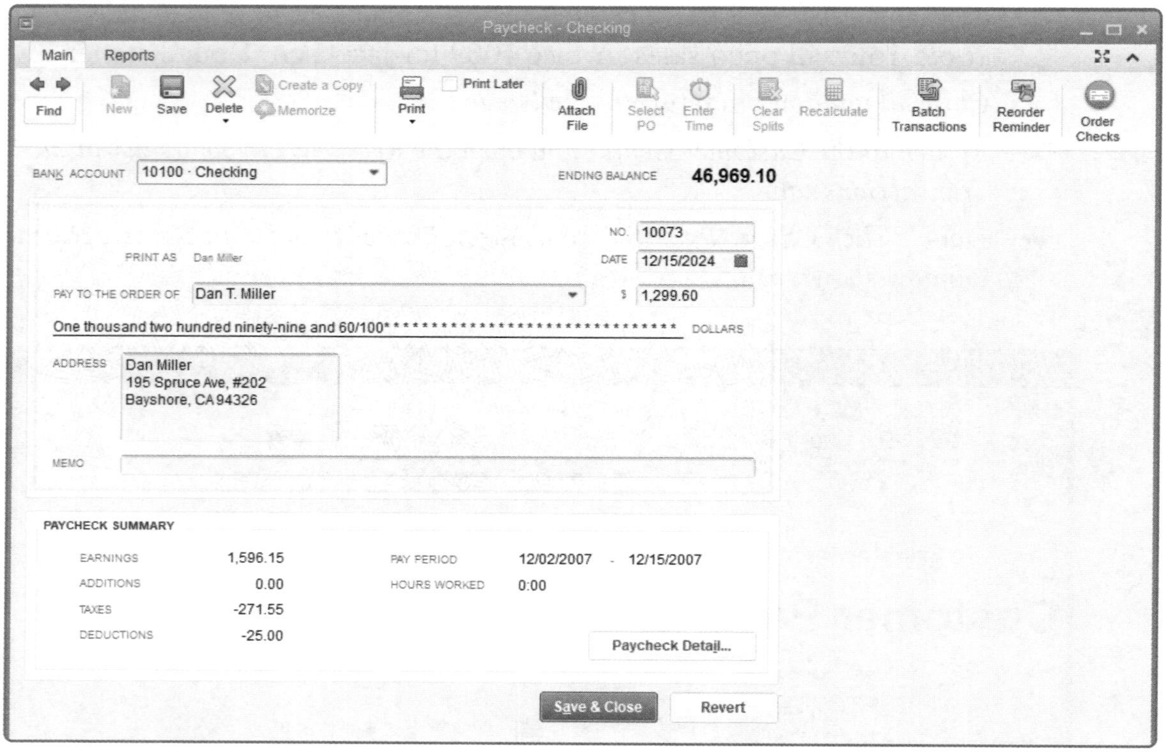

▶ *Click the Paycheck Detail button to open the Review Paycheck window for Dan Miller.* This illustrates another way to do double drill down.

▶ *Practice the drill-down feature for different lists and reports using the methods you learned in this section until you feel comfortable obtaining information this way.*

Custom Transaction Detail Reports

QuickBooks has a unique feature that enables users to obtain a wide variety of detailed information about transactions in a company's database. This section provides practice obtaining that information.

▶ *Make sure Rock Castle Construction is open. Click Reports on the Menu Bar (not the Reports icon) → Custom Reports → Transaction Detail → select This Fiscal Quarter in the Dates box to open the window shown below.*

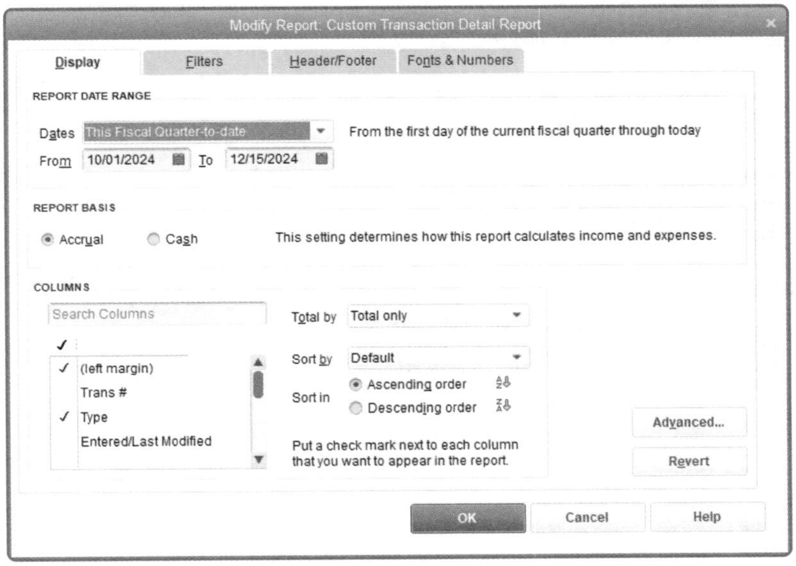

▶ *Click the Filters tab to open the window that appears below.*

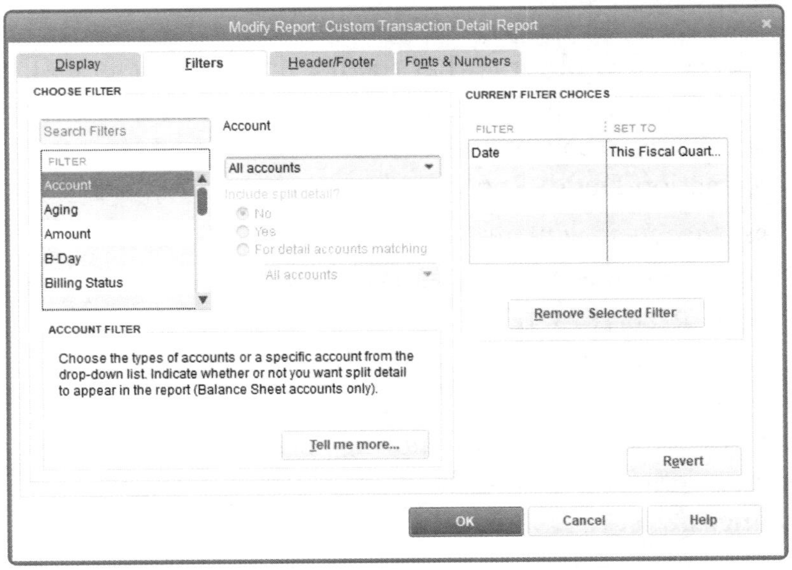

Account is highlighted in the Filter box and All accounts is shown in the Account filter box.

▶ *Scroll down the Account drop-down list and observe the large number of options available. Click All current assets and the window now appears as shown below.*

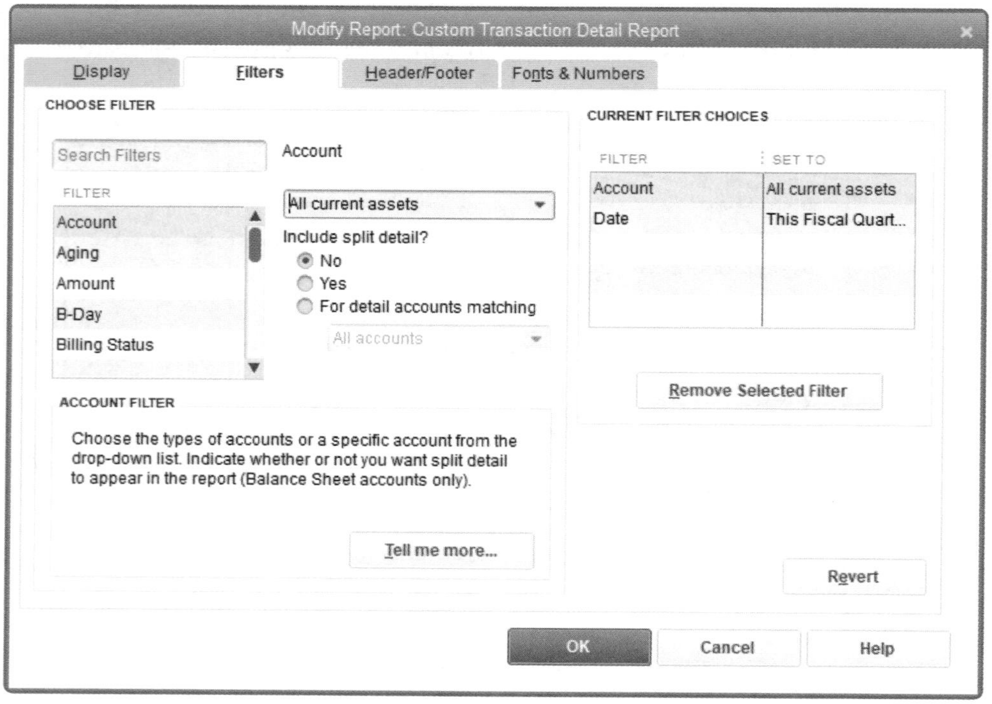

Notice that the window under Current Filter Choices now includes both the account you selected and also the date you selected earlier.

▶ *Click OK.* Now observe that the list does not include all current assets for the period, but all transactions for the period that affected any current assets. This is consistent with the title of the Menu Bar item — Custom Transaction Detail Report.

▶ *Close the report window.*

▶ *Open the Custom Transaction Detail Report again (Reports menu item → Custom Reports → Transaction Detail), but set the Dates to Last week → click the Filters tab → scroll down the list in the Filter box and again see the large number of options available → click Amount in the Choose Filter box to open the window shown on the following page. Amount now appears directly to the right of the Filter box and the information in the window also changes.*

Modify Report: Custom Transaction Detail Report

> Click the radio button circled in red in the preceding window illustration and
> type 2000 in the box to the right → press the Tab key. Click Transaction
> Type in the Choose Filter box and select Invoice under Transaction Type. Your
> window should now look like the one below.

Modify Report: Custom Transaction Detail Report

Examine the Current Filter Choices box and observe that you will be filtering for three things. (You can remove any of those filter choices by highlighting the line and clicking the Remove Select Filter button, but do not do that.)

▷ *Click OK.* The result should look like the window below. Using this feature allows you to obtain a large amount of information about transactions.

▷ *Close the report and then open the Modify Report: Custom Transaction Detail Report window again (Reports menu → Custom Reports → Transaction Detail) and leave the Dates as This Month-to-date and again click the Filters tab → select Transaction Type in the Choose Filter box and Journal on the Transaction Type drop-down list → click OK.* There should be no transactions in the window.

▷ *Do not close the report, but change the setting to This Fiscal Year in the Dates box at the top of the report.* The list of journal transactions now includes a large number of transactions. Observe in the left column that the Type is General Journal for general journal entries, which are covered in Chapter 8.

▷ *Double-click one of the lines for Num 1108 to open the Make General Journal Entries window.* You can now see that the entry was the monthly allocation of prepaid insurance to insurance expense. This is another example of drill down.

▷ *Practice using the Custom Transaction Detail Report window until you are comfortable obtaining transaction information.* The most important part is using alternative filters in the Filter box and the related information immediately to the right of that box.

Reports

Reports are the output of the accounting data and are typically all that information users see. Some of the reports are only for management within the company, such as an aged trial balance, whereas other reports are useful to both management and outsiders, such as banks and unions. These include the income statement and balance sheet. There is a wide variety of reports available in *QuickBooks*. First, there is a brief introduction to a few of the most important reports and then a followup with practice in accessing various reports.

General Ledger Balances (Trial Balance)

The general ledger balances are the accounts in an organization's chart of accounts that have balances at any designated point in time. They are the basis for preparing financial statements and the result of all transaction processing to the point where the trial balance is prepared.

A trial balance is a report that lists the general ledger accounts, including account balances on a given date.

Subsidiary Ledger Balances (Master Files)

A subsidiary ledger maintains detailed records for certain general ledger accounts. They are frequently referred to as master files. An example is accounts receivable. The accounts receivable general ledger records all transactions affecting accounts receivable and includes the total balance on a specific date. The subsidiary ledger for accounts receivable does the same thing for each customer making up the accounts in accounts receivable. The subsidiary ledger includes the balance due from each customer on a specific date. The total of all customer balances equals the general ledger balance for accounts receivable.

There is a variety of information included in *QuickBooks* for each of the following four subsidiary ledger accounts:

- Accounts Receivable
- Accounts Payable
- Payroll
- Inventory

Financial Statements

Three financial statements that are commonly created for most companies are the balance sheet, income statement, and statement of cash flows. Companies typically print monthly, quarterly, and annual financial statements.

Accessing Reports

There are several ways to access reports. The only method discussed is the one introduced earlier.

> ▶ *Make sure Rock Castle Construction is open and that all windows are closed except the Home Page.*

> ▶ *Click the Reports icon on the Icon Bar → then select Company & Financial (if not already selected) to open the window partially shown below.*

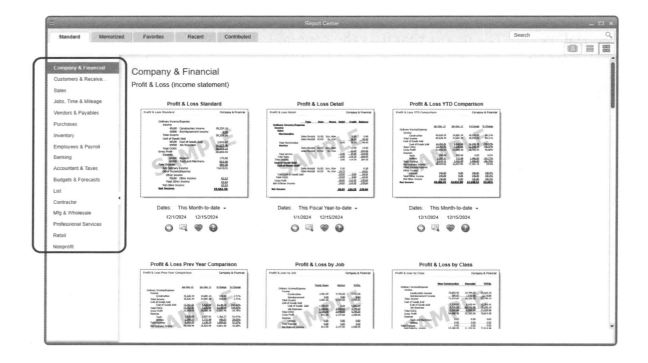

The above circled listing on the left includes categories of available reports. These are used to access the reports included in *QuickBooks*.

> ▶ *Click Customers & Receivables on the left to display all Customers & Receivables related reports on the right.*

▷ *Click Vendor & Payables in the Reports listing and observe how a new set of reports is included in the main section on the right.*

▷ *Click other titles in the Reports listing until you feel comfortable with selecting reports.*

▷ *Click Customers & Receivables again to open the window shown below.*

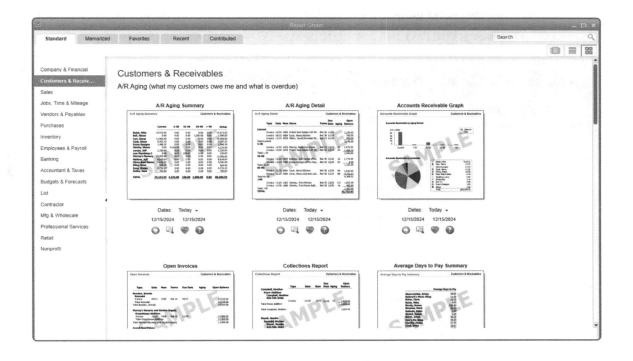

The Customers & Receivables window has several categories related to accounts receivable starting with A/R Aging, which includes seven reports. The right side of the screen includes a brief illustration/explanation of each report to help the user decide which report best meets his or her needs.

▷ *Move your cursor over the Open Invoices (due but not received) report, which opens more information about this report near the bottom of the report description.*

▷ *Click the Info button at the bottom of the report illustration to open an information window about the report.* In the lower part of the information window is a description of what the report tells you.

▷ *Close the information window to return to the Customers & Receivables Reports window.*

▷ *Scroll down and double-click the Customer Balance Detail report under the Customer Balance category to see a listing of customer balances, including the detailed transactions that make up each customer balance due.*

▷ *Close the Customer Balance Detail window.*

▷ *Click Company & Financial on the Reports listing → double-click Profit & Loss Standard to access the Profit & Loss report for December 1–15, 2024, the top portion of which is shown below.* Do not be concerned if your window shows slightly different numbers.

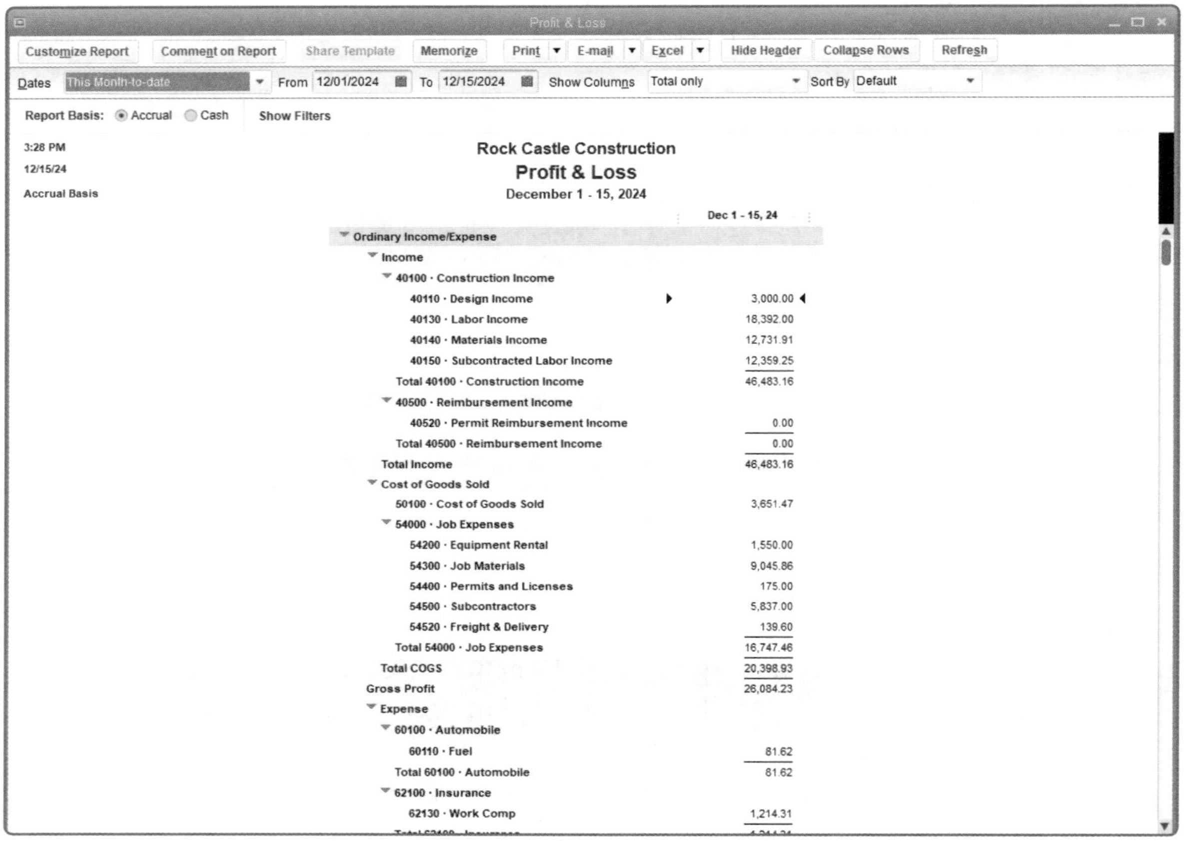

Selecting Report Dates and Other Options

QuickBooks provides users the option to select an accounting period or date for each report and to also select other display options. This section includes discussion of three options:

- **Dates:** Permits selecting different accounting periods or ending dates for a report.

- **Columns:** Permits selecting different totals or subtotals for a report.
- **Expand/Collapse:** Permits a different appearance when there are subtotals.

Dates

▶ *With the Profit & Loss report open, click the drop-down list arrow next to the Dates box and observe the many options for accounting periods available to users → select This Fiscal Year-to-date to open a year-to-date income statement.* Again, your screen may contain different amounts, but do not be concerned about that.

						Profit & Loss				_ □ ×	

Customize Report	Comment on Report	Share Template	Memorize	Print ▼	E-mail ▼	Excel ▼	Hide Header	Collapse Rows	Refresh

Dates This Fiscal Year-to-date ▼   From 01/01/2024 🗓 To 12/15/2024 🗓   Show Columns Total only ▼   Sort By Default ▼

Report Basis: ⦿ Accrual ◯ Cash   Show Filters

3:30 PM
12/15/24
Accrual Basis

Rock Castle Construction
Profit & Loss
January 1 through December 15, 2024

	Jan 1 - Dec 15, 24
▼ **Ordinary Income/Expense**	
▼ **Income**	
▼ **40100 · Construction Income**	
40110 · Design Income ▶	36,729.25 ◀
40130 · Labor Income	206,239.42
40140 · Materials Income	120,610.67
40150 · Subcontracted Labor Income	79,608.35
40199 · Less Discounts given	-48.35
40100 · Construction Income - Other	0.00
Total 40100 · Construction Income	443,139.34
▼ **40500 · Reimbursement Income**	
40520 · Permit Reimbursement Income	1,223.75
40530 · Reimbursed Freight & Delivery	896.05
Total 40500 · Reimbursement Income	2,119.80
Total Income	445,259.14
▼ **Cost of Goods Sold**	
50100 · Cost of Goods Sold	16,950.36
▼ **54000 · Job Expenses**	
54200 · Equipment Rental	1,850.00
54300 · Job Materials	96,935.90
54400 · Permits and Licenses	700.00
54600 · Subcontractors	63,217.95
54520 · Freight & Delivery	867.10
54599 · Less Discounts Taken	-201.81
Total 54000 · Job Expenses	165,369.14
Total COGS	182,319.50
Gross Profit	262,939.64
▼ **Expense**	
▼ **60100 · Automobile**	

Whenever selecting any of the options to change a report window, develop the habit of also clicking the Refresh button (Refresh). In most cases, the window refreshes automatically, but not always.

▶ *Select different date options to observe the changes in the income statement.*

Columns

▶ *Click the drop-down list arrow next to the Show Columns box and observe the many options for different information available to users → select Quarter and observe the new quarterly as well as the previous total information provided.*

▶ *Select Employee in the drop-down list in the Show Columns box.* The information provided is the payroll expense for each employee.

▶ *Select different items in the Show Columns drop-down list to see the large amount of information available to users when this box is selected.*

Expand/Collapse

▶ *Select Month in the drop-down list in the Show Column box.* Notice that there are sub-account details showing in addition to the main account. Notice that there is a Collapse Rows button (Collapse Rows) to the left of the Refresh button. By clicking the Collapse Rows button, the sub-accounts are no longer visible.

▶ *Click the Collapse Rows button and it changes to an Expand Rows button (Expand Rows). Click on the Expand Rows button to show the report with the sub-accounts again.*

Additional Practice for Reports

▶ *Return to the main Report Center window → click Accountant & Taxes in the Reports list → double-click the Trial Balance report under Account Activity → select Custom in the drop-down list for the Dates box.*

▶ *Change the From Box date to 07/01/2024 and the To box date to 08/01/2024 → click the Refresh button.* Notice that the amounts all changed.

▶ *Change the Dates box to This Fiscal Year-to-date. Drill down on account 15000, Furniture and Equipment by double-clicking on the dollar amount for this account. (Make sure This Fiscal Year-to-date is still in the Dates box.)* What were the two additions to this account during the year? The answer is two purchases from Kershaw Computer Services.

▶ *Drill down on the $6,500 transaction to examine the original Enter Bills transaction.*

▶ *Close all windows to return to the Report Center.*

▶ *Open the Journal report in the Accountants & Taxes Reports under Account Activity → select Today in the Dates box.* This is a useful window to determine if you have correctly recorded a transaction that you recorded on that day. For this project you often record a transaction on a date other than the current date, but you want to examine the transaction in the journal to make sure it was correctly recorded. One way to do that is to select any period in the Dates box that includes the date you are processing data, and then scroll to the appropriate transaction. An alternative that makes it easier to find the transaction is to change the dates to include only the date you are interested in.

Assume you processed a transaction to Sergeant Insurance on 12/07/2024 and want to determine if it was correctly recorded.

> ▶ *While you are in the Journal report, select Custom for the Dates box →*
> *12/07/2024 for the From box → 12/07/2024 for the To box → Refresh.* It is now easy to find and review the transaction because there were only four transactions recorded on that date.

> ▶ *Select This Fiscal Year-to-date for the Dates box in the Journal report → select Date in the Sort By box → click the AZ button to the right of Sort By. Now scroll down to the 12/07/2024 date to find Sergeant Insurance a different way.* You will be locating transactions you have just recorded several times in later chapters. There are alternative ways to locate them.

Chapter Summary

After completing Chapter 4, you have now learned:

- ✔ how to obtain information from your accounting system using lists and drill down.
- ✔ how to export information to Excel.
- ✔ what information is available in Company Snapshot.
- ✔ how to modify information obtained through Custom Transaction Detail Reports.
- ✔ how to generate reports.

You should now save your work by making periodic backups of Rock Castle Construction and Larry's Landscaping & Garden Supply using the instructions in the E-Materials you downloaded from the Armond Dalton Resources website. Be sure to use descriptive file names, such as "Rock Castle after Ch 4" or something similar.

Before starting the homework for Chapter 4, you should restore both Rock Castle Construction and Larry's Landscaping & Garden Supply using the initial backups you downloaded from the Armond Dalton Resources website. Restore both companies before proceeding to the Chapter 4 homework assigned by your instructor, which is available on the Armond Dalton Resources website at www.armonddaltonresources.com.

If you cannot recall how to make a periodic backup or restore a backup, refer to the E-Materials located at www.armonddaltonresources.com.

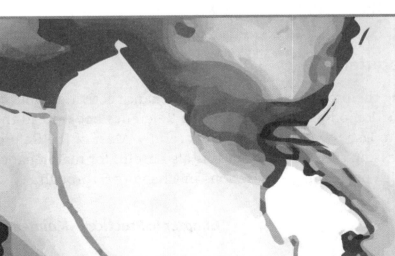

5 Chapter

PRACTICE— MAINTENANCE ACTIVITIES

Introduction

Maintenance activities were introduced in Chapter 2 and further expanded in Chapter 3. This chapter's material provides a review, a more detailed study of maintenance, and introduces use of the Reference book. Additional practice is provided.

Maintenance Overview

When a transaction is recorded in a *QuickBooks* window, one of the most useful features of the program is the default information stored in the system. For example, after a customer name is selected in the Create Invoices window for a credit sale, the software automatically completes many areas of the window, such as the customer's name, address, and the discount terms for sales to that customer.

Default information is stored in the system through maintenance. As discussed in Chapter 3, there are five maintenance windows, and for each of the five there are three possible maintenance tasks that can be performed with the window. These are as follows:

Five Maintenance Windows
1. Vendors
2. Customers & Jobs
3. Inventory Items & Services
4. Employees
5. Chart of Accounts

Three Types of Maintenance Tasks
1. Add a new record
2. View and change information in an existing record
3. Delete a record

> Maintenance tasks have no effect on transactions already recorded, but certain maintenance tasks affect the amounts recorded in subsequent transactions. For example, changing an inventory item's cost and selling price has no effect on previously recorded sales transactions, but it will affect the amount of sales revenue and cost of goods sold posted to the general ledger for future sales of the item.

Reference Material

Before beginning the practice section for maintenance activities, you should read the introduction on pages 3 and 4 of the Reference book. Read the section Suggested Way to Use the Reference Book carefully. Most of the Reference book is used for processing transactions, but it is also useful for maintenance activities. You will deal with processing transactions in Chapters 6 through 8.

Instructions for using each of the five maintenance windows to perform the three types of maintenance tasks are on pages 58 through 85 of the Reference book. The reference material for maintenance is less detailed than for the other reference sections because there is a wider variety of information that may or may not be entered or changed in each window.

Read and understand the overview material in the Perform Maintenance Activities section on pages 58 and 59 of the Reference book before practicing maintenance.

In this section, you will practice working with each of the five types of maintenance windows shown in the Reference book. All maintenance tasks are processed through one or more of the maintenance windows listed previously.

Practice Tasks

As discussed previously and in the Reference book, maintenance windows are used to (1) add a new record, (2) view and change information in an existing record, and (3) delete a record.

Maintenance Practice Task #1 — Add a New Vendor Record

When a company makes a purchase from a new vendor, a new record must be created in *QuickBooks*. During this part of the practice section, you are to add a new vendor record for the sample company, Jackson Supply Company, using the New Vendor window.

Jackson Supply Company has a new vendor, XYZ Warehouse, from which it purchases inventory.

> ▶ *Open Jackson Supply Company and add a new vendor record for XYZ Warehouse using the Reference book instructions on page 64 and the information in the box that follows, but do not save the new record yet.* **Note:** All default information is correct for the vendor unless otherwise noted. Also remember that not all boxes in the New Vendor window are applicable to this vendor.

- **Vendor Name:** XYZ Warehouse
- **Opening Balance:** 0
- **As of:** 2/18/2021

Address Info Tab
- **Company Name:** XYZ Warehouse
- **Main Phone:** (201) 235-0039
- **Main Email:** xyzw@xyzwarehouse.com
- **Website:** www.xyzwarehouse.com
- **Fax:** (201) 234-9002
- **Addresses: (Billed From & Shipped From — use Copy button)** XYZ Warehouse
  500 Westland Park Dr.
  Upper Saddle River, NJ 07458

Payment Settings Tab
- **Account No.:** XYZ0001
- **Terms:** 2% 10, Net 30
- **Print on Check as:** XYZ Warehouse

Account Settings Tab
- **First Prefill:** 10400 Inventory
- **Second Prefill:** 30700 Purchases Discounts
- **Third Prefill:** 30800 Freight Costs

Maintenance Practice Transaction #1. Add a New Vendor Record

Maintenance Practice Transaction #1. Add a New Vendor Record *(continued)*

New Vendor

VENDOR NAME **XYZ Warehouse**

OPENING BALANCE [ ] AS OF 02/18/2021 ▦ How do I determine the opening balance?

- Address Info
- **Payment Settings**
- Tax Settings
- Account Settings
- Additional Info

ACCOUNT NO. XYZ0001

PAYMENT TERMS 2% 10 Net 30 ▼

PRINT NAME ON CHECK AS XYZ Warehouse

CREDIT LIMIT [ ]

BILLING RATE LEVEL [▼] [?]

☐ Vendor is inactive

[OK] [Cancel] [Help]

New Vendor

VENDOR NAME **XYZ Warehouse**

OPENING BALANCE [ ] AS OF 02/18/2021 ▦ How do I determine the opening balance?

- Address Info
- Payment Settings
- Tax Settings
- **Account Settings**
- Additional Info

Tell us which expense accounts to prefill when you enter bills for this vendor.

Spending a little time here can save you time later on.

Accounts you select here show up automatically in the accounts field when you enter a bill for this vendor. Example: Bills from the phone company would be assigned to the Telephone Utilities expense account.

10400 · Inventory ▼

30700 · Purchases Discounts ▼

30800 · Freight Costs ▼

[Clear All]

How do Account Prefills work with Bank Feeds?

☐ Vendor is inactive

[OK] [Cancel] [Help]

The preceding diagrams show the completed tabs of the New Vendor window.

▶ *If the windows on your screen are consistent with the diagrams, click OK to save the new vendor record. If there are errors, correct them before saving the record.*

Review After the New Vendor Record is Saved

▶ *Click Vendors in the Home Page → Vendors tab → right-click vendor XYZ Warehouse, which should now appear in the list of Active Vendors → select Edit Vendor to open the Edit Vendor window. Review the information for the new vendor and correct the information if it is wrong.*

The purpose of the Maintenance procedure you just completed is to review the addition of a new vendor and verify that the information you added was correct. You should follow this procedure for any new maintenance activity or change of maintenance information to determine if the information was entered and saved correctly. *Note:* This subsequent review is not repeated in this or later chapters for new maintenance or change in maintenance information.

Maintenance Practice Task #2 — Change Information in an Existing Customer Record

Adding a customer record is similar to adding a vendor record and is therefore not repeated here.

Often, it is necessary to change information in an existing customer's record. Examples include changing a customer's address and modifying the default general ledger accounts for a customer. Edits to existing records are made using the Edit Customer window.

▶ *Change the customer record for Sunway Suites using the Reference book instructions on page 61 and the following information, but do not save the revised record yet.*

Sunway Suites, an existing customer, added a new website of www.sunwaysuites.com. In addition, Jackson Supply Company's management no longer wants to extend an early payment discount to the customer. The new payment terms will be Net 30. Also, Jackson Supply Company's credit manager has decided to place a $15,000 credit limit on Sunway Suites' account.

Maintenance Practice Transaction #2. Change Information in an Existing Customer Record

Edit Customer

CUSTOMER NAME **Sunway Suites**

CURRENT BALANCE 0.00   How do I adjust the current balance?

Address Info	COMPANY NAME	Sunway Suites
Payment Settings	FULL NAME	Mr./Ms./... First M.I. Last
Sales Tax Settings	JOB TITLE	
Additional Info	Main Phone ▾ (614) 897-4400	Main Email ▾
Job Info	Work Phone ▾	CC Email ▾
	Mobile ▾	Website ▾ www.sunwaysuites.com
	Fax ▾	Other 1 ▾

ADDRESS DETAILS

INVOICE/BILL TO

Sunway Suites
5000 East Sun Blvd.
Columbus, OH 43215

Copy >>

SHIP TO Ship To 1 ▾

Sunway Suites
5000 East Sun Blvd.
Columbus, OH 43215

✓ Default shipping address

☐ Customer is inactive   OK   Cancel   Help

Edit Customer

CUSTOMER NAME **Sunway Suites**

CURRENT BALANCE 0.00   How do I adjust the current balance?

Address Info	ACCOUNT NO.	SUNW0001
Payment Settings	PAYMENT TERMS	Net 30
Sales Tax Settings	PREFERRED DELIVERY METHOD	None
Additional Info	PREFERRED PAYMENT METHOD	
Job Info		

CREDIT LIMIT 15,000.00

PRICE LEVEL ▾ ?

CREDIT CARD INFORMATION

CREDIT CARD NO.

EXP. DATE   /

NAME ON CARD

ADDRESS

ZIP / POSTAL CODE

Can I save the Card Security Code?

ONLINE PAYMENTS
Let this customer pay you by:

☐ Credit Card VISA ...

☐ Bank Transfer (ACH) Bank

☐ Customer is inactive   OK   Cancel   Help

▶ *If the windows on your screen are consistent with the preceding diagrams, click OK to save the changes to the customer record.*

Maintenance Practice Task #3 — Delete a Customer Record

It is often desirable to remove an existing customer record from *QuickBooks*. An example is a customer to which the company no longer sells goods or services. Deletion is possible only if customer accounts have no active transactions or account balances.

▷ *Delete Traver's Bed & Breakfast Customer ID using the Reference book instructions on page 61.*

Maintenance Practice Transaction #3. Delete a Customer Record

Review After the Customer is Deleted

▷ *Click Customers on the Home Page → Customers & Jobs tab, if it is not already open. As shown on the next page, notice that Traver's Bed & Breakfast no longer exists in the list of customers. If the customer is still listed, select it again and repeat the steps to delete the record for Traver's Bed & Breakfast.*

Maintenance Practice Transaction #3. Delete a Customer Record *(continued)*

You should follow this same review procedure for any deletion maintenance activity to determine if the information was deleted. This subsequent review is not repeated in this or subsequent chapters for deletion maintenance activities.

Hide Inactive Names

Jackson Supply Company is planning to no longer do business with an existing customer, Ameristay International. Practice deleting the customer record using the Customer Maintenance window as follows:

▶ *Attempt to delete Ameristay International's customer record using the Reference book instructions on page 61.*

Maintenance Practice Transaction #3. Hide Inactive Names

Maintenance Practice Transaction #3. Hide Inactive Names *(continued)*

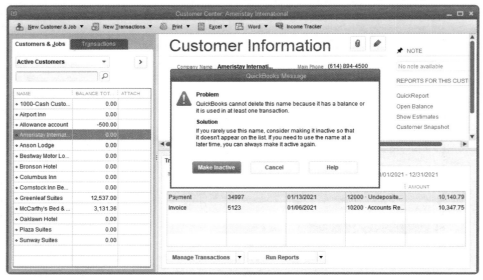

A warning message appears in the QuickBooks Message window saying that you cannot delete this record because it has a balance or it is used in at least one transaction. Transactions and balances from an existing customer must be cleared before the software will allow that customer to be deleted.

Observe in the QuickBooks Message window that a solution is provided. Hide the inactive customer so they don't appear on the list of customers.

> ▶ *Click the Make Inactive button and click Yes if you receive a message saying the customer has an outstanding balance.* Ameristay International's name should no longer be included in the Customers & Jobs window because the View box indicates only Active Customers are shown.

> ▶ *Click the drop-down list arrow next to the first box in the Customers & Jobs tab, and then click All Customers. Ameristay International is now included, this time with an X in the left margin.*

After completing the first three maintenance practice tasks, you have practiced performing all three types of maintenance tasks with either the Vendor or Customer maintenance window, which are two of the five maintenance windows. Next, you will complete various maintenance tasks with the three remaining maintenance windows: Chart of Account Maintenance, Employees Maintenance, and Item & Services Maintenance. You will not practice all three types of maintenance tasks with each of the remaining maintenance windows because the procedures for adding, changing, and deleting records are similar among maintenance windows. The five remaining maintenance practice tasks are representative of tasks that you will be required to complete in later chapters.

Maintenance Practice Task #4 — Add a General Ledger Account

The next maintenance task is to add a new general ledger account for Jackson Supply Company.

▶ *Add a new general ledger account record using the Reference book instructions on page 82 and the information that follows, but do not save the new record yet.*

- **Account Type:** Other Current Liability
- **Number:** 20210
- **Account Name:** 401K Deductions Payable
- **Description:** Liability for employee 401K deductions from gross pay
- **Tax-Line Mapping:** B/S-Liabs/Eq: Other current liabilities

Maintenance Practice Transaction #4. Add New Account

Add New Account

| Account Type | Other Current Liability | Number | 20210 |

Account Name 401K Deductions Payable

☐ Subaccount of

OPTIONAL

Description Liability for employee 401K deductions from gross pay

Account No.

Routing Number

Tax-Line Mapping B/S-Liabs/Eq.: Other current li... ▼ How do I choose the right tax line?

Enter Opening Balance... Should I enter an opening balance?

Save & Close   Save & New   Cancel

The preceding diagram includes the completed Add New Account window for the new general ledger account. Do not be concerned if the general ledger account numbers and balances on your screen differ slightly from those shown.

▶ *If the window on your screen is consistent with the diagram, save the new record. If there are errors, correct them before saving the record.*

Changing or deleting an existing general ledger account is relatively simple when you follow the instructions on page 83 of the Reference book. No practice exercises are considered necessary.

Maintenance Practice Task #5 — Change an Inventory Item's Cost and Selling Price

The next maintenance task is to edit an inventory item's record for changes in the item's cost and selling price.

▶ *Change the inventory item record for Item No. 103 using the Reference book instructions on page 69 and the following information, but do not save the revised record yet.*

■	**Item Number:**	103
■	**Description:**	Washcloths – 100 pack
■	**Old Cost:**	$85.00
■	**New Cost:**	$87.00
■	**Old Sales Price:**	$110.50
■	**New Sales Price:**	$113.00

Maintenance Practice Transaction #5. Change an Inventory Item's Cost and Selling Price

The preceding diagram includes the revised Edit Item maintenance window for Item No. 103. Ignore the contents of the On Hand box; your window may contain a different quantity.

> ▶ *If the window on your screen is consistent with the diagram, click the OK button to save the revised inventory item record. If there are errors, correct them before saving the record.*

Maintenance Practice Task #6 — Add an Inventory Item

The next maintenance task is to add a new inventory item's record.

> ▶ *Add an inventory item record for Item No. 118 using the Reference book instructions on page 68 and the following information, but do not save the new record yet.*

■	Type:	Inventory Part
■	Item Name/Number:	118
■	Description on Purchase Transactions:	Hair conditioner – box of 50
■	Description on Sales Transactions:	Hair conditioner – box of 50
■	Cost:	$24.25
■	Sales Price:	$49.75
■	COGS Account:	50000 Cost of Goods Sold
■	Tax Code:	Tax
■	Preferred Vendor:	Omni Incorporated
■	Income Account:	30100 Sales
■	Asset Account:	10400 Inventory
■	On Hand:	0.00
■	As of:	2/15/2021

Maintenance Practice Transaction #6. Add an Inventory Item

The preceding diagram includes the New Item maintenance window for Item No. 118.

> ▶ *If the window on your screen is consistent with the diagram, click the OK button to save the new item record. If there are errors, correct them before saving the record.*

Maintenance Practice Task #7 — Increase an Employee's Pay Rate

The sample company, Jackson Supply Company, increased the hourly and overtime pay rates for Mark Phelps, an employee.

▶ *Change Mr. Phelps' employee record to reflect his increased hourly pay rate, using the Reference book instructions on page 75 and the following information, but do not save the information yet.*

▪	**Employee Name:**	Mark C Phelps
	Payroll Info Tab	
▪	**Old hourly rates:**	$14.00 hourly, $21.00 overtime
▪	**New hourly rates:**	$15.00 hourly, $22.50 overtime

Maintenance Practice Transaction #7. Increase an Employee's Pay Rate

The preceding diagram includes the revised Edit Employee Payroll and Compensation Info tab window for Mr. Phelps.

▶ *If the window on your screen is consistent with the diagram, click the OK button to save the hourly pay rate increase. If there are errors, correct them before saving.*

Maintenance Practice Task #8 — Perform Maintenance "On the Fly"

It is common for the person entering sales invoice information in the Create Invoices window to find no name in the Customer drop-down list because it is a new customer. The same situation occurs when entering information for transactions related to the other four maintenance activities. *QuickBooks* solves this by allowing the person to add the new customer or other maintenance activity while the transaction is being processed. This is often called maintenance "on the fly."

▶ *Click Create Invoices on the Home Page → click the drop-down list arrow next to Customer: Job box. Observe that the top item is <Add New>.*

▶ *Click <Add New> to access the New Customer window.* This is the same window in which you entered data earlier for a new customer.

▶ *Type ABCD in the Customer Name box and click OK. You have returned to the Create Invoices window and can now continue entering data.* (Normally, in practice, the person entering data enters information for all tabs in the New Customer window but, to avoid repetition of what you did earlier, only the name is included.)

▶ *Click the drop-down list arrow in the Item box. Observe that the top item is <Add New>.*

▶ *Click <Add New> to access the New Item window.* This is the same window in which you entered data earlier for a new inventory item.

▶ *Leave the default setting for Type as Service.* (A new inventory item would have been added during purchases.) *Type 137 in the Item Name/Number box, 30400 in the Account box, then click OK to return to the Create Invoices window again.* (Again, in practice, the person entering data completes the entire window.)

▶ *Close the Create Invoices window and do not record the transaction.*

▶ *Delete both customer ABCD and Item 137 from the maintenance activity records.* You will not be using them again.

The same approach you just completed is equally applicable to new vendors, employees, and account numbers.

No illustrative windows are included for Maintenance "on the fly."

Chapter Summary

After completing Chapter 5, you have now learned how to perform detailed maintenance activities for customers, vendors, inventory, employees, and general ledger accounts. You have practiced the five types of maintenance activities and the three types of changes for each activity. This knowledge is essential for the remaining chapters in the book.

You should back up your data files for Jackson Supply Company using the instructions in the E-Materials. Be sure use a descriptive file name, such as "Jackson after Ch 5" or something similar.

If you do not feel comfortable with your ability to complete each of these purchases and cash disbursements activities, you can practice further in one of two ways.

1. You can do the entire chapter again by following the instructions in the E-Materials to restore the Jackson Supply Company dataset from the initial backup you downloaded and extracted to your QB Backup Files folder in the E-Materials. Doing so will return all data to its original form and permit you to practice all procedures again.

2. You can do additional practice by completing any or most of the sections in this chapter again. You can continue to use Jackson Supply Company.

There are no problems for Chapter 5. There will be questions dealing with maintenance in subsequent chapters as you learn to process transactions. Next, you will move on to learn and practice processing a wide variety of transactions and doing other activities in the next three chapters, starting with purchases and cash disbursements cycle activities in Chapter 6.

This page is intentionally blank.

PRACTICE— PURCHASES AND CASH DISBURSEMENTS CYCLE ACTIVITIES

Introduction

In Chapters 6 through 8, you will learn how to record transactions and perform other activities commonly done using *QuickBooks*. You will use Jackson Supply Company to complete these chapters. For each of the practice exercises summarized in Chapters 6 through 8 you will be given information about a transaction or other activity and Reference book pages that provide a summary to help you complete the practice exercise. You are already familiar with the Reference book from the last chapter, but for the next three chapters more detail is provided. Windows showing the relevant information are provided to help your learning.

Chapters 6 through 8 are organized by the transaction cycle approach. The transaction cycle approach means that related transactions and account balances are included in the same cycle. For example, sales transactions, collections on accounts receivable, sales returns, and write-offs, as well as the account balances associated with those transactions, are included in the sales and cash receipts cycle. Systems designers develop accounting systems using cycles. Similarly, auditors perform audits following a cycle approach.

The following three cycles are included in the next three chapters:

- Chapter 6 — Purchases and cash disbursements cycle
- Chapter 7 — Sales and cash receipts cycle
- Chapter 8 — Payroll cycle and other activities

Before beginning the practice section, you should reread the introduction on pages 3 and 4 of the Reference book. Read the section Suggested Way to Use the Reference Book especially carefully. You should do all of the practice exercises in the order listed in Chapters 6 through 8. The knowledge you gain in these practice chapters will be applied to subsequent chapters.

The transaction cycle included in Chapter 6 is the purchases and cash disbursements. The beginning process for operating a business that sells inventory for a profit is to purchase inventory and turn it into saleable commodities.

▶ *Open Jackson Supply Company if it is not already open.*

▶ *Open the Home Page if it is not already open.* Observe in the top-left corner of the flow diagram that the first step is Purchase Orders, which is used to order inventory or services. Following to the right is the receipt of inventory, entering bills, and then paying those bills. You will follow that process in this chapter and learn how to complete each major task in the cycle using *QuickBooks*. You will be dealing with all of the processes on the Home Page in the next three chapters. Even though the flow diagram shows purchase orders as the first step, the process is ongoing, with purchases & cash disbursements, sales & cash receipts, and payroll working simultaneously and continuously.

Be sure to carefully read the following considerations before you begin processing transactions to avoid making mistakes.

Several considerations are relevant for Chapters 6 through 8.

- Throughout Chapters 6 through 8, 2021 has been adopted as the business year for purposes of demonstrating transaction entry and report generation. You will need to pay close attention to dates to ensure that you enter the correct 2021 date. (Of course, when companies process information using *QuickBooks* in real time, the current date usually is the proper default date for the entry window.)
- You will be given a specific date for processing each practice transaction. Unless otherwise noted, use this same date throughout the entire transaction.
- Before starting to process transactions for Chapters 6 through 8, you should make sure that the "Use the last entered date as default" radio button is selected in the General Preferences window (Edit → Preferences → General). Then make sure that each time you open Jackson Supply Company and record a practice transaction you use the correct date for that transaction. As long as the company remains open, that same date will be used as the default date for other transactions. Even if you forget to change the date to another date in February 2021, at least the transaction will be recorded in the correct month. When you close Jackson Supply Company and open it back up again, the date defaults to 12/15/2021. You will have to be careful to enter the correct date for the first transaction you record when opening the company again.
- The only company that is used to process practice transactions is Jackson Supply Company. The problem material for Chapters 6 through 8 often uses a different company.
- Recall from Chapter 5 that if a box is not mentioned in the Reference book, you do not have to do anything with that box.
- You can make most corrections prior to saving a transaction by clicking the appropriate boxes and correcting the errors.

- Do not be concerned about making mistakes during any of the practice sections until you get to the problems at the end of each chapter. These practice sections are for your benefit only and any errors that you make will not affect the graded assignments.
- If, at any time, you decide that you want to start the chapter over, you may do so by restoring the Jackson Supply Company dataset using the instructions in Chapter 1. You may want to do so if you believe that you do not understand the material in the chapter.

For the purchases and cash disbursements cycle, the following activities are included in this chapter:

- Prepare a purchase order
- Receive goods on a purchase order
- Purchase inventory without a purchase order — no payment made at time of purchase
- Purchase non-inventory items or services without a purchase order — no payment made at time of purchase
- Pay a vendor's outstanding invoice
- Purchase inventory without a purchase order — payment made at time of purchase
- Purchase non-inventory items or services without a purchase order — payment made at time of purchase
- Return inventory from a purchase

Prepare a Purchase Order

Reference Material

A purchase order is prepared through the Create Purchase Orders window, an example of which is shown on page 7 of the Reference book. Read and understand the Prepare a Purchase Order overview on page 6 of the Reference book before processing the transaction. Then follow the instructions on pages 6 and 7 as you complete the practice section.

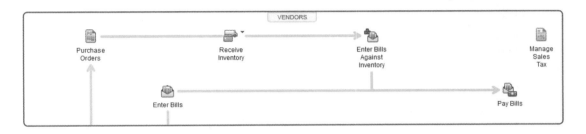

Practice Transaction #1. Prepare a Purchase Order For Inventory Items

▶ *Process the first purchase order using the following information, but do not save it yet.*

- **Vendor:** Omni Incorporated
- **Date:** February 11, 2021
- **PO No.:** 5877
- **Inventory items ordered:**

Item	Description	Qty.	Rate
114	Soap – box of 50	25	$21.15
117	Hand Lotion – 50 pack	15	9.00

- **Purchase Order Total (check figure):** $663.75

Practice Transaction #1. Create Purchase Orders Window

The preceding window shows the Purchase Orders entry window with Purchase Order No. 5877 entered.

▶ *If your Create Purchase Orders window is consistent with the one shown, click Save & Close. If there are errors, correct them before saving.*

Purchase Order Review After the Transaction Is Saved

▶ *Click Vendors on the Home Page → Transactions tab – Purchase Orders → double-click Purchase Order 5877. Review the information for Purchase Order No. 5877 on the same Create Purchase Orders window that you just prepared and correct the information if there are errors.*

Practice Transaction #2. Prepare a Purchase Order With a Different Shipping Location and With Item Cost Other than Standard

▶ *Process the second purchase order using the following information, but do not save it yet.* Because this transaction is for a shipment to a different location than the default one and the purchase price of the products is not the standard price charged by American Linen, both must be changed. This is a one-time change in both the price negotiated with American Linen and the shipping location.

- ■ **Vendor:**   American Linen Supply
- ■ **Date:**   February 12, 2021
- ■ **PO No.:**   5878
- ■ **Shipping Address:** Jackson Supply Company
                          1726 Carbon Lane
                          Cincinnati, Ohio 43196 (no phone number)
- ■ **Inventory items ordered:**

Item	Description	Qty.	Rate
105	Queen sheet set	30	$22.75
109	Standard comforter	15	31.50

- ■ **Purchase Order Total (check figure):** $1,155.000

Practice Transaction #2. Create Purchase Orders Window

> *If your Create Purchase Orders window is consistent with the one shown, click Save & Close. If there are errors, correct them before saving. Click No if asked if you want to change the shipping address for future purchases.*

Purchase Order Review After the Transaction Is Saved

> *Click Vendors on the Home Page → Transactions tab – Purchase Orders → double-click Purchase Order 5878. Review the information for Purchase Order No. 5878 on the same Create Purchase Orders window that you just prepared and correct the information if there are errors.*

Receive Goods on a Purchase Order

Reference Material

The receipt of inventory and other goods when a purchase order has been prepared is processed through the Enter Bills window, an example of which is shown on page 9 of the Reference book. Read and understand the Receive Goods on a Purchase Order overview on page 8 of the Reference book before processing the transaction. Then follow the instructions on pages 8 and 9 of the Reference book as you complete the practice section.

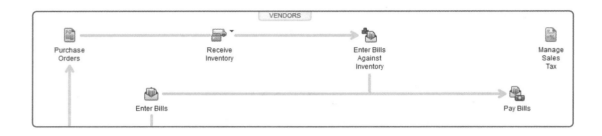

Practice Transaction #1. Receive Goods On a Purchase Order

▶ *Process a receipt of inventory transaction where a purchase order had been prepared using the information that follows, but do not save it yet.* You processed the purchase order in the Prepare a Purchase Order for inventory practice section on pages 6-5 and 6-6 (Practice Transaction #1).

On February 15, 2021, a shipment from Purchase Order No. 5877 is received from Omni Incorporated, along with an invoice. Other details of the transaction follow.

■	**Vendor:**	Omni Incorporated
■	**Purchase Order No.:**	5877
■	**Date:**	February 15, 2021
■	**Ref. No. (Vendor Invoice No.):**	X21478
■	**Terms:**	2% 10 Net 30
■	**Goods received:**	

Item	Description	Qty.	Rate
114	Soap – box of 50	25	$21.15
117	Hand Lotion – 50 pack	15	9.00
■ Invoice Total (check figure):		$663.75	

Practice Transaction #1. Enter Bills Window

The preceding window shows the Enter Bills windows immediately before the Save & Close button is clicked.

▶ *If your Enter Bills window is consistent with the one shown, click Save & Close to save the transaction. If there are errors, correct them before saving.*

Transaction Review After the Transaction Is Saved

▶ *Click Vendors on the Home Page → Transactions tab – Bills → double-click Vendor Invoice X21478 (Num). Review the information for Vendor Invoice No. X21478 on the same Enter Bills window that you just prepared and correct the information if there are errors.*

Practice Transaction #2. Receive Goods On a Purchase Order

▶ *Process a receipt of inventory using the following information, but do not save it yet.* You processed the purchase order in the Prepare a Purchase Order practice section on pages 6-6 and 6-7 (Practice Transaction #2).

On February 18, 2021, a partial shipment from Purchase Order No. 5878 is received from American Linen Supply, along with an invoice. Due to special pricing, the selling price to Jackson Supply Company was reduced even further. Other details of the transaction follow. *Note:* Answer No when asked if you want to make these price changes permanent.

■	**Vendor:**		American Linen Supply
■	**Purchase Order No.:**		5878
■	**Date:**		February 18, 2021
■	**Ref. No. (Vendor Invoice No.):**		ALS2663
■	**Terms:**		2/10, Net 30
■	**Goods received:**		

Item	Description	Qty.	Rate
105	Queen sheet set	20	$21.25
109	Standard comforter	10	28.50

■	**Invoice Total (check figure):**		$710.00

Practice Transaction #2. Enter Bills Window

The preceding window includes the Enter Bills windows immediately *before* the Save & Close button is clicked.

▶ *If your Enter Bills window is consistent with the one shown, save the transaction. If there are errors, correct them before saving.*

Transaction Review

▶ *Click Vendors on the Home Page → Transactions tab – Bills → double-click Vendor Invoice ALS2663 (Num). Review the information for Vendor Invoice No. ALS2663 on the same Enter Bills window that you just prepared and correct the information if there are errors.*

Purchase Inventory Without a Purchase Order — No Payment Made At Time of Purchase

Reference Material

A purchase of inventory without a purchase order and without a corresponding cash disbursement is processed through the Enter Bills window, an example of which is shown on page 11 of the Reference book. Read and understand the Purchase Inventory Without a Purchase Order — No Payment Made At Time of Purchase overview on page 10 of the Reference book before processing the transaction. Then follow the instructions on pages 10 and 11 of the Reference book as you complete the practice section.

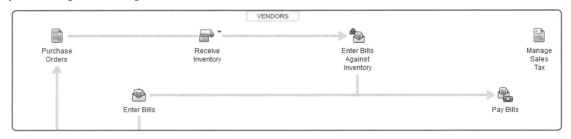

Practice Transaction. Purchase Inventory Without a Purchase Order — No Payment Made At Time of Purchase

▶ *Process a vendor's invoice using the following information, but do not save it yet.*

On February 22, 2021, Jackson Supply Company received an invoice from American Linen Supply for inventory delivered on the same day. Other details are in the box that follows.

▪	Vendor:	American Linen Supply
▪	Date:	February 22, 2021
▪	Ref. No. (Vendor Invoice No.):	ALS2714
▪	Terms:	2/10, Net 30
▪	Goods received:	

Item	Description	Qty.	Rate
103	Washcloths – 100 pack	40	$87.00 *
107	Pillows set of 2	10	22.25
112	Draperies	20	56.00
▪ Invoice Total (check figure):		$4,822.50	

* Recall that this item's cost and selling price were updated in Maintenance Practice Task # 5 in the previous chapter.

Practice Transaction. Enter Bills Window

The preceding window shows the Enter Bills window with Invoice No. ALS2714 entered.

▷ *If your window is consistent with the one shown, save the transaction. If there are errors, correct them before saving.*

Transaction Review After the Transaction Is Saved

▷ *Click Vendors on the Home Page → Transactions tab – Bills → double-click Vendor Invoice ALS2714 (Num). Review the information for Vendor Invoice No. ALS2714 on the same Enter Bills window that you just prepared and correct the information if there are errors.*

Purchases Non-Inventory Items or Services Without a Purchase Order — No Payment Made At Time of Purchase

Reference Material

A purchase of non-inventory items or services without a purchase order and without a corresponding cash disbursement is processed through the Enter Bills window, an example of which is shown on page 13 of the Reference book. Read and understand the Purchase of Non-Inventory Items or Services Without a Purchase Order—No Payment at Time of Purchase overview on page 12 of the Reference book before processing the transaction. Then follow the instructions on pages 12 and 13 of the Reference book as you complete the practice section.

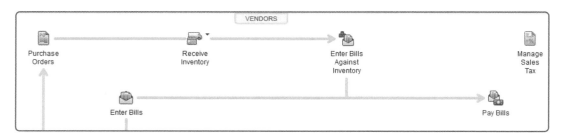

Practice Transaction #1. Purchase of Non-Inventory or Services Without a Purchase Order—No Payment Made At Time of Purchase

▶ *Process the following vendor's invoice using the following information, but do not save it yet.*

On February 25, 2021, Jackson Supply Company received an invoice from Standard Office Supplies for two color laser printers delivered on the same day. Other details are in the box that follows.

■ Vendor:	Standard Office Supplies	
■ Date:	February 25, 2021	
■ Ref. No. (Vendor Invoice No.):	26978	
■ Terms:	2/10, Net 30 (one-time change)	
■ Goods received:		

Account	Amount	Memo
10800 Fixed Assets	$1,290.50	XPL612C Color Laser Printer
40300 Office Supplies	126.15	25 reams of printer paper
■ Invoice Total (check figure):	$1,416.65	

Practice Transaction #1. Enter Bills Window

The window above shows the Enter Bills window with Invoice No. 26978 entered.

▶ *If your window is consistent with the one shown, save the transaction. If there are errors, correct them before saving. Click No when asked if you want to save the payment terms for future transactions.*

Transaction Review After the Transaction Is Saved

▶ *Click Vendors on the Home Page → Transactions tab – Bills → double-click Vendor Invoice 26978 (Num). Review the information for Vendor Invoice No. 26978 on the same Enter Bills window that you just prepared and correct the information if there are errors.*

Practice Transaction #2. Purchase of Non-Inventory or Services Without a Purchase Order—No Payment Made At Time of Purchase

▶ *Process the following vendor's invoice using the following information, but do not save it yet.*

On February 26, 2021, Jackson Supply Company received an invoice from Ohio Power & Light for electric and gas utilities for the month. Other details are in the box that follows.

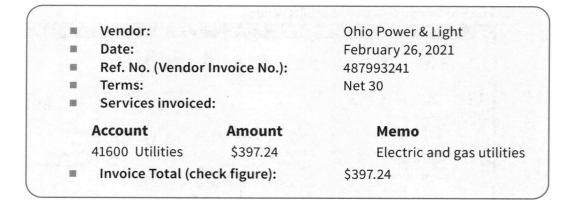

Vendor:	Ohio Power & Light
Date:	February 26, 2021
Ref. No. (Vendor Invoice No.):	487993241
Terms:	Net 30
Services invoiced:	

Account	Amount	Memo
41600 Utilities	$397.24	Electric and gas utilities
Invoice Total (check figure):	$397.24	

Practice Transaction #2. Enter Bills Window

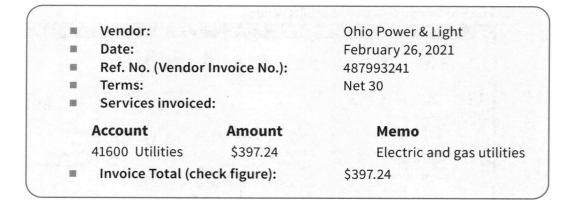

The preceding window shows the Enter Bills window with Invoice No. 487993241 entered.

▶ *If your window is consistent with the one shown, save the transaction. If there are errors, correct them before saving.*

Transaction Review After the Transaction Is Saved

▶ *Click Vendors on the Home Page → Transactions tab – Bills → double-click Vendor Invoice 487993241 (Num). Review the information for Vendor Invoice No. 487993241 on the same Enter Bills window that you just prepared and correct the information if there are errors.*

Pay a Vendor's Outstanding Invoice

Reference Material

Payment of a vendor's outstanding invoice is processed through the Pay Bills window, an example of which is shown on page 15 of the Reference book. Read and understand the Pay a Vendor's Outstanding Invoice overview on page 14 of the Reference book before processing the transaction. Then follow the instructions on pages 14 through 16 as you complete the practice section.

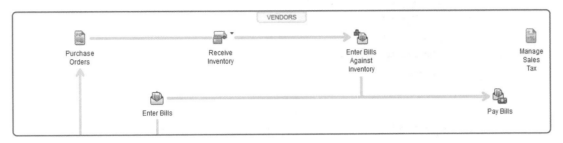

Practice Transaction #1. Full Payment of Vendor's Outstanding Invoice

▶ *Process a cash disbursement using the following information, but do not save it yet.*

On February 25, 2021, the company issued a check to American Linen Supply in payment of an outstanding invoice within the discount period. Recall that the invoice being paid was recorded earlier.

■ **Vendor ID:**	American Linen Supply
■ **Check amount:**	$695.80
■ **Ref. No. (Invoice paid):**	ALS2663, totaling $710.00
■ **Amt. Due:**	$710.00
■ **Disc. Used:**	$14.20
■ **Amt. To Pay:**	$695.80
■ **Discount Account:**	30700 - Purchases Discounts
■ **Check Number:**	513

Practice Transaction #1. Discount and Credits Window

Discount and Credits

BILL

Vendor	American Linen Supply		
Ref. No.	ALS2663	Amount Due	710.00
Date	02/18/2021	Discount Used	**14.20**
Original Amt.	710.00	Credits Used	**0.00**
		Amt. To Pay	695.80

Discount   Credits

Discount Date	02/28/2021
Terms	2% 10 Net 30
Suggested Discount	14.20
Amount of Discount	14.20
Discount Account	30700 · Purchases Discounts
Discount Class	

Done   Cancel   Help

Practice Transaction #1. Pay Bills Window

Pay Bills

SELECT BILLS TO BE PAID

Show bills   ○ Due on or before   12/25/2021

      ● Show all bills

Filter By

Sort By   Vendor

☑	DATE DUE	VENDOR	REF. NO.	DISC. DATE	AMT. DUE	DISC. USED	CREDITS USED	AMT. TO PAY
☐	02/27/2021	American Linen...	RCT5720	02/07/2021	8,796.25	0.00	0.00	0.00
☑	03/20/2021	American Linen ...	ALS2663	02/28/2021	710.00	14.20	0.00	695.80
☐	03/24/2021	American Linen...	ALS2714	03/04/2021	4,822.50	0.00	0.00	0.00
☐	03/28/2021	Ohio Power & L...	487993241		397.24	0.00	0.00	0.00
				Totals	16,806.39	14.20	0.00	695.80

Clear Selections

DISCOUNT & CREDIT INFORMATION FOR HIGHLIGHTED BILL

Vendor	**American Linen Supply**	Terms	**2% 10 Net 30**	Number of Credits	**0**
Bill Ref. No.	**ALS2663**	Sugg. Discount	**14.20**	Total Credits Available	**0.00**

Go to Bill   Set Discount   Set Credits

PAYMENT

Date	Method		Account
02/25/2021	Check	○ To be printed	10100 · Cash-General Account
		● Assign check number	**Ending Balance** 10,701.03

Pay Selected Bills   Cancel

Practice Transaction #1. Assign Check Numbers Window

Assign Check Numbers

Payment Account   **10100 · Cash-General Account**

How do you want to assign check numbers?
- ○ Let QuickBooks assign check numbers.
- ● Let me assign the check numbers below.

CHECK NO.	DATE	PAYEE	AMOUNT
513	02/25/2021	American Linen Sup...	695.80

OK   Cancel   Help

Practice Transaction #1. Payment Summary Window

Payment Summary

PAYMENT DETAILS

Payment Date	02/25/2021
Payment Account	10100 · Cash-General Account
Payment Method	Check

Payment has been successfully recorded for the following bill:

CHECK NO.	DATE DUE	VENDOR	AMOUNT PAID
513	03/20/2021	American Linen Supply	695.80
		Total	695.80

How do I find and change a bill payment?

Pay More Bills   Done

The preceding three windows show the Pay Bills, Assign Check Numbers, and Payment Summary windows with the practice transaction entered. Do not be concerned if your window shows some miscellaneous differences in the other transactions included or the ending cash balance shown in the window as long as the current transaction information is correct.

▷ *If your windows are consistent with the ones shown, save the transaction in the Pay Bills window. If there are errors, correct them.*

Transaction Review After the Transaction Is Saved

▷ *Click Vendors on the Home Page → Transactions tab – Bill Payments → double-click check number 513 (Num). Review the information for check number 513 on the same Bill Payments window that you just prepared and correct the information if there are errors.*

Practice Transaction #2. Partial Payment of Vendor's Outstanding Invoice

▶ *Process a cash disbursement using the following information, but do not save it yet.*

On February 20, 2021, the company issued a check to Omni Incorporated in partial payment of an outstanding invoice. There are no discounts on partial payments. *Note:* You may need to change the discount amount to 0 in the Discounts and Credits window.

■ **Vendor ID:**	Omni Incorporated
■ **Check amount:**	$400.00
■ **Ref. No. (Invoice paid):**	X21478, totaling $663.75
■ **Amt. Due:**	$663.75
■ **Disc. Used:**	None
■ **Amt. To Pay:**	$400.00
■ **Check Number:**	514

Practice Transaction #2. Discount and Credits Window

Discount and Credits

BILL

Vendor	Omni Incorporated		
Ref. No.	X21478	Amount Due	663.75
Date	02/15/2021	Discount Used	0.00
Original Amt.	663.75	Credits Used	0.00
		Amt. To Pay	663.75

Discount / Credits

Discount Date	02/25/2021
Terms	2% 10 Net 30
Suggested Discount	13.28
Amount of Discount	0.00
Discount Account	
Discount Class	

Done   Cancel   Help

Practice Transaction #2. Pay Bills Window

Pay Bills

SELECT BILLS TO BE PAID

Show bills ○ Due on or before 12/25/2021 🔲
● Show all bills

Filter By ▼
Sort By Vendor ▼

☑	DATE DUE	VENDOR	REF. NO.	DISC. DATE	AMT. DUE	DISC. USED	CREDITS USED	AMT. TO PAY
☐	02/27/2021	American Linen...	RCT5720	02/07/2021	8,796.25	0.00	0.00	0.00
☐	03/24/2021	American Linen...	ALS2714	03/04/2021	4,822.50	0.00	0.00	0.00
☐	03/28/2021	Ohio Power & L...	487993241		397.24	0.00	0.00	0.00
☑	03/17/2021	Omni Incorporat...	X21478	02/25/2021	663.75	0.00	0.00	400.00
				Totals	16,096.39	0.00	0.00	400.00

Clear Selections

DISCOUNT & CREDIT INFORMATION FOR HIGHLIGHTED BILL

Vendor **Omni Incorporated**   Terms   **2% 10 Net 30**   Number of Credits   **0**
Bill Ref. No. **X21478**   Sugg. Discount   **13.28**   Total Credits Available   **0.00**

Go to Bill   **Set Discount**   **Set Credits**

PAYMENT

Date   Method   ○ To be printed   Account
02/20/2021 🔲   Check ▼   ● Assign check number   10100 · Cash-General Account ▼

Ending Balance   **10,301.03**

Pay Selected Bills   **Cancel**

Practice Transaction #2. Assign Check Numbers Window

Assign Check Numbers

Payment Account   **10100 · Cash-General Account**

How do you want to assign check numbers?

○ Let QuickBooks assign check numbers.
● Let me assign the check numbers below.

CHECK NO.	DATE	PAYEE	AMOUNT
514	02/20/2021	Omni Incorporated	400.00

OK   **Cancel**   **Help**

The two preceding windows show the Pay Bills and the Assign Check Numbers windows with the practice transaction entered. Do not be concerned if your windows show some miscellaneous differences in the other transactions included in the window as long as the current transaction information is correct.

▶ *If your windows are consistent with the ones shown, click OK in the Assign Check Numbers window. If there are errors, correct them before clicking OK.*

After clicking OK in the Assign Check Numbers window, the Payment Summary window shown below appears.

Practice Transaction #2. Payment Summary Window

▶ *Click Done to close the Payment Summary window.*

Transactions Review After Transaction Is Saved

▶ *Click Vendors on the Home Page → Transactions tab – Bill Payments → double-click check number 514 (Num). Review the information for check number 514 on the same Bill Payments window that you just prepared and correct the information if there are errors.*

Purchase Inventory Without a Purchase Order — Payment Made At Time of Purchase

Reference Material

A purchase of and payment for inventory without a purchase order is processed through the Write Checks window, an example of which is shown on page 19 of the Reference book. Read and understand the Purchase Inventory Without a Purchase Order — Payment Made at Time of Purchase overview on page 18 of the Reference book before processing the transaction. Then follow the instructions on pages 18 and 19 as you complete the practice section.

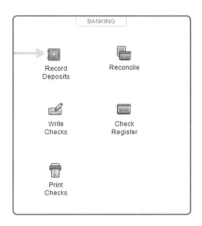

Practice Transaction. Purchase Inventory Without a Purchase Order — Payment Made At Time of Purchase

▶ *Process the following invoice and its corresponding payment using the following information, but do not save it yet.*

On February 26, 2021, Jackson Supply Company received an invoice from American Linen Supply for inventory delivered on the same day. Jackson Supply Company issued a check for payment at the time of delivery. Other details are in the box that follows.

■	**Vendor ID:**		American Linen Supply
■	**Check No.:**		515
■	**Date:**		February 26, 2021
■	**Memo:**		Invoice #6788
■	**Check Amount:**		$2,607.50
■	**Goods shipped/invoiced:**		

Item	Description	Qty.	Rate
106	King sheet set	35	$28.50
111	King comforter	40	40.25

Practice Transaction. Write Checks–Cash-General Account Window

The preceding window shows the Write Checks – Cash-General Account window with the practice transaction entered. Do not be concerned if your screen shows a different Ending Balance (cash) near the top of the window.

▶ *If your window is consistent with the one shown, save the transaction. If there are errors, correct them before saving.*

Transaction Review After the Transaction Is Saved

▶ *Click Vendors on the Home Page → Transactions tab – Checks → double-click check number 515 (Num). Review the information for check number 515 on the same Write Checks – Cash-General Account window that you just prepared and correct the information if there are errors.*

Purchase Non-Inventory Items or Services Without a Purchase Order — Payment Made At Time of Purchase

Reference Material

A purchase of and payment for non-inventory items or services without a purchase order is processed through the Write Checks window, an example of which is shown on page 21 of the Reference book. Read and understand the Purchase of Non-Inventory Items or Services Without a Purchase Order — Payment Made at Time of Purchase overview on page 20 of the Reference book before processing the transaction. Then follow the instructions on pages 20 and 21 as you complete the practice section.

Practice Transaction. Purchase of Non-Inventory or Services Without a Purchase Order — Payment Made At Time of Purchase

▶ *Process the following invoice and its corresponding payment using the following information, but do not save it yet. Use Quick Add so that you do not have to enter anything into the system for the vendor except the name.*

On February 26, 2021, Jackson Supply Company received an invoice from Hawkins Web Design for designing a web page for the company. Jackson Supply Company issued a check on the same day in full payment of the invoice. Other details about the invoice and payment follow.

■	**Vendor ID:**	Hawkins Web Design
■	**Check No.:**	516
■	**Invoice and Check Amount:**	$1,250.00
■	**Memo:**	Invoice #115890
■	**General ledger account:**	41700 Professional Fees

Practice Transaction. Name Not Found Window

▶ *Select Quick Add.*

Practice Transaction. Select Name Type Window

▶ *Click Ok.*

Practice Transaction. Write Checks–Cash-General Account Window

The preceding window shows the Write Checks – Cash-General Account window with the practice transaction entered. Do not be concerned if your window shows a different cash balance as long as the current transaction is correct.

▶ *If your window is consistent with the one shown, save the transaction. If there are errors, correct them before saving.*

Transaction Review After the Transaction Is Saved

▶ *Click Vendors on the Home Page → Transactions tab – Checks → double-click check number 516 (Num). Review the information for check number 516 on the same Write Checks – Cash-General Account window that you just prepared and correct the information if there are errors.*

Return Inventory From a Purchase

Reference Material

A purchase return is processed through the Enter Bills window, an example of which is shown on page 23 of the Reference book. Read and understand the Return Inventory from a Purchase overview on page 22 of the Reference book before processing the transaction. Then follow the instructions on pages 22 and 23 as you complete the practice section.

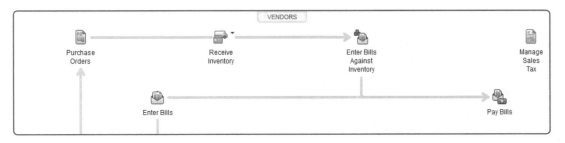

Practice Transaction. Return Inventory From a Purchase

▶ *Process the purchase return using the following information, but do not save it yet.*

On February 26, 2021, Jackson Supply Company returned inventory items that were originally purchased from American Linen Supply on February 22, 2021. Other details about the purchase return follow.

- **Vendor ID:** American Linen Supply
- **Date:** February 26, 2021
- **Ref. No.:** 445877 (debit memo number)
- **Vendor's Invoice No.**
  for original purchase: ALS2714 (Memo box)
- **Items returned:**

Item	Description	Qty. Returned
103	Washcloths – 100 pack	15
112	Draperies	5

- **Credit Amount (check figure):** $1,585.00

Practice Transaction. Enter Bills

The preceding window shows the Enter Bills window with the purchase return entered.

▶ *If your window is consistent with the one shown, save the transaction. If there are errors, correct them before saving.*

Transaction Review

▶ *Click Vendors on the Home Page → Transactions tab – Bills → double-click Vendor Credit 445877 (Num). Review the information for the credit to Vendor Credit 445877 on the same Enter Bills window that you just prepared and correct the information if there are errors.*

Chapter Summary

After completing Chapter 6, back up your data files for Jackson Supply Company using the instructions in the E-Materials you downloaded from the Armond Dalton Resources website. Be sure to use a descriptive file name, such as "Jackson after Ch 6."

You have now practiced processing transactions for the eight purchases and cash disbursements cycle activities. If you are satisfied with your understanding of the purchases and cash disbursements transactions in this chapter, you should now proceed to the Chapter 6 homework assigned by your instructor, which is available on the Armond Dalton Resources website at www.armonddaltonresources.com.

Because of practice exercises and chapter problems in previous chapters, each of you may have different transactions and balances in the company datasets used in the homework. **To ensure consistent answers across everyone in the class, please restore both the Rock Castle Construction and Larry's Landscaping & Garden Supply datasets using the initial backups you downloaded from the Armond Dalton Resources website. Restore both companies before proceeding to the Chapter 6 homework assigned by your instructor.**

If you do not feel comfortable with your ability to complete each of these purchases and cash disbursements activities, you can practice further in one of two ways.

1. You can do the entire chapter again by following the instructions in the E-Materials to restore the Jackson Supply Company dataset from the initial backup you downloaded from the Armond Dalton Resources website. Doing so will return all data to its original form and permit you to practice all procedures again.
2. You can do additional practice by completing any or most of the sections in this chapter again. You can continue to use Jackson Supply Company.

Document numbers will, of course, be different if you redo sections without restoring the dataset. In addition, there are certain activities that you cannot do without first recording other information. For example, you cannot complete the Pay a Vendor's Outstanding Invoice section without first recording receipt of the goods in the Receive Inventory on a Purchase Order section. All practice sections that are dependent upon the completion of an earlier practice section are clearly identified in this chapter.

If you cannot recall how to make a periodic backup or restore a backup, refer to the E-Materials located at www.armonddaltonresources.com.

This page is intentionally blank.

PRACTICE — SALES AND CASH RECEIPTS CYCLE ACTIVITIES

Introduction

Next you will learn about activities in the sales and cash receipts cycle. The approach is similar to those followed in the purchases and cash disbursements cycle. The following seven activities are included:

- Make a credit sale
- Collect an account receivable and make a deposit
- Make a cash sale
- Process a sales return or allowance (credit memo)
- Write off an uncollectible account receivable
- Receive a miscellaneous cash receipt
- Prepare a monthly accounts receivable statement

> The same considerations included in Chapter 6 (pages 6-3 and 6-4) are equally relevant for Chapter 7. Carefully read these considerations again before you begin processing transactions in this chapter to avoid making mistakes.

Make a Credit Sale

Reference Material

A credit sale is processed through the Create Invoices–Accounts Receivable window, an example of which is shown on page 25 of the Reference book. Read and understand the Make a Credit Sale overview on page 24 of the Reference book before processing the transaction. Then follow the instructions on pages 24 and 25 as you complete the practice section.

The first practice transaction involves the sale of inventory items at the standard price level.

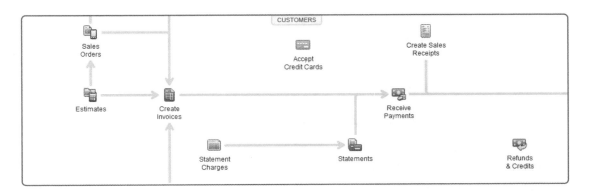

Practice Transaction #1. Sale of Inventory Items at Standard Price Level

▶ *Process a credit sale invoice using the information that follows, but do not save it.*

▪	**Customer:**	Columbus Inn	
▪	**Date:**	February 1, 2021	
▪	**Invoice No.:**	5128	
▪	**PO No.:**	63921	
▪	**Terms:**	2% 10, Net 30	
▪	**Products sold:**		

Qty.	Item	Description	Rate
15	112	Draperies	$72.50
10	116	Shower cap – 25	3.40

▪	**Ohio Sales Tax:**	5%	
▪	**Invoice Total (check figure):**	$1,177.58	

Practice Transaction #1. Create Invoices–Accounts Receivable Window

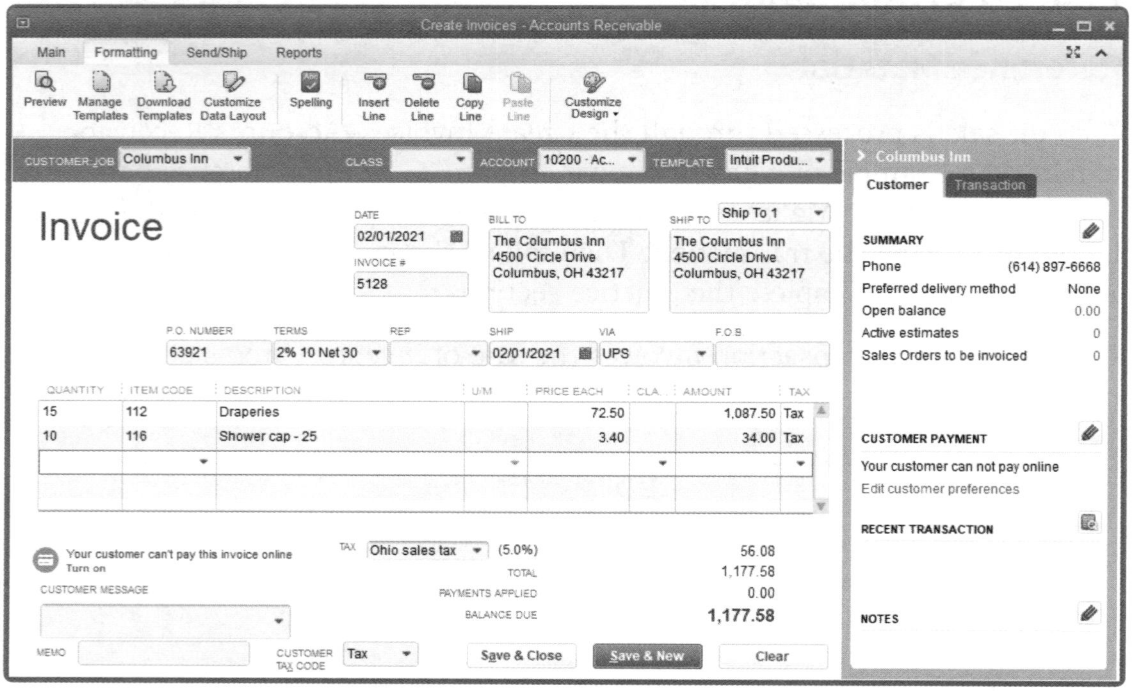

The previous diagram shows the Create Invoices–Accounts Receivable window with Practice Transaction #1 entered.

▶ *If your window is consistent with the diagram, save the transaction. If there are errors, correct them before saving.*

Transaction Review after the Transaction is Saved

▶ *Click Customers in the Home Center → Transactions tab → Invoices → double-click Invoice No. 5128. Review the information for Invoice No. 5128 on the same Create Invoices–Accounts Receivable window that you just prepared and correct the information if it is wrong.*

Practice Transaction #2. Sale of Inventory with Change in Price Level

The second practice transaction involves the sale of inventory items at a different price level for the inventory items sold.

▶ *Process another credit sale invoice using the information that follows, but do not save it yet.*

■ **Customer:**		Oaklawn Hotel
■ **Date:**		February 8, 2021
■ **Invoice No.:**		5129
■ **PO No.:**		40297
■ **Terms:**		2% 10, Net 30
■ **Products sold:**		

Qty.	Item	Description	Rate
25	114	Soap – box of 50	$22.50
15	117	Hand lotion – 50 pack	11.25

■ **Ohio Sales Tax:**	5%	
■ **Invoice Total (check figure):**	$767.81	

Practice Transaction #2. Create Invoices–Accounts Receivable Window

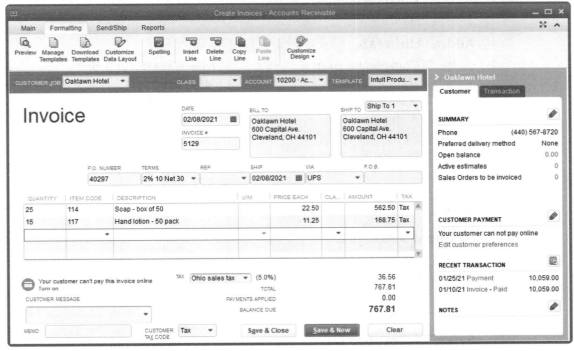

The previous window shows the Create Invoices–Accounts Receivable window with Practice Transaction #2 entered.

▶ *If your window is consistent with the diagram, save the transaction. If there are errors, correct them before saving.*

Transaction Review after the Transaction is Saved

▶ *Click Customers in the Home Center → Transactions tab → Invoices → double-click Invoice No. 5129. Review the information for Invoice No. 5129 on the same Create Invoices–Accounts Receivable window that you just prepared and correct the information if it is wrong.*

Practice Transaction #3. Sale of Inventory to a New Customer

The third practice transaction involves the sale of inventory items for a new customer.

▶ *Perform the required maintenance for a new customer and then process the credit sale invoice using the information that follows, but do not save it yet.*

New Customer Information
- Customer Name: New Place Motor Lodge
- Opening Balance: $0
- As of: 02/12/2021

Address Info tab
- Company Name: New Place Motor Lodge
- Main Phone: (404) 543-2117
- Main Email: newplace@newplacemotor.com
- Website: www.newplacemotorlodge.com
- Fax: (404) 543-7002
- Invoice/Bill To: New Place Motor Lodge
  1622 New Place Road
  Cleveland, OH 44101
- Ship To 1:   Same address

Payment Settings tab
- Account No.:   New01
- Credit Limit: $20,000
- Payment Terms: 1% 10, Net 30
- Preferred Delivery Method: E-Mail

Sales Tax Settings tab
- Tax Code: Tax
- Tax Item: Ohio sales tax

Practice Transaction #3. New Customer Window — Address Info Tab

New Customer

CUSTOMER NAME **New Place Motor Lodge**

OPENING BALANCE `0.00` AS OF `02/12/2021` How do I determine the opening balance?

Address Info

Payment Settings

Sales Tax Settings

Additional Info

Job Info

COMPANY NAME	New Place Motor Lodge
FULL NAME	First · M.I. · Last
JOB TITLE	

Main Phone ▼	(404) 543-2117	Main Email ▼	newplace@newplacemotor.com
Work Phone ▼		CC Email ▼	
Mobile ▼		Website ▼	www.newplacemotorlodge.com
Fax ▼	(404) 543-7002	Other 1 ▼	

ADDRESS DETAILS

INVOICE/BILL TO

New Place Motor Lodge
1622 New Place Road
Cleveland, OH 44101

Copy >>

SHIP TO Ship To 1 ▼

New Place Motor Lodge
1622 New Place Road
Cleveland, OH 44101

☑ Default shipping address

☐ Customer is inactive   OK   Cancel   Help

Practice Transaction #3. New Customer Window — Payment Settings Tab

New Customer

CUSTOMER NAME **New Place Motor Lodge**

OPENING BALANCE `0.00` AS OF `02/12/2021` How do I determine the opening balance?

Address Info

Payment Settings

Sales Tax Settings

Additional Info

Job Info

ACCOUNT NO.	New01	CREDIT LIMIT	20,000.00
PAYMENT TERMS	1% 10 Net 30 ▼	PRICE LEVEL	▼
PREFERRED DELIVERY METHOD	E-mail ▼		
PREFERRED PAYMENT METHOD	▼		

CREDIT CARD INFORMATION

CREDIT CARD NO.

EXP. DATE /

NAME ON CARD

ADDRESS

ZIP / POSTAL CODE

Can I save the Card Security Code?

ONLINE PAYMENTS

Let this customer pay you by:

☐ Credit Card VISA

☐ Bank Transfer (ACH) Bank

☐ Customer is inactive   OK   Cancel   Help

Practice Transaction #3. New Customer Window — Sales Tax Settings Tab

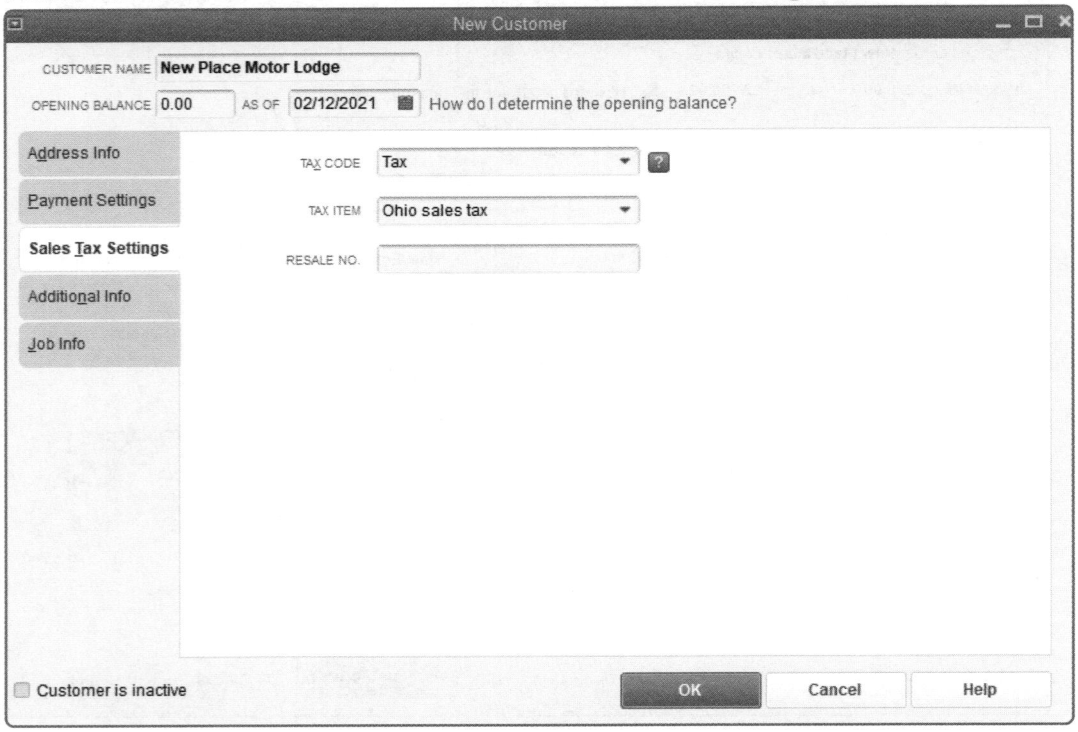

New Customer	— □ ×

CUSTOMER NAME **New Place Motor Lodge**

OPENING BALANCE 0.00   AS OF 02/12/2021 📅   How do I determine the opening balance?

- Address Info
- Payment Settings
- **Sales Tax Settings**
- Additional Info
- Job Info

TAX CODE Tax ▾ ❓

TAX ITEM Ohio sales tax ▾

RESALE NO. _____

☐ Customer is inactive

[OK] [Cancel] [Help]

Sale information for Practice Transaction #3 follows:

- **Customer:** New Place Motor Lodge
- **Date:** February 12, 2021
- **Invoice No.:** 5130
- **P.O. No.:** P4487
- **Terms:** 1% 10, Net 30
- **Products sold:**

Qty.	Item	Description	Rate
5	109	Standard comforter $44.50	

- **Ohio Sales Tax:** 5%
- **Invoice Total (check figure):** $233.63

Practice Transaction #3. Create Invoices–Accounts Receivable Window

The preceding window shows the Create Invoices–Accounts Receivable window with Practice Transaction #3 entered.

▶ *If your window is consistent with the diagram, save the transaction.*
If there are errors, correct them before saving.

Transaction Review after the Transaction is Saved

▶ *Click Customers in the Home Center → Transactions tab → Invoices → double-click Invoice No. 5130. Review the information for Invoice No. 5130 on the same Create Invoices–Accounts Receivable window that you just prepared and correct the information if it is wrong.*

Collect an Account Receivable and Make a Deposit

Reference Material

A collection of an account receivable is processed through the Receive Payments window, an example of which is shown on page 27 of the Reference book. Both processing and applying cash receipts are necessary for each collection. Read and understand the Collect an Account Receivable overview on page 26 of the Reference book before processing the transaction. Then follow the instructions on pages 26 through 28 of the Reference book as you complete the practice section. You will also be making a bank deposit using the Reference Book instructions on pages 30 through 32.

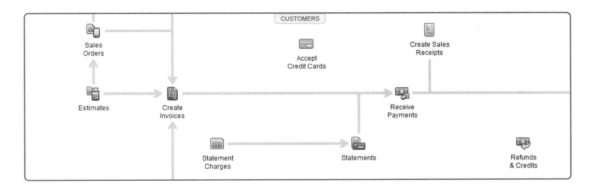

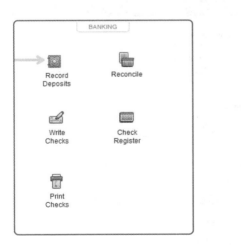

Practice Transaction #1. Collection Within the Discount Period

The first practice transaction illustrates an account receivable collection made within the early payment discount period.

▶ *Record Practice Transaction #1 using the following information, but do not save it yet.*

On February 1, 2021, Jackson Supply Company received a check from Greenleaf Suites in payment of Invoice No. 5127, which was dated January 24, 2021. Jackson Supply Company's payment terms for Greenleaf is 2% 10, Net 30.

- **Customer:** Greenleaf Suites
- **Date:** February 1, 2021
- **Invoice No.:** 5127
- **Terms:** 2% 10, Net 30
- **Amount:** $12,286.26
  (early payment discount = $250.74)
- **Discount Account:** 30300 Sales Discounts
- **Pmt. Method:** Check
- **Customer's Check:** 8421

Practice Transaction #1. Discount and Credits Window

	Discount and Credits	
INVOICE		
Customer:Job	Greenleaf Suites	
Number	5127	Amount Due 12,537.00
Date	01/24/2021	Discount Used **250.74**
Original Amt.	12,537.00	Credits Used **0.00**
		Balance Due 12,286.26

Discount	Credits

Discount Date   02/03/2021
Terms   2% 10 Net 30
Suggested Discount   250.74
Amount of Discount   [250.74]
Discount Account   [30300 · Sales Discounts ▼]
Discount Class   [▼]

[Done] [Cancel] [Help]

Practice Transaction #1. Receive Payments Window

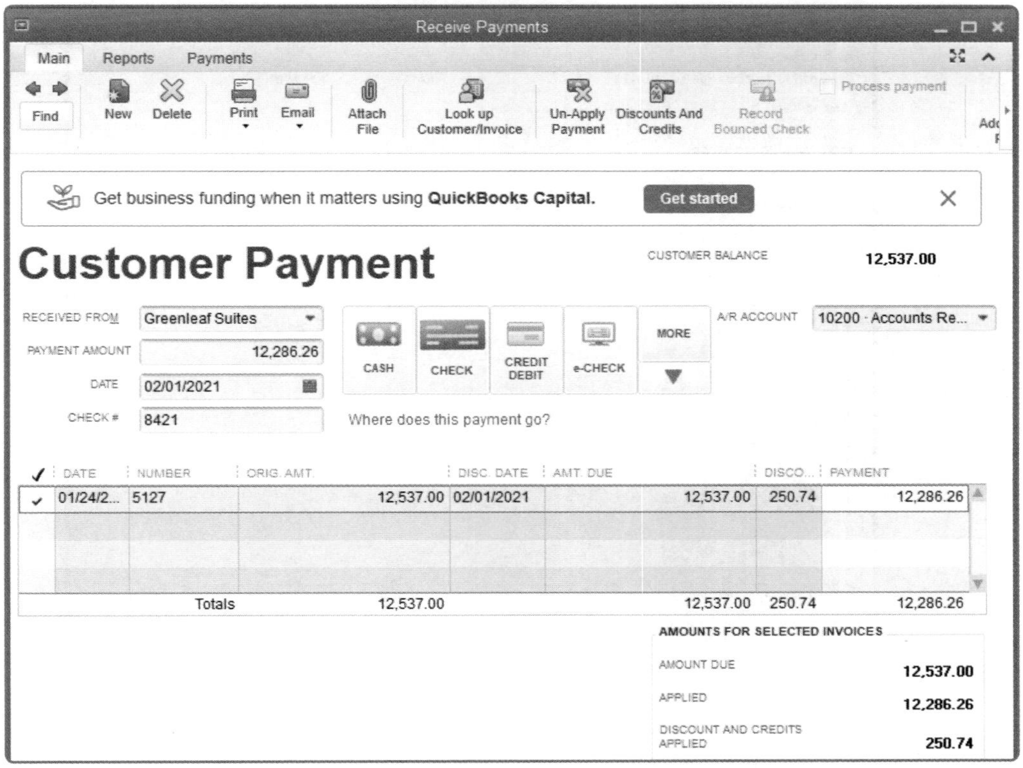

The preceding diagram shows the Receive Payments window with Practice Transaction #1 entered.

▶ *If your window is consistent with the diagram, save the transaction. If there are errors, correct them before saving.*

Transaction Review after the Transaction is Saved

▶ *Click Customers in the Home Center → Transactions tab → Received Payments → double-click Customer Payment for Check No. 8421. Review the information for Check No. 8421 on the same Receive Payments window that you just prepared and correct the information if it is wrong.*

Make a Bank Deposit for Practice Transaction #1

Record the bank deposit for the check received from Greenleaf Suites.

▶ *Process the bank deposit of $12,286.26 on 02/01/2021 in the general cash account (#10100 Cash - General Account) following the instructions on pages 30 through 32 of the Reference book, but do not save it yet.*

Practice Transaction #1. Payments to Deposit Window

Payments to Deposit

SELECT VIEW

View payment method type　　All types　　　　　What are payment method views?

Sort payments by　　　　　Payment Method

SELECT PAYMENTS TO DEPOSIT

✓	DATE	TIME	TYPE	NO	PAYMENT METHOD	NAME	AMOUNT
✓	02/01/2021		PMT	8421	Check	Greenleaf Suites	12,286.26

1 of 1 payments selected for deposit　　　　　　**Payments Subtotal**　　12,286.26

Select All　　Select None

OK　　Cancel　　Help

Practice Transaction #1. Make Deposits Window

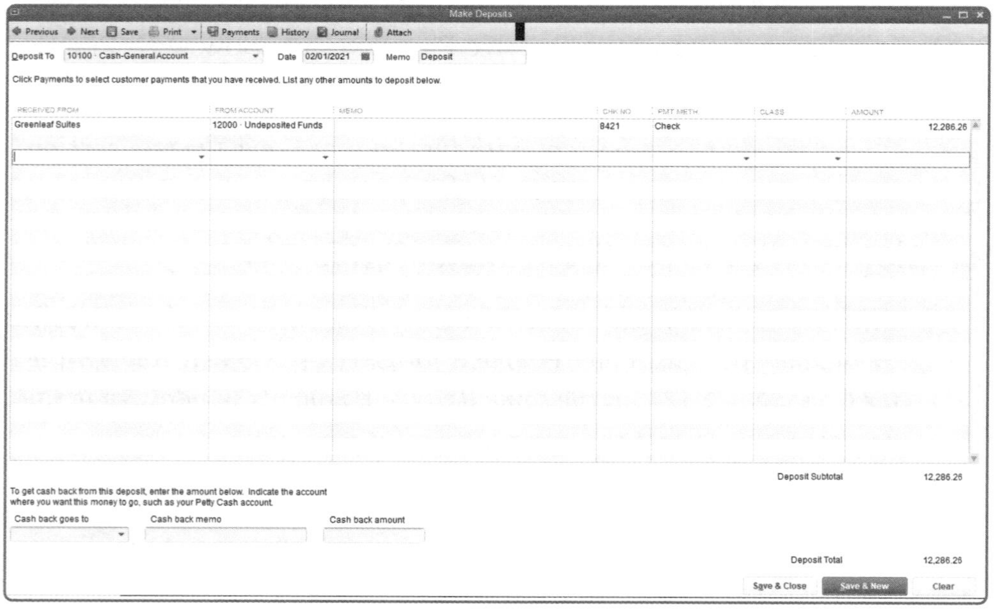

Make Deposits

◆ Previous　◆ Next　🖫 Save　🖨 Print ▾　🖫 Payments　🖫 History　🖫 Journal　🖫 Attach

Deposit To　10100 · Cash-General Account　　Date　02/01/2021　　Memo　Deposit

Click Payments to select customer payments that you have received. List any other amounts to deposit below.

RECEIVED FROM	FROM ACCOUNT	MEMO	CHK NO	PMT METH	CLASS	AMOUNT
Greenleaf Suites	12000 · Undeposited Funds		8421	Check		12,286.26

Deposit Subtotal　　12,286.26

To get cash back from this deposit, enter the amount below. Indicate the account where you want this money to go, such as your Petty Cash account.

Cash back goes to　　Cash back memo　　Cash back amount

Deposit Total　　12,286.26

Save & Close　　Save & New　　Clear

The previous diagram shows the Make Deposits window with the deposit completed.

▶ *If your window is consistent with the diagram, save it. If there are errors, correct them before saving it.*

Transaction Review After the Transaction Is Saved

▶ *Click Report Center → Banking → Deposit Detail → select This Fiscal Year in the Dates box → scroll to the last deposit, which is for Greenleaf Suites. If the deposit is for an amount other than $12,286.26, click on the transaction and make the correction.*

Practice Transaction #2. Partial Collection

The second practice transaction is a partial payment of an outstanding invoice.

▶ *Record the account receivable collection for Practice Transaction #2 using the information that follows, but do not post the transaction yet.*

On February 8, 2021, McCarthy's Bed & Breakfast sent a check in partial payment of Invoice No. 5126. The payment was outside the discount period.

■	Customer:	McCarthy's Bed & Breakfast
■	Date:	February 8, 2021
■	Invoice No.:	5126
■	Amount:	$2,500.00
■	Pmt. Method:	Check
■	Customer's Check:	7563

Practice Transaction #2. Receive Payments Window

The preceding diagram shows the Receive Payments window with Practice Transaction #2 entered.

▶ *If your window is consistent with the diagram, save the transaction and close the window. If there are errors, go back and correct them before saving.*

Transaction Review After the Transaction Is Saved

▶ *Click Customers in the Home Center → Transactions tab → Received Payments → double-click Customer Payment for Check No. 7563. Review the information for Check No. 7563 on the same Receive Payments window that you just prepared and correct the information if it is wrong.*

Make a Bank Deposit for Practice Transaction #2

Record the bank deposit for the check received from McCarthy's Bed & Breakfast.

▶ *Process the bank deposit of $2,500 on 02/08/2021 in the general cash account (#10100 Cash - General Account) following the instructions on pages 30 through 32 of the Reference book, but do not save it yet.*

Practice Transaction #2. Payments to Deposit Window

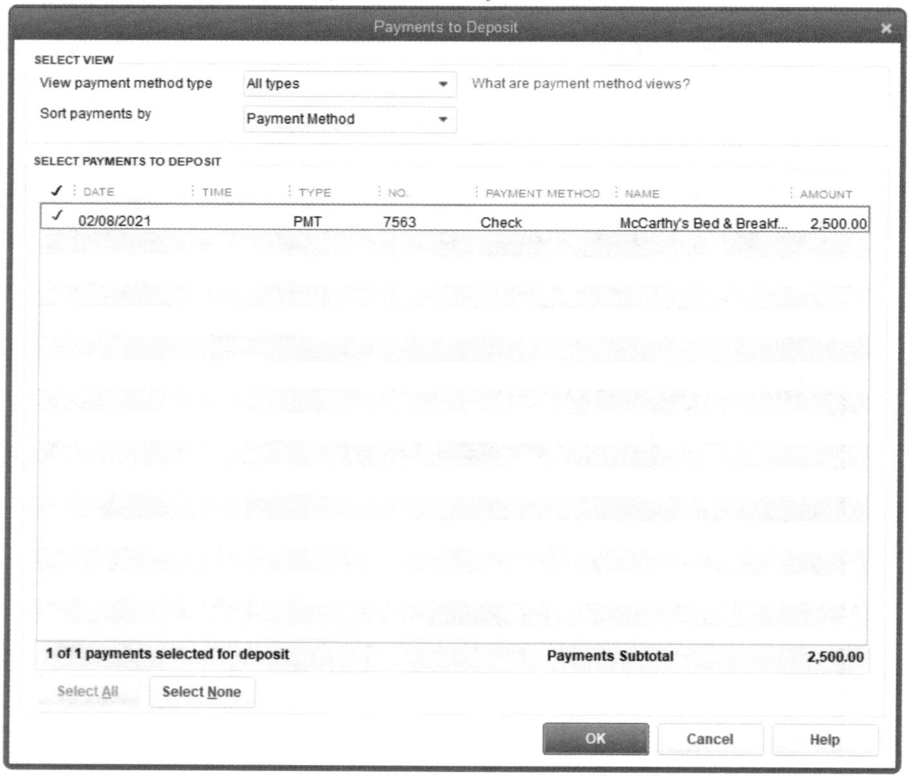

Payments to Deposit							✕
SELECT VIEW							
View payment method type	All types	▾	What are payment method views?				
Sort payments by	Payment Method	▾					
SELECT PAYMENTS TO DEPOSIT							
✓ DATE	TIME	TYPE	NO.	PAYMENT METHOD	NAME	AMOUNT	
✓ 02/08/2021		PMT	7563	Check	McCarthy's Bed & Breakf...	2,500.00	
1 of 1 payments selected for deposit				Payments Subtotal		2,500.00	
Select All Select None							
				OK	Cancel	Help	

Practice Transaction #2. Make Deposits Window

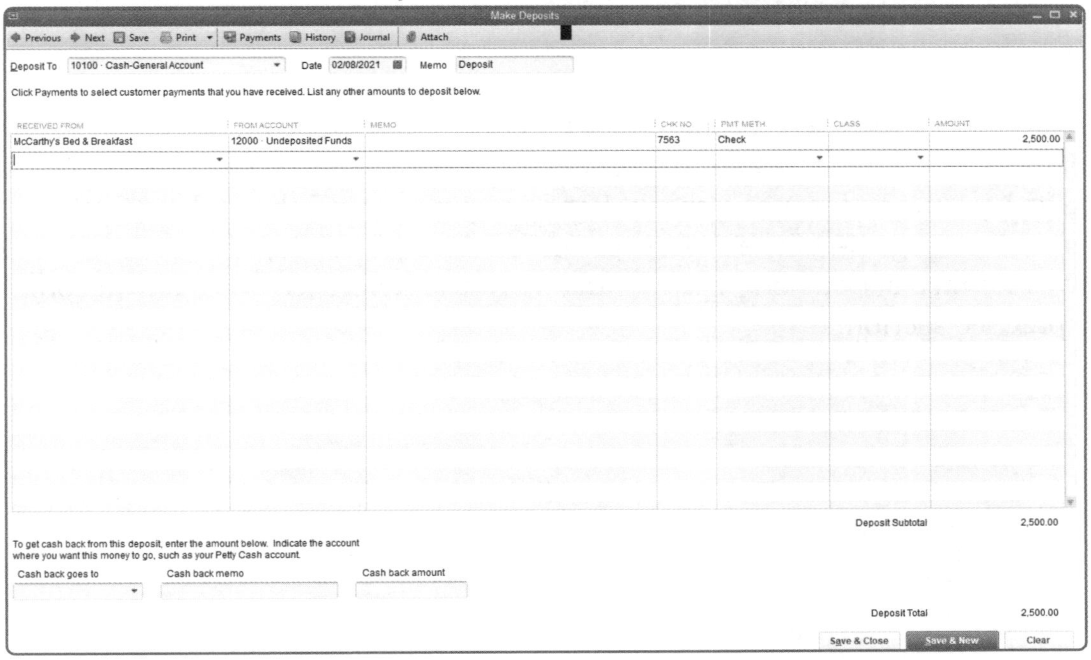

The previous diagram shows the Make Deposits window with the deposit completed.

> ▶ *If your window is consistent with the diagram, save it. If there are errors, correct them before saving it.*

Transaction Review After the Transaction Is Saved

> ▶ *Click Report Center → Banking → Deposit Detail → select This Fiscal Year in the Dates box → scroll to the last deposit for McCarthy's Bed & Breakfast. If the deposit is for an amount other than $2,500.00, click on the transaction and make the correction.*

Make a Cash Sale

Reference Material

A cash sale is processed through the Enter Sales Receipts window, an example of which is shown on page 35 of the Reference book. In this project, all payments received are in the form of a check. Read and understand the Make a Cash Sale overview on page 34 of the Reference book before processing the transaction. Then follow the instructions on pages 34 and 35 of the Reference book as you complete the practice section.

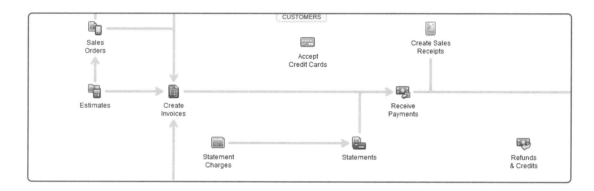

Practice Transaction. Make a Cash Sale Receipt

▶ *Process a cash sale invoice using the following information, but do not save it yet.*

- Customer: 1000–Cash Customer (10Cash Cust)
- Payment Method: Check
- Date: February 12, 2021
- Sale No.:   CASH549
- Sold To: Rockview Inn
  6117 Green Blvd.
  Cleveland, OH 44101
- Check No.:   78645
- Products sold:

Item	Description	Qty.	Rate
105	Queen sheet set	10	$35.75
110	Queen comforter	15	49.25

- Ohio Sales Tax: 5%
- Amount Received: $1,151.06

Practice Transaction. Enter Sales Receipts Window — 10Cash Cust

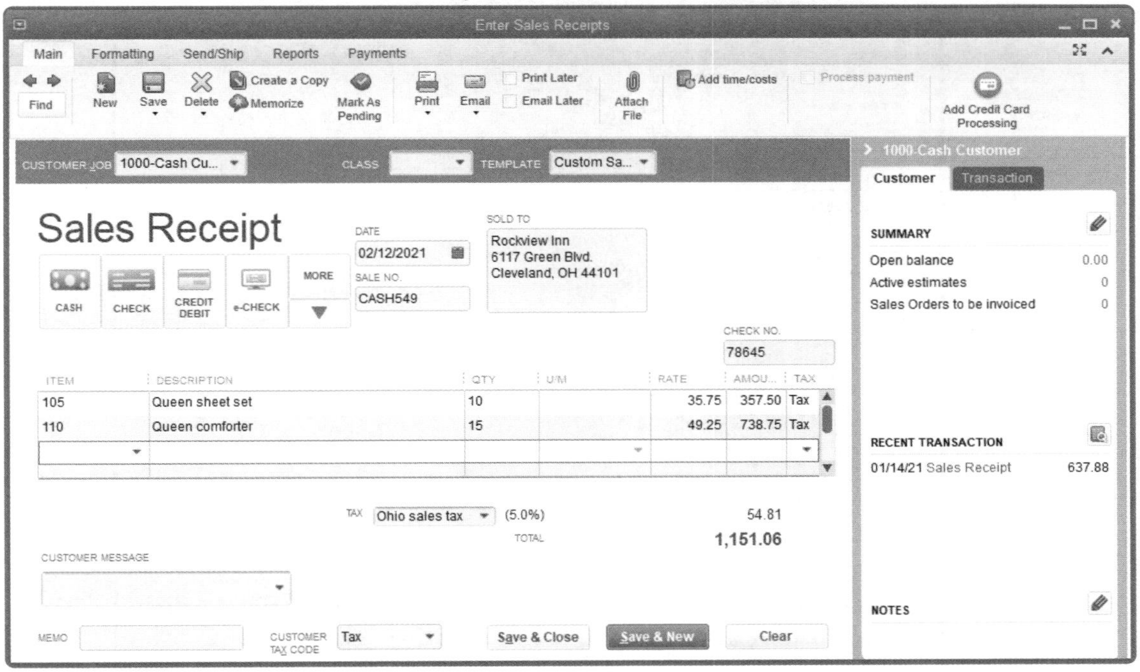

The preceding diagram shows the Enter Sales Receipts window with the practice transaction entered.

▶ *If your window is consistent with the diagram, save the transaction. If there are errors, correct them before saving. Click No if asked if you want to change all future cash sales billing addresses to Rockview's.*

Transaction Review After the Transaction Is Saved

▶ *Click Customers in the Home Center → Transactions tab → Sales Receipts → double-click Customer Payment for Sale No. CASH549. Review the information for CASH549 on the same Receive Payments window that you just prepared and correct the information if it is wrong.*

Make a Bank Deposit for the Practice Transaction

▶ *Process the bank deposit of $1,151.06 on 2/12/2021 in the General Account following the instructions on pages 30 through 32 of the Reference book, but do not save it yet.*

Practice Transaction. Payments to Deposit Window

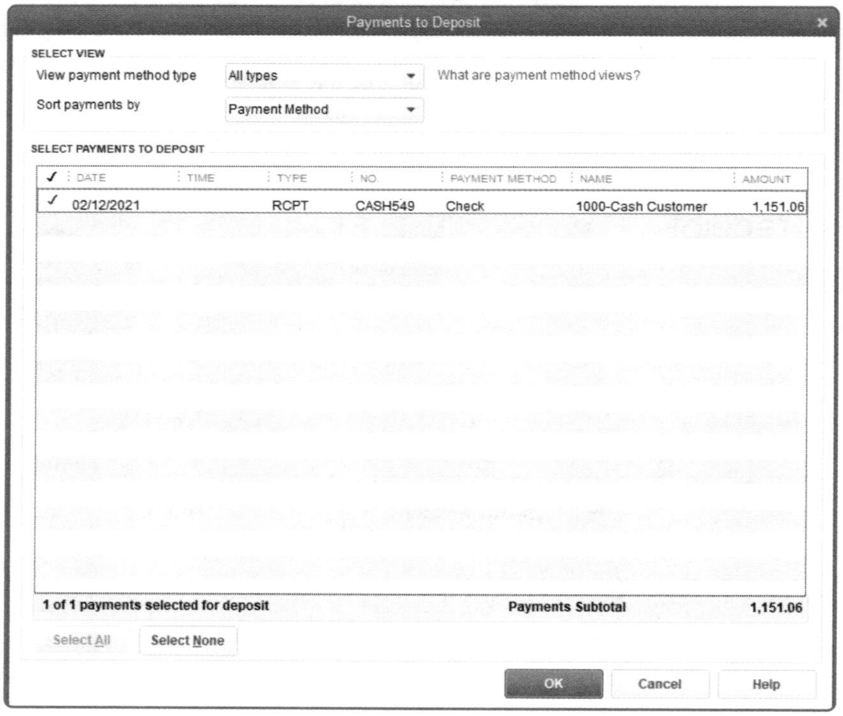

Payments to Deposit

SELECT VIEW

View payment method type: All types | What are payment method views?

Sort payments by: Payment Method

SELECT PAYMENTS TO DEPOSIT

✓	DATE	TIME	TYPE	NO.	PAYMENT METHOD	NAME	AMOUNT
✓	02/12/2021		RCPT	CASH549	Check	1000-Cash Customer	1,151.06

1 of 1 payments selected for deposit   Payments Subtotal   1,151.06

Select All   Select None

OK   Cancel   Help

Practice Transaction. Make Deposits Window

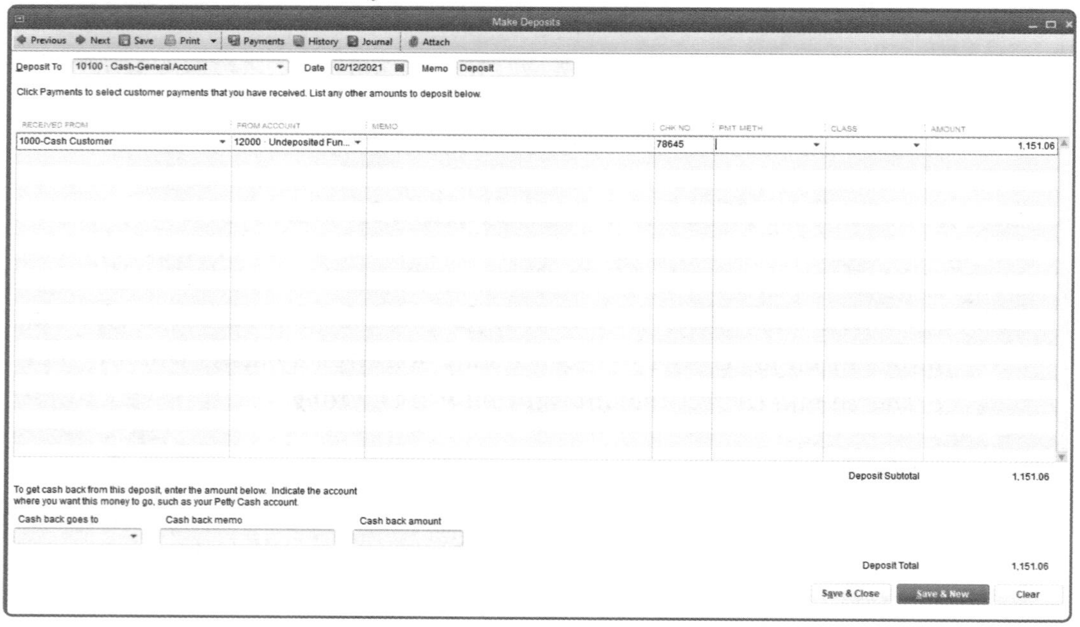

Make Deposits

◆ Previous ◆ Next 🖫 Save 🖨 Print ▾ 🖳 Payments 🕘 History 📄 Journal 📎 Attach

Deposit To: 10100 · Cash-General Account   Date 02/12/2021   Memo Deposit

Click Payments to select customer payments that you have received. List any other amounts to deposit below.

RECEIVED FROM	FROM ACCOUNT	MEMO	CHK NO.	PMT METH.	CLASS	AMOUNT
1000-Cash Customer	12000 · Undeposited Fun...		78645			1,151.06

Deposit Subtotal   1,151.06

To get cash back from this deposit, enter the amount below. Indicate the account where you want this money to go, such as your Petty Cash account.

Cash back goes to   Cash back memo   Cash back amount

Deposit Total   1,151.06

Save & Close   Save & New   Clear

The preceding diagram shows the Make Deposits window with the deposit completed.

▶ *If your window is consistent with the diagram, save the deposit. If there are errors, correct them before saving.*

Process a Sales Return or Allowance (Credit Memo)

Reference Material

A sales return or allowance is processed through the Create Credit Memos/Refunds–Accounts Receivable window, an example of which is shown on page 37 of the Reference book. Read and understand the Process a Sales Return or Allowance (Credit Memo) overview on page 36 of the Reference book before processing the transaction. Then follow the instructions on pages 36 and 37 of the Reference book as you complete the practice section.

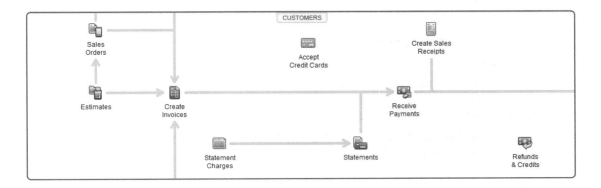

Practice Transaction #1. Create Credit Memo/Refund

▶ *Process a sales return, but do not save it yet.* Use the following information to record the sales return.

This sales return transaction is related to the February 1, 2021, sale to Columbus Inn. You processed the original sale in the Make a Credit Sale practice section on pages 7-3 and 7-4 (Practice Transaction #1). On February 12, 2021, the customer returned some of the items purchased on Invoice No. 5128. Details of the sales return are shown below and on the following page.

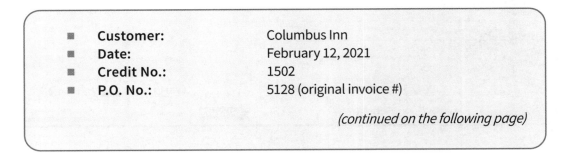

▪ **Customer:**　　　Columbus Inn
▪ **Date:**　　　　　February 12, 2021
▪ **Credit No.:**　　 1502
▪ **P.O. No.:**　　　 5128 (original invoice #)

(continued on the following page)

> *(continued from previous page)*
>
> ■ Items returned:
>
> | Item | Description | Qty. | Rate |
> |------|-------------|------|------|
> | 112 | Draperies | 5 | $72.50 |
> | 116 | Shower cap – 25 | 4 | 3.40 |
>
> ■ Ohio Sales Tax: 5%
> ■ Sales Return Total (check figure): $394.91
>
> **Available Credit window**
>
> ■ What would you like
>   to do with this credit?:   Apply to an invoice
>
> **Apply Credit to Invoices window**
>
> ■ Number: 5128

The following diagrams show the Create Credit Memos/Refunds–Accounts Receivable, Available Credit, and Apply Credit to Invoices windows with the preceding information included.

Practice Transaction #1. Create Credit Memos/Refunds–Accounts Receivable

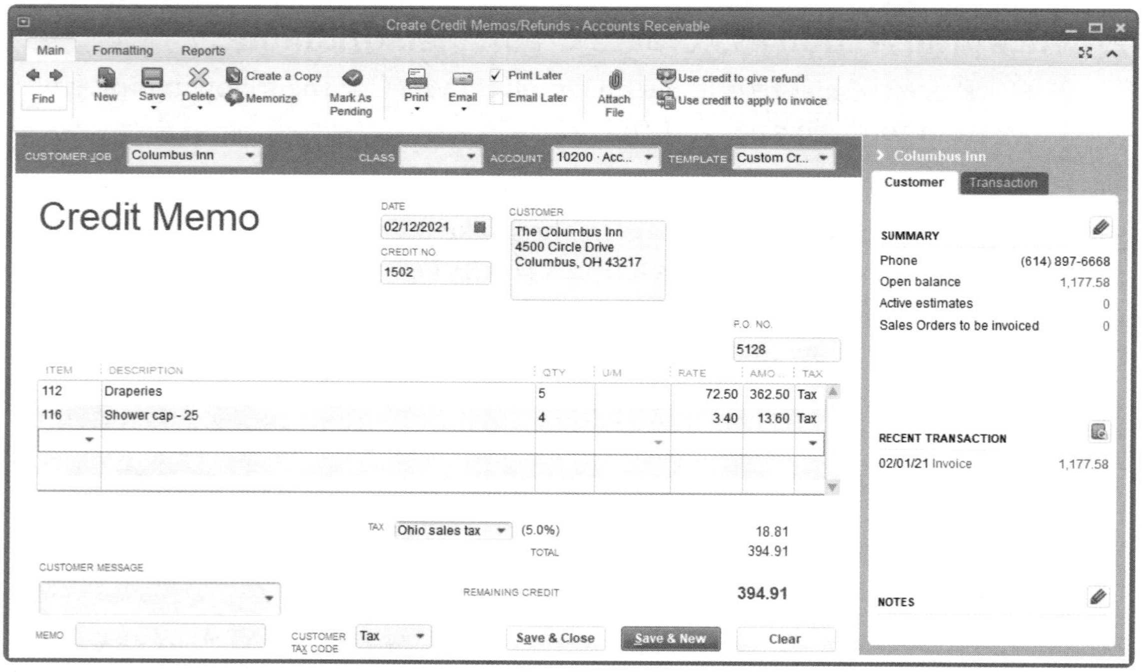

Practice Transaction #1. Available Credit Window

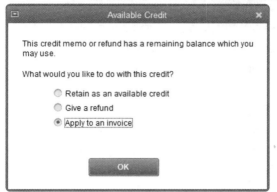

Practice Transaction #1. Apply Credit to Invoices Window

Apply Credit to Invoices						✕
CREDIT MEMO						
Customer:Job	Columbus Inn					
Ref. No.	1502		Original Amt.		394.91	
Date	02/12/2021		Remaining Credit		0.00	

✓	DATE	JOB	NUMBER	ORIG. AMT.	AMT. DUE	AMT. APPLIED
✓	02/01/2021		5128	1,177.58	1,177.58	394.91
		Totals		1,177.58	0.00	394.91

Clear Selections

Done   Cancel

▶ *If your windows are consistent with the diagrams, save the transaction. If there are errors, correct them before saving.*

Transaction Review After the Transaction Is Saved

▶ *Click Customers in the Home Center → Transactions tab → Credit Memos → double-click Credit Memo No. 1502. Review the information for Credit Memo No. 1502 on the same Create Credit Memos/Refunds → Accounts Receivable window that you just prepared and correct the information if it is wrong.*

Practice Transaction #2. Grant a Sales Allowance

This sales allowance transaction is also related to the February 1, 2021, sale to Columbus Inn. You processed the original sale in the Make a Credit Sale practice section on pages 7-3 and 7-4. On February 12, 2021, you processed a credit memo for the customer's return of some of the items purchased on Invoice No. 5128. After considerable discussion, Jackson's management has agreed to grant an allowance of $300.00 for the remaining draperies, which Columbus Inn management contends are lower in quality than was expected. Credit Memo No. 1503 was approved on February 15, 2021, for the allowance.

▶ *Process a credit memo for the sales allowance to Columbus Inn using the preceding information and other information from Practice Transaction #1, but do not save it yet.*

▪	**Customer:**	Columbus Inn
▪	**Date:**	February 15, 2021
▪	**Credit No.:**	1503
▪	**P.O. No.:**	5128 (original invoice #)
▪	**Item:**	112 - Draperies
▪	**Amount Discounted:**	$300.00
▪	**Credit Memo Total (check figure):**	$315.00

Available Credit window

▪	**What would you like to do with this credit?:**	Apply to an invoice

Apply Credit to Invoices window

▪	**Number:**	5128

The following diagrams show the Create Credit Memos/Refunds–Accounts Receivable, Available Credit, and Apply Credit to Invoices windows with the preceding information included.

Practice Transaction #2. Create Credit Memos/Refunds–Accounts Receivable Window

Practice Transaction #2. Available Credit Window

Practice Transaction #2. Apply Credit to Invoices Window

	Apply Credit to Invoices						✕
CREDIT MEMO							
Customer:Job	Columbus Inn						
Ref. No.	1503			Original Amt.		315.00	
Date	02/15/2021			Remaining Credit		0.00	

✓	DATE	JOB	NUMBER	ORIG. AMT.	AMT. DUE	AMT. APPLIED
✓	02/01/2021		5128	1,177.58	782.67	315.00
			Totals	1,177.58	0.00	315.00

Clear Selections

Done   Cancel

▶ *If your windows are consistent with the diagrams, save the transaction. If there are errors, correct them before saving.*

Transaction Review After the Transaction Is Saved

▶ *Click Customers in the Home Center → Transactions tab → Credit Memos → double-click Credit Memo No. 1503. Review the information for Credit Memo No. 1503 on the same Create Credit Memos/Refunds → Accounts Receivable window that you just prepared and correct the information if it is wrong.*

Write Off an Uncollectible Account Receivable

Direct and Allowance Methods of Accounting for Bad Debts and Write-off of an Uncollectible Accounts Receivable

There are two ways to write off an uncollectible accounts receivable:

- **Direct method.** In this method, the write-off of an uncollectible account receivable is a debit to bad debt expense and a credit to account receivable. Although this method is simple, it is acceptable for accrual accounting only when the potential uncollectible accounts receivable balance is immaterial at year-end. This method is used for both sample companies in *QuickBooks*. (Rock Castle Construction and Larry's Landscaping & Garden Supply).

- **Allowance method.** In this method, an estimate is made of the potential uncollectible receivables at year-end. The accounting entry for this estimate is a debit to bad debt expense and a credit to allowance to uncollectible accounts, which is a contra-account to accounts receivable. When an account becomes uncollectible, one option for the accounting entry is a debit to allowance for uncollectible accounts and a credit to accounts receivable. Another option that is common in practice is to follow the direct method for the write-off of the uncollectible accounts and then adjust the allowance to the appropriate amount at year-end. The allowance method is used in this chapter for Jackson Supply Company and in Chapter 9 for Waren Sports Supply. In both cases you will follow the direct method to write off uncollectible accounts and adjust the allowance at year-end.

When the allowance method is used in *QuickBooks*, the Account Type in Chart of Account maintenance must be Accounts Receivable for the allowance for uncollectible accounts to be included as a contra-account to accounts receivable on the balance sheet. When an account is labeled Accounts Receivable, *QuickBooks* requires that there is also a subsidiary account. In both Jackson Supply Company and Waren Sports Supply, there is a customer in the Customer & Jobs subsidiary record called Allowance account with a credit balance even though it is not an account receivable. This is illustrated below.

▶ *For Jackson Supply Company, click Home Page → Chart of Accounts. Right-click Account No. 10300, Allowance for Uncoll Accts. → Edit Account to access the chart of accounts maintenance account for the allowance.* Observe that the Account Type is Accounts Receivable and the Subaccount box is checked, which makes it a contra-account to accounts receivable.

> Save and close all open windows and return to the Home Page. Click the Customers icon → Customers and Jobs tab. Observe that there is a customer called Allowance account with a credit balance of $500, even though it is not a customer.

> Click Report Center → Company & Financial → double-click on Balance Sheet Standard under Balance Sheet & Net Worth. Change the "As of" date to 01/31/2021. Observe that both accounts receivable and the allowance are shown, with net accounts receivable also included.

> Click Report Center → Customers & Receivables → double-click on A/R Aging Summary. Change the date to 01/31/2021. Observe that the allowance is again shown as a negative amount.

Reference Material

A write-off of an uncollectible account receivable is processed through the Receive Payments window, an example of which is shown on page 39 of the Reference book. Read and understand the Write-off an Uncollectible Account Receivable overview on page 38 of the Reference book before processing the transaction. Then follow the instructions on pages 38 through 40 of the Reference book as you complete the practice section.

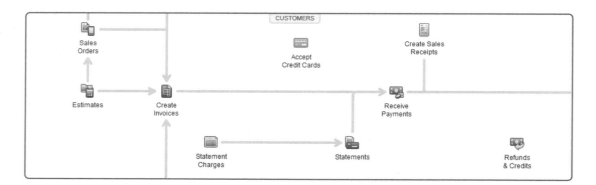

Practice Transaction. Receipts — Write-off

> Process an account receivable write-off transaction following the allowance method using the following information, but do not save the transaction yet.

McCarthy's Bed & Breakfast filed for bankruptcy protection and is unable to pay its outstanding receivable balance from Invoice No. 5126. Recall from the previous practice section that the customer remitted $2,500.00 of the invoice balance on February 8, 2021 (Practice Transaction #2 on pages 7-15 through 7-17). The remaining balance is uncollectible and is to be written off. Other details of the write-off transaction follow:

- **Customer Name:** McCarthy's Bed & Breakfast
- **Reference No.:** Write-off
- **Date:** February 25, 2021
- **Invoice No. written off:** 5126
- **Amount written off:** $631.36 (balance outstanding)
- **General ledger account information:**
  - Dr. A/C No. 40900 Bad Debt Expense
  - Cr. A/C No. 10200 Accounts Receivable

Practice Transaction. Discounts and Credits Window

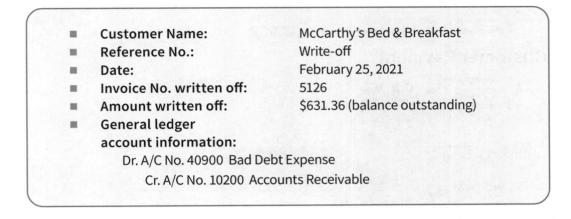

Practice Transaction. Receive Payments Window

The preceding diagrams show the Discount and Credits and Receive Payments windows with the write-off practice transaction entered.

▶   *If your windows are consistent with the diagrams, save the transaction. If there are errors, correct them before saving.*

Transaction Review After the Transaction Is Saved

▶   *Click Customers in the Home Center → Transactions tab → Received Payments → double-click customer McCarthy's Bed & Breakfast for Amount - $631.36. Review the information for Amount - $631.36 on the same Receive Payments window that you just prepared and correct the information if it is wrong.*

Receive a Miscellaneous Cash Receipt

Reference Material

Miscellaneous cash receipts, such as loan proceeds or sales of fixed assets or marketable securities, are processed through the Make Deposits window. An example of the window is shown on page 43 of the Reference book. Read and understand the Receive a Miscellaneous Cash Receipt overview on page 42. Then follow the instructions on pages 42 and 43 of the Reference book as you complete the practice section.

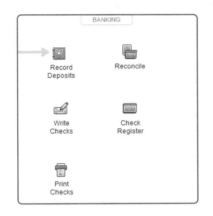

Practice Transaction. Receive a Miscellaneous Cash Receipt

▶ *Process a miscellaneous cash receipt transaction using the following information, but do not save the transaction yet.*

On February 15, 2021, the company received Check No. 83206 for $10,000 from Sun Bank for a note payable that is due February 15, 2023. The general ledger account for the debt is 21100, Long-Term Debt. *Note:* Sun Bank is not included in *QuickBooks* for Jackson. You will therefore need to add Sun Bank with the Make Deposits window open.

▶ *In Received From, type Sun Bank and press Enter. That will open the Name Not Found window. Click Quick Add. In the Select Name Type window click Other and then click Ok.*

Practice Transaction. Customer: Job Not Found Window

Name Not Found

Sun Bank is not in the Name list.

To automatically add Sun Bank to the Name list, click Quick Add.
You can enter more detailed information later.

To enter the detailed information now, click Set Up (usually not required).

[Quick Add]   [Set Up]   [Cancel]

Practice Transaction. Make Deposits Window

RECEIVED FROM	FROM ACCOUNT	MEMO	CHK. NO.	PMT. METH.	CLASS	AMOUNT
Sun Bank	21100 · Long-term Debt	Note payable	83206	Check		10,000.00

Deposit To: 10100 · Cash-General Account   Date 02/15/2021   Memo: Deposit

Click Payments to select customer payments that you have received. List any other amounts to deposit below.

Deposit Subtotal — 10,000.00

To get cash back from this deposit, enter the amount below. Indicate the account where you want this money to go, such as your Petty Cash account.

Cash back goes to   Cash back memo   Cash back amount

Deposit Total — 10,000.00

[Save & Close]   [Save & New]   [Clear]

The preceding diagram shows the Make Deposits window with the bank loan transaction entered.

▶ *If your window is consistent with the diagram, save the transaction. If there are errors, correct them before saving.*

Transaction Review After the Transaction Is Saved

▶ *Click Reports Center → Accountant & Taxes → click on Journal. Select 02/15/21 in both the From and To date boxes. Scroll to the last transaction on the list to make sure it is recorded as a debit to Cash and a credit to Long-term Debt for $10,000. If any of the information is wrong, drill down on the transaction to access the Make Deposits window and correct the information.*

Prepare a Monthly Statement for Accounts Receivable

Reference Material

Accounts receivable statements are prepared using the Create Statements window, an example of which is shown on page 45 of the Reference book. Read and understand the Prepare a Statement for Accounts Receivable overview on page 44 of the Reference book before preparing the accounts receivable statements. Then follow the instructions on pages 44 through 46 of the Reference book as you complete the practice section.

Practice Transaction. Create a Statement

▶ *Prepare and preview an accounts receivable statement at February 28, 2021, for the period January 1, 2021, to February 28, 2021, for McCarthy's Bed & Breakfast. If the statement is the same as the one shown on page 7-34, print it. If it is not the same, make corrections in the Create Statements window. If it is still not the same, you have made errors in recording the transactions for McCarthy's Bed & Breakfast. You can make those corrections by first comparing the transactions in your window to those shown below and then correcting the transactions you have recorded.*

Practice Transaction. Create Statements Window

Statement

Jackson Supply Company

6211 Washburn Ave.
Columbus, OH 43216

Date
2/28/2021

To:
McCarthy's B&B
511 Mansion
Columbus, OH 43216

Amount Due	Amount Enc.
$0.00	

U/M	Date	Transaction	Amount	Balance
	12/31/2020	Balance forward		0.00
	01/20/2021	INV #5126. Due 02/19/2021.	3,286.50	3,286.50
	01/20/2021	CREDMEM #1501.	-155.14	3,131.36
	02/08/2021	PMT #7563.	-2,500.00	631.36
	02/25/2021	Discount #write off.	-631.36	0.00

CURRENT	1-30 DAYS PAST DUE	31-60 DAYS PAST DUE	61-90 DAYS PAST DUE	OVER 90 DAYS PAST DUE	Amount Due
0.00	0.00	0.00	0.00	0.00	$0.00

Chapter Summary

After completing Chapter 7, back up your data files for Jackson Supply Company using the instructions in the E-Materials you downloaded from the Armond Dalton Resources website. Be sure to use a descriptive file name, such as "Jackson after Ch 07."

You have now practiced processing transactions for the seven sales and cash receipts activities. If you are satisfied with your understanding of the sales and cash receipts transactions in this chapter, you should now proceed to Chapter 7 homework assigned by your instructor, which is available on the Armond Dalton Resources website at www.armonddaltonresources.com.

Because of practice exercises and chapter problems in previous chapters, each of you may have different transactions and balances in the company datasets used in the homework. **To ensure consistent answers across everyone in the class, please restore both the Rock Castle Construction and Larry's Landscaping & Garden Supply datasets using the initial backups you downloaded from the Armond Dalton Resources website. Restore both companies before proceeding to the Chapter 7 homework assigned by your instructor.**

If you do not feel comfortable with your ability to complete each of these sales and cash receipts activities, you can practice further in one of two ways.

1. You can do the entire chapter again by following the instructions in the E-Materials to restore the Jackson Supply Company dataset from the initial backup you downloaded from the Armond Dalton Resources website. Doing so will return all data to its original form and permit you to practice all procedures again.
2. You can do additional practice by completing any or most of the sections in this chapter again. You can continue to use Jackson Supply Company.

Document numbers will, of course, be different if you redo sections without restoring the company data. In addition, there are certain activities that you cannot do without first recording other information. For example, you cannot complete the Receive Goods on a Sales Return practice section without first recording the original sale in the Make a Credit Sale section. All practice sections that are dependent upon the completion of an earlier practice section are clearly identified in this chapter.

If you cannot recall how to make a periodic backup or restore a backup, refer to the E-Materials located at www.armonddaltonresources.com.

This page is intentionally blank.

PRACTICE — PAYROLL CYCLE AND OTHER ACTIVITIES

Introduction

In this chapter you will first learn about paying employees. Following that, you will learn about three other activities. The same approach is followed for the payroll cycle (pay employees) and other activities that was followed for the purchases and cash disbursements and sales and cash receipts cycles. After the completion of the pay employees section, the following three activities are included:

- Prepare a general journal entry
- Adjust perpetual inventory records
- Prepare a bank reconciliation

The same considerations included in Chapter 6, pages 6-3 and 6-4, are equally relevant for Chapter 8. You should carefully read these considerations again before you begin processing transactions in this chapter to avoid making mistakes.

Pay Employees

Reference Material

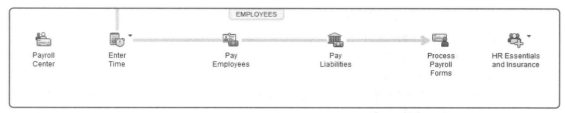

A payroll transaction is processed starting with the Employee Center: Payroll Center window. Although payroll is easy to process, there are several windows involved:

- Employee Center: Payroll Center
- Enter Payroll Information
- Review and Create Paychecks
- Preview Paycheck
- Confirmation and Next Steps

Read and understand the Pay Employees overview on page 48 of the Reference book before processing the transaction. Then follow the instructions on pages 48 through 51 as you complete the practice section.

Practice Transaction—Pay Employees

> Recall that in Chapter 5 you increased Mark Phelps's regular pay rate to $15 and his overtime pay rate to $22.50. If you have restored the Jackson Supply Company dataset since processing this maintenance task in Chapter 5 (maintenance task #7), you will need to update his pay rates again now using the Edit Employee window.

▷ *Process the February 15, 2021, semi-monthly payroll for Jackson Supply Company using the information below by completing all steps in the Quick Reference Table on pages 48 and 49 of the Reference book.*

▷ *As you complete each window, compare the information to the relevant window that follows before continuing to the next window.* **Note:** The windows shown here assume you completed the maintenance task in Chapter 5 that updated Mark Phelps's regular pay rate to $15.00 and his overtime pay rate to $22.50. If you did not do this maintenance task in Chapter 5, either complete it now or realize that your windows will have slightly different information.

Enter Employee Information window

- **Pay Period Ends:** 02/15/2021
- **Check Date:** 02/15/2021
- **First Check No.:** 517
- **Bank Account No.:** 10100 Cash–General Account
- **Employees Selected To Pay:** 3 (all)
- **Employee Information:**

Employee	Regular Pay	Overtime Pay	Salary	Total Hours
Jennifer Brownell			*	
Kenneth Jorgensen	88 (88.00)	8.50 hrs.		96.50 hrs.
Mark Phelps	88 (88.00)	5.00 hrs.		93.00 hrs.

Totals

- **Gross Pay:** $ 6,749.00
- **Taxes:** $ 1,209.44 withheld**
- **Net Pay:** $ 5,539.56**
- **Employer Taxes:** $ 725.25**

* Leave salary blank in this window. It will appear in the final version after you preview the paychecks.
** Because the *QuickBooks* program periodically updates for changes in federal and state taxes, you may have slightly different numbers for taxes or the resulting net pay. There may be slight differences, depending on when you load *QuickBooks* and when the periodic updates happen after initial installation.

▷ *If the contents of your windows are the same as the ones shown on pages 8-5 through 8-8, go ahead and click the Create Paychecks button in the Review and Create Paychecks window per step M in the Quick Reference Table. If there are errors, go back and correct them before clicking the Create Paychecks button. See the illustrations that follow for the multiple payroll windows you will be processing. Do not be concerned if any of the payroll taxes and/ or the bank account balance shown on your screen are different from the window illustrations.*

Practice Transaction. Employee Center: Payroll Center Window

Practice Transaction. Enter Payroll Information Window

Practice Transaction. Review and Create Paychecks Window

Practice Transaction. Preview Paycheck Window

Chapter 8: Practice — Payroll Cycle and Other Activities

Practice Transaction. Preview Paycheck Window

Kenneth J Jorgensen

PAY PERIOD 02/01/2021 - 02/15/2021

☐ Use Direct Deposit   CLASS

Earnings

ITEM NAME	RATE	HOURS	WC CODE	CUSTOMER:JOB
Regular Pay	22.00	88.00		
Overtime	33.00	8.50		
TOTALS		2,216.50	96.50 hrs	

SICK AVAILABLE   48.00
VACATION AVAIL.   71.25
SICK ACCRUED
VAC. ACCRUED   6.75
☐ Do not accrue sick/vac

Other Payroll Items

ITEM NAME	RATE	QUANTITY

Company Summary

How are these items calculated?

ITEM NAME	AMOUNT	YTD
Social Security Company	137.43	366.58
Medicare Company	32.14	85.73
Federal Unemployment	13.30	35.48
OH - Unemployment	59.85	159.64

Employee Summary

How are these items calculated?

ITEM NAME	AMOUNT	YTD
Regular Pay	1,936.00	5,632.00
Overtime	280.50	280.50
Medicare Employee Addl Tax	0.00	0.00
OH - School District	0.00	0.00
Federal Withholding	-128.00	-293.00
Social Security Employee	-137.43	-366.58
Medicare Employee	-32.14	-85.73
OH - Withholding	-61.05	-151.63
Check Amount:	1,857.88	

Save & Previous | Save & Next | Save & Close | Cancel | Help | ☐ Enter net/Calculate gross

---

Practice Transaction. Preview Paycheck Window

Mark C Phelps

PAY PERIOD 02/01/2021 - 02/15/2021

☐ Use Direct Deposit   CLASS

Earnings

ITEM NAME	RATE	HOURS	WC CODE	CUSTOMER:JOB
Regular Pay	15.00	88.00		
Overtime	22.50	5.00		
TOTALS		1,432.50	93.00 hrs	

SICK AVAILABLE   40.00
VACATION AVAIL.   63.25
SICK ACCRUED
VAC. ACCRUED   6.75
☐ Do not accrue sick/vac

Other Payroll Items

ITEM NAME	RATE	QUANTITY

Company Summary

How are these items calculated?

ITEM NAME	AMOUNT	YTD
Social Security Company	88.82	234.64
Medicare Company	20.78	54.88
Federal Unemployment	8.60	22.71
OH - Unemployment	38.68	102.18

Employee Summary

How are these items calculated?

ITEM NAME	AMOUNT	YTD
Regular Pay	1,320.00	3,672.00
Overtime	112.50	112.50
Medicare Employee Addl Tax	0.00	0.00
OH - School District	0.00	0.00
Federal Withholding	-124.00	-309.00
Social Security Employee	-88.82	-234.64
Medicare Employee	-20.78	-54.88
OH - Withholding	-32.79	-79.85
Check Amount:	1,166.11	

Save & Previous | Save & Next | Save & Close | Cancel | Help | ☐ Enter net/Calculate gross

Practice Transaction. Confirmation and Next Steps Window

Transaction Review After the Transactions Are Saved

▶ *Click Report Center → Employees & Payroll → Payroll Item Detail. Select "This Calendar Year" in the Dates column. Click the check number for each of the three employees and compare the amounts to the amounts in the Preview Paycheck windows. If there are errors it is possible to correct them, but it typically requires preparing a new check and retrieving it from the employee if it has already been issued. If state or federal tax forms have already been sent, the change may require an amendment of these forms. It is therefore essential that processing payroll be done with extreme care.*

Prepare a General Journal Entry

General journal entries are transactions that can affect any of the three cycles. In *QuickBooks*, a general journal entry is used only when a transaction cannot be recorded with any of the activities already discussed in the previous chapters. For example, the write-off of an uncollectible accounts receivable is processed by completing a discount to bad debt expense in the Receive Payments window that was shown in the revenue cycle section of this book. The monthly or annual provision for bad debt expense is processed with a Make General Journal Entries activity because it is not included as a separate activity.

Reference Material

A general journal entry is posted through the Make General Journal Entries window, an example of which is shown on page 53 of the Reference book. Read and understand the Prepare a General Journal Entry overview on page 52 of the Reference book before processing the transaction. Then follow the instructions on pages 52 and 53 of the Reference book as you complete the practice section.

Practice Transaction #1. Accrue Interest Expense on Long-Term Debt

On February 28, 2021, Jackson Supply Company records interest expense on its long-term debt.

▶ Record a general journal entry at 2/28/2021 for two months interest on long-term debt of $625.00 (5% annually for two months on an $75,000 note). The general journal entry is number 1.

▪ **Date:**	02/28/2021	
▪ **General Journal Entry No.:**	909	
▪ **Account:**		
	Amount	**Memo**
Debit: 40800 Interest Expense	$625.00	Interest Pmt LT Debt
Credit: 21000 Interest Payable	625.00	Interest Pmt LT Debt
▪ **Name:**	leave blank	

The diagram at the top of the following page shows the Make General Journal Entries window with the interest expense general journal entry displayed. Note that a descriptive entry was made in the Memo box to clearly identify the general journal entry.

Practice Transaction #1. Make General Journal Entries Window—Quarterly Interest Expense

> If your window is consistent with the diagram, save the general journal entry. If there are errors, correct them before saving. Don't be concerned if your window shows a different number in the Entry No. box.

General Journal Entry Review After the Journal Entry Is Saved

> Click Report Center → Accountant & Taxes in the left column → Adjusting Journal Entries. Change the From & To dates to 2/28/2021, and then locate the journal entry you just processed. Determine that the information is correct in the journal listing. If any of the information is wrong, drill down on the entry to access the Make General Journal Entries window and correct the information.

Practice Transaction #2. Adjust Bad Debt Expense

Jackson Supply Company management wants to adjust bad debt expense and the allowance for uncollectible accounts at 2/28/2021. Bad debt expense on the first two months sales is estimated to be 1.75% of sales (Account No. 30100).

► *Record the general journal entry for bad debts at 2/28/2021. You must also select the subsidiary account named "Allowance account" in the name column on the same line as the credit for the allowance for uncollectible accounts. (See pages 7-27 through 7-30 in Chapter 7 for an explanation of the treatment of bad debt expense and the allowance for uncollectible accounts.)*

Note: Regardless of the balance in your general ledger account for sales and bad debt expense, assume that sales has a balance of $51,811.40 and bad debt expense of $631.36. One percent of sales of $51,811.40 is $906.70. Since the existing balance is $138.75, the adjustment is for the difference, which is $275.34 ($906.70 - $631.36). The general journal entry is therefore a debit to bad debt expense of $275.34 and a credit to the allowance for uncollectible accounts of the same amount.

■ Date:	02/28/2021	
■ General Journal Entry No.:	910	
■ Account:		

	Amount	Memo
Debit: 40900 Bad Debt Expense	$275.34	Bad Debt Expense Adj.
Credit: 10300 Allowance Uncoll Accts	$275.34	Bad Debt Expense Adj.
■ Name:		Leave blank for debit but select Allowance account using the Name drop-down list for the credit.

The diagram that follows shows the Make General Journal Entries window with the bad debt expense general journal entry displayed. Note that a descriptive entry was made in the Memo box to clearly identify the general journal entry. If you cannot see account # 10300, you might have to expand the Make General Journal Entries window to see it.

Practice Transaction #2. Make General Journal Entries Window

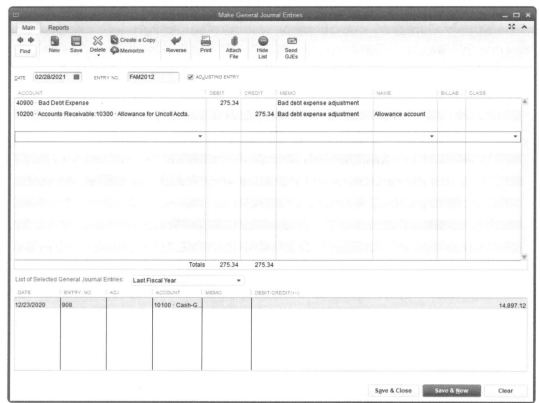

> ▶ *If your window is consistent with the diagram, save the general journal entry. If there are errors, correct them before saving.* Don't be concerned if your window shows a different number in the Entry No. box.

General Journal Entry Review After the Journal Entry Is Saved

> ▶ *Follow the same procedure that you used for the first general journal entry. If any of the information is wrong, drill down on the entry to access the Make General Journal Entries window and correct the information.*

Adjust Perpetual Inventory Records

Reference Material

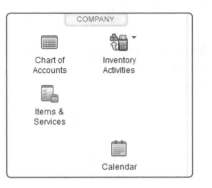

An adjustment of the perpetual inventory records is processed through the Adjust Quantity/Value on Hand window, an example of which is shown on page 55 of the Reference book. Inventory adjustments are usually made to make the perpetual records equal a physical count, but they can also be made for such things as inventory transfers, returned goods, and discarding obsolete inventory. Read and understand the Adjust Perpetual Inventory Records overview on page 54 of the Reference book before processing the transaction. Then follow the instructions on pages 54 and 55 of the Reference book as you complete the practice section.

Practice Transaction

▶ *Record an adjustment to the perpetual inventory records in QuickBooks using the following information, but do not save it yet.*

On February 28, 2021, a physical inventory count was taken by company personnel. There were differences between the physical count and the perpetual quantities recorded in *QuickBooks* for two inventory items. The physical count is the correct quantity for each of the items. The adjustment account is Cost of Goods Sold.

	Adjustment Date:	02/28/2021		
	Reference No.:	1		
	Adjustment Account:	30400 Cost of Goods Sold		

Item	Description	Current Qty.	New Qty.	Qty. Difference
104	Standard sheet set	190	182	– 8
108	Blanket	207	214	7

| | Total Value of Adjustment: | ($65.50) |
| | Memo: | Physical count adjustment |

The diagram below shows the Adjust Quantity/Value on Hand window for the two inventory adjustments. Don't be concerned if your window contains different current quantities as long as the new quantities are correct.

Practice Transaction. Adjust Quantity/Value on Hand Window

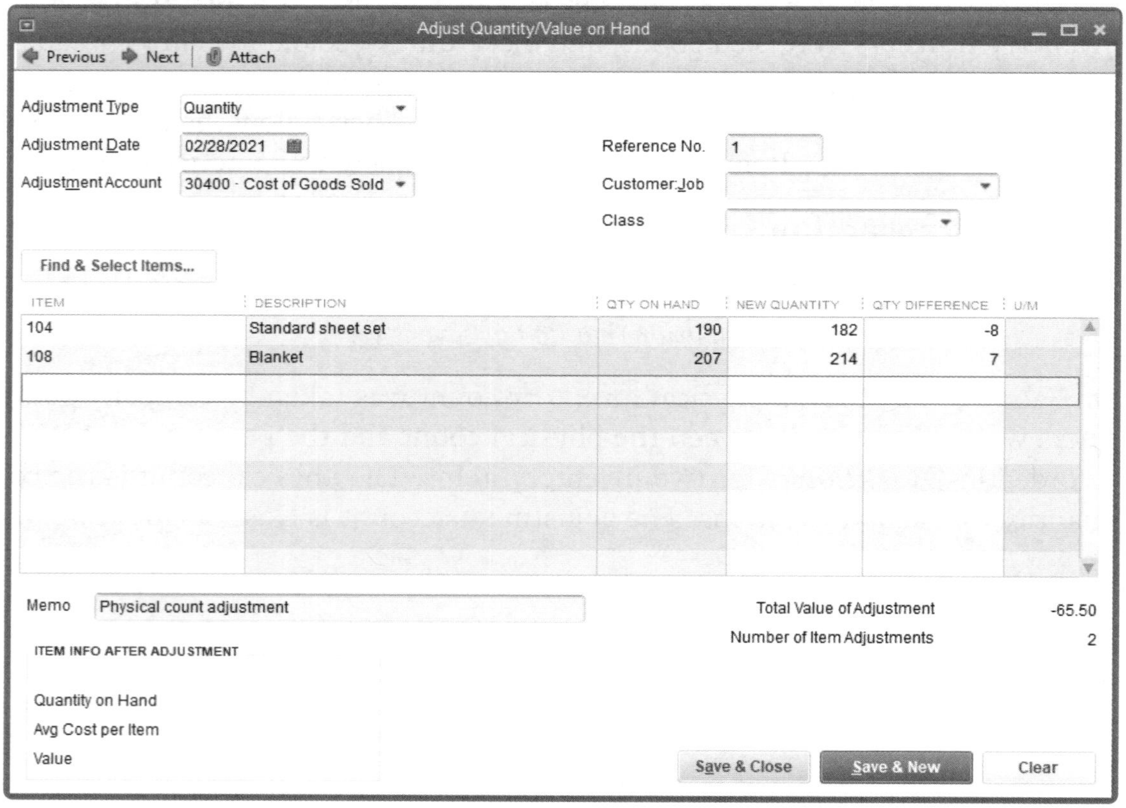

▶ *If your window is consistent with the diagram for each item, Save & Close the transaction. If there are errors, correct them before saving.*

Transaction Review After the Inventory Adjustment Is Saved

▶ *Click Lists on the Menu Bar → Item List to open the Item List window. Examine the two inventory items you adjusted to determine if the correct quantities are now included.* If any of the information is wrong, return to the Adjust Quantity/Value on Hand window and make corrections.

Prepare a Bank Reconciliation

Reference Material

Bank reconciliations are prepared through the Begin Reconciliation and Reconcile windows, examples of which are shown on page 57 of the Reference book. Read and understand the Prepare a Bank Reconciliation overview on page 56 of the Reference book before you perform the activity. Then follow the instructions on pages 56 and 57 of the Reference book as you complete the practice section.

There is no way for *QuickBooks* to know which deposits, checks, and other bank transactions have cleared the bank. Therefore, the person preparing the bank reconciliation must determine whether recorded *QuickBooks* transactions have or have not cleared the bank and whether any transactions that have cleared the bank were not recorded in *QuickBooks*. This is done by the person preparing the bank reconciliation examining all bank statement transactions and comparing them to the amounts included on the *QuickBooks* account reconciliation window. In some cases this may result in additions or changes to recorded amounts in the *QuickBooks* records.

You are to prepare the bank reconciliation for the month of January 2021. The transactions processed in this chapter do not affect the bank reconciliation because they are all in February, not in the period you are doing the bank reconciliation. Keep in mind that you can make most corrections prior to reconciling the bank statement by clicking the appropriate box and correcting the error.

Practice Activity

▶ *Prepare the January bank reconciliation for the 10100 Cash–General Account in QuickBooks using the information on the following page.* **Note:** Select the check box next to "Hide transactions after the statement end date" in the upper-right corner of the Reconcile–Cash–General Account window to hide transactions after 1/31/21.

■	Account:	10100 Cash–General Account
■	Bank Statement Date:	01/31/2021
■	Beginning Balance:	$14,897.12
■	Ending Balance:	$17,281.88
■	Deposits In Transit:	None
■	Checks Not Clearing the Bank (outstanding checks):	

Check No.	Amount
506	$ 392.00
509	562.50
510	2,436.06
511	1,736.80
512	1,064.88

■	Service Charge on Bank Statement, not yet recorded in G/L:	$27.50
■	Date:	01/31/2021
■	G/L Posting Account for Service Charge:	A/C No. 41800 Miscellaneous

Practice Activity. Bank Reconciliation—Begin Reconciliation Window

Begin Reconciliation

Select an account to reconcile, and then enter the ending balance from your account statement.

Account   10100 · Cash-General Acc... ▼   last reconciled on 12/31/2020.

Statement Date   01/31/2021
Beginning Balance   14,897.12   What if my beginning balance doesn't match my statement?
Ending Balance   17,281.88

Enter any service charge or interest earned.

Service Charge	Date	Account	Class
27.50	01/31/2021	41800 · Miscellaneous ▼	▼
Interest Earned	Date	Account	Class
0.00	01/31/2021	▼	▼

Locate Discrepancies   Undo Last Reconciliation   Continue   Cancel   Help

The diagram on the following page shows the Account Reconciliation window before the "Reconcile Now" button is clicked.

Practice Activity. Reconcile—Cash–General Account Window

Reconcile - Cash-General Account									_ □ ×

For period: 01/31/2021   ☑ Hide transactions after the statement's end date

Checks and Payments

✓	DATE ▲	CHK #	PAYEE	AMOUNT
✓	01/03/2021	501	American Linen S...	14,048.30
✓	01/07/2021	502	National Insuranc...	1,502.00
✓	01/15/2021	503	Jennifer M Brownell	2,521.27
✓	01/15/2021	504	Kenneth J Jorgen...	1,647.43
✓	01/15/2021	505	Mark C Phelps	1,013.49
	01/17/2021	506	Ohio Power & Lig...	392.00
✓	01/21/2021	507	Omni Incorporated	1,609.65
✓	01/25/2021	508	American Linen S...	22,475.00
	01/26/2021	509	Ohio National Bank	562.50
	01/29/2021	510	Jennifer M Brown...	2,521.27
	01/29/2021	511	Kenneth J Jorgen...	1,510.25
	01/29/2021	512	Mark C Phelps	926.53

Deposits and Other Credits

✓	DATE ▲	CHK #	PAYEE	TYPE	AMOUNT
✓	01/07/2021		American Line...	BILL	
✓	01/10/2021			DEP	1,557.65
✓	01/13/2021			DEP	10,140.79
✓	01/14/2021			DEP	637.88
✓	01/19/2021			DEP	1,089.38
✓	01/20/2021			DEP	11,602.50
✓	01/21/2021			DEP	12,142.20
✓	01/25/2021			DEP	10,059.00

☑ Highlight Marked   Mark All   Unmark All   Go To   Columns to Display...

Beginning Balance	14,897.12		Service Charge	-27.50
Items you have marked cleared		Modify	Interest Earned	0.00
8 Deposits and Other Credits	47,229.40		Ending Balance	17,281.88
7 Checks and Payments	44,817.14		Cleared Balance	17,281.88
			Difference	0.00

                                                        Reconcile Now   Leave

▷ *If your window is consistent with the diagram for each item, click the Reconcile Now button. If there is a problem, click the Leave button. You can then go back to correct the reconciliation in process by selecting the Reconcile button from the Home Page and making the necessary corrections.*

Bank Reconciliation Review After the Bank Reconciliation Is Saved

After clicking the Reconcile Now button when the reconciliation is complete, *QuickBooks* allows you to view and print the reconciliation reports immediately. If you want to view them later, complete the following step.

▷ *You can review your bank reconciliation at any time by navigating to Reports → Report Center → Banking → Previous Reconciliation. Select A/C No. 10100 (Cash–General Account), select Summary, Detail, or Both, and then select the statement ending date for the reconciliation you want to review. Review the bank reconciliation. If any of the information is wrong, go back and correct it.*

Chapter Summary

After completing Chapter 8, you should again back up your data files for Jackson Supply Company using the instructions in the E-Materials you downloaded from the Armond Dalton Resources website. Be sure to give the file a descriptive name, such as "Jackson after Ch 08."

You have now practiced all of the primary transactions and other activities included in Chapters 6 through 8. You will use the knowledge you have gained in these chapters as you do Chapters 9 and 10. You are not, however, expected to be able to process transactions and do other activities without the use of the Reference book. You should plan to use the Reference book for all remaining parts of the project.

One way for you to summarize the information you have learned is to reread the brief overview in the Reference book for each section. This overview emphasizes what is being accomplished using *QuickBooks*, not how to do the activity.

You should now proceed to Chapter 8 homework assigned by your instructor, which is available on the Armond Dalton Resources website at www.armonddaltonresources.com. **Because of practice exercises and chapter problems in previous chapters, each of you may have different transactions and balances in the company datasets used in the homework. To ensure consistent answers across everyone in the class, please restore both the Rock Castle Construction and Larry's Landscaping & Garden Supply datasets using the initial backups that you downloaded from the Armond Dalton Resources website. Restore both companies before proceeding to the Chapter 8 homework assigned by your instructor.**

If you are satisfied with your understanding of the payroll transactions and other activities in this chapter and have completed all of this chapter's problems assigned by your instructor, continue to Chapter 9, which applies the knowledge about *QuickBooks* that you have learned in the first eight chapters.

If you do not feel comfortable with your ability to complete each of the transactions and other activities in this chapter, you can practice further in one of two ways.

1. You can do the entire chapter again by following the instructions in the E-Materials to restore the Jackson Supply Company data. Doing so will return all data to its original form and permit you to practice all procedures again.

2. You can do additional practice by completing any or most of the sections in this chapter again. You can continue to use Jackson Supply Company.

Document numbers will, of course, be different if you redo sections without restoring the company data.

If you cannot recall how to make a periodic backup or restore a backup, refer to the E-Materials located at www.armonddaltonresources.com.

This page is intentionally blank.

9 Chapter

RECORDING TRANSACTIONS, PERFORMING MONTH-END PROCEDURES, RECORDING YEAR-END ADJUSTING ENTRIES, AND PRINTING REPORTS

Overview of Options A, B, and C

This chapter has three options depending upon your instructor's preference and your previous experience with a project called the *Systems Understanding Aid*: either the 10th edition manual version (*SUA*) or the 1st edition electronic cloud version (*E-SUA*), both published by Armond Dalton Publishers. You will only do one of the three options. Your instructor will inform you which option to do.

- **Option A** — normally assigned to students who have already completed either the *SUA* or the *E-SUA* using Transactions List Ⓐ (Document No. 1). This version of the Transactions List has an Ⓐ in the bottom left corner of each page.
- **Option B** — normally assigned to students who have already completed the *SUA* or the *E-SUA* using Transactions List Ⓑ (Document No. 1). This version of the Transactions List has a Ⓑ in the bottom left corner of each page.
- **Option C** — normally assigned to students who have not used either the *SUA* or the *E-SUA*.

Option A — Introduction

Waren Sports Supply Dataset

As described in the E-Materials, you should have downloaded an initial backup file for Waren Sports Supply to either your hard drive or to a USB flash drive after registering on the Armond Dalton Resources website (www.armonddaltonresources.com). If you correctly followed the instructions in the E-Materials, then Waren Sports Supply has been successfully restored into *QuickBooks*.

If you haven't yet completed these tasks from the E-Materials, complete the following step.

> ▶ *Follow the instructions in the E-Materials for downloading and restoring the Waren Sports Supply initial company backup file.*

Chapter Overview

In this chapter, you will record the same December 16–31, 2022, transactions for Waren Sports Supply that you did in the *Systems Understanding Aid*: either the 10th edition manual version (*SUA*) or the 1st edition electronic cloud version (*E-SUA*). You will also complete other activities commonly done with accounting software and print several items to submit to your instructor.

An important difference in this assignment compared to previous ones is the lack of detailed instructions for using *QuickBooks* to record transactions and perform other activities. You are expected to use the Reference book for guidance if you need any.

If, at any time, you decide that you want to start the chapter over, you may do so by restoring the Waren Sports Supply dataset using the initial backup you downloaded from the Armond Dalton Resources website (armonddaltonresources.com). If you have not downloaded this initial backup yet, take the time to do that now, following the instructions in the E-Materials. You may restore this backup at any time during your work on this chapter if you have made errors that are too difficult to correct or if you believe that you do not understand the material in this chapter.

In recording the transactions and performing the other activities for Waren Sports Supply, you will need several things:

1. **Optional Items from the SUA/E-SUA** (not required; all necessary information from the *SUA/E-SUA* has been incorporated into this chapter):

    - Instructions & Flowcharts book
    - Ledgers book
    - Journals book
    - All year-end financial statements and schedules you prepared for Waren Sports Supply in the *SUA/E-SUA*.

2. **Information in this chapter.** The material instructs you what to record or do.

3. **Reference Book Guide** (see inside front cover of Reference book). Use this to locate the appropriate pages in the Reference book for recording transactions or doing other activities.

4. **Reference book.** Open the Reference book to the appropriate pages for the transaction you are recording or other activity you are doing and follow the instructions. In some cases, you will not have practiced using a Reference book section. You should not be concerned about this lack of practice.

5. **Online Homework.** After you have completed the transactions and other requirements for Waren Sports Supply, you may access the questions for Chapter 9 online at the Armond Dalton Resources website. Either print a hard copy to complete and submit to your instructor or answer the questions online along with the other requirements of this chapter. Consult your instructor about which method to use.

6. *QuickBooks* **software and company data sets.**

7. **A printer connected to your computer and/or the ability to print reports to PDF format.**

When you have completed this chapter, you will also submit several reports to your instructor, along with the homework questions for Chapter 9 available on the Armond Dalton Resources website. Consult your instructor as to whether you should submit these items using the online grading page of the Armond Dalton Resources website or in hard copy.

Jim Adams has recorded all transactions for the year 2022 through December 15, 2022, using *QuickBooks*. This is consistent with the *SUA/E-SUA*. For this assignment, you will do the following using *QuickBooks*:

- Perform maintenance for inventory sales prices.
- Record December 16–31 transactions and perform related maintenance.
- Perform December 2022 month-end procedures.
- Record 2022 year-end adjusting entries.
- Print financial statements and other reports.

When you are finished, the financial statements and other results will be comparable to the correct solution for the *SUA/E-SUA*.

Perform Maintenance for Inventory Sales Prices

The price list on page 9-6, taken from the *SUA/E-SUA*, reflects the current selling prices for Waren's thirty products. In this section, you will compare the selling price of each product to the amount included in *QuickBooks* and update the software for any differences.

▶ *If you are not already working in QuickBooks, open the program and open Waren Sports Supply.*

▶ *Perform maintenance for inventory sales prices (Sales Information section in the Edit Item Window) for each inventory item, following the guidance on page 69 of the Reference book. Be sure to click the OK button after each inventory item is changed before proceeding to the next inventory item.*

Alternative Method

▶ *Perform maintenance for inventory sales prices for multiple inventory items by first highlighting any of the Inventory Part items in the Item List. Then, select the Add/Edit Multiple Items function from the Item drop-down list in the lower-left corner of the Item List. Edit the entries in the Sales Price column that need to be changed, using the directional buttons to move from item to item for editing. When you have finished editing your sales prices, make sure you select the Save Changes button in the lower-right corner of the Item List.*

PRICE LIST
As of December 15, 2022

Item No.	Description	Selling Price
BA-054 & RET BA-054	Premium aluminum bat	$198.00
BA-158 & RET BA-158	Baseballs–12 game balls	60.00
BA-199 & RET BA-199	Fielding glove	72.00
BA-281 & RET BA-281	60 lb. dry line marker	99.00
BA-445 & RET BA-445	Catcher's mask	67.00
BA-507 & RET BA-507	Baseball equipment bag	41.00
BA-667 & RET BA-667	Ball bucket with seat–set of 3	35.00
BA-694 & RET BA-694	Batting gloves–1 pair	38.00
BA-807 & RET BA-807	Pitching machine	260.00
BA-859 & RET BA-859	Set of bases	179.00
BB-008 & RET BB-008	Basketball	35.00
BB-019 & RET BB-019	Basketball pole pad	135.00
BB-113 & RET BB-113	Scoreboard and timer	400.00
BB-267 & RET BB-267	Goal and rim set	138.00
BB-358 & RET BB-358	Backboard	127.00
BB-399 & RET BB-399	Basketball net	15.00
BB-431 & RET BB-431	Whistle and lanyard–set of 6	35.00
BB-538 & RET BB-538	Basketball bag	39.00
BB-688 & RET BB-688	Portable inflation pump	102.00
BB-926 & RET BB-926	Trainer's first aid kit	43.00
FB-027 & RET FB-027	Shoulder pad set	132.00
FB-091 & RET FB-091	Hip, tail, arm pad set	58.00
FB-225 & RET FB-225	Football helmet	89.00
FB-344 & RET FB-344	Football	29.00
FB-513 & RET FB-513	Portable storage locker	209.00
FB-573 & RET FB-573	Kicking tees–set of 6	21.00
FB-650 & RET FB-650	Football post pad	149.00
FB-812 & RET FB-812	Collapsible cones–set of 8	37.00
FB-874 & RET FB-874	Sideline repair kit	127.00
FB-952 & RET FB-952	Portable hand warmer	38.00

As shown in the first column of the table above, be sure that you also adjust the 'RET' (Inventory Return Items) sales prices to the correct amounts as you just did for the regular inventory items. *QuickBooks* handles returns as separate inventory items for Waren, so if you have to change the sales price of an item, you will need to do it twice: once for the item and once for the 'RET' of that same item.

After you complete inventory sales price maintenance, the *QuickBooks* files will contain the correct default sales price for each inventory item. These sales prices are used for all sales of inventory between December 16 and December 31, 2022. You should recheck the amounts to make sure they are all correct before you proceed.

Record December 16-31 Transactions and Perform Related Maintenance

The transactions on pages 9-8 through 9-15 for December 16 – 31 are the same as the transactions you recorded in the *SUA/E-SUA*, except where noted. Events and information that are not necessary to process the transactions in *QuickBooks* have been removed. In addition, supplemental information from the *SUA/E-SUA* documents has been incorporated into the *QuickBooks* transactions list so that you do not need the transactions list or the documents from the *SUA/E-SUA* to complete this section. Deal with each transaction in the order listed. Some transactions must be recorded whereas others require only maintenance.

The information you have already learned about *QuickBooks* in Chapters 2 through 8 is used throughout the rest of this chapter. You should use the *QuickBooks* Reference book and information from prior chapters to the extent you need it. Also, if you want to check whether information was recorded and correctly included, use the Home Page buttons (for Centers), the Icon Bar, or the Company, Customer, Vendor, or Employee lists menu to view transactions, as you did in earlier chapters. You can also compare each transaction you record in *QuickBooks* to the result you obtained in the *SUA/E-SUA* journals book, although this is not required.

All default general ledger distribution accounts are correct for Waren's December 16 – 31 transactions unless otherwise noted on pages 9-8 through 9-15.

WAREN SPORTS SUPPLY TRANSACTIONS FOR DECEMBER 16–31, 2022

▶ *Record each of the following transactions (No. 1 through 18) using QuickBooks.*

■ Hints are provided in boxed areas like this.

Use care in recording each transaction. **You should follow each step in the Quick Reference Table for each transaction.** It may take slightly more time, but it will almost certainly help you avoid serious errors. Find the appropriate Quick Reference Table for each transaction or other activity by using the Reference Book Guide located on the inside front cover of the Reference book.

Trans. No.	Dec.	
1	16	**Make a credit sale:** Received customer Purchase Order No. 53426 in the mail from Rosemont University (Customer 406), approved their credit, prepared Invoice No. 731 totaling $15,490 and shipped the goods from the warehouse. The following goods were shipped (only 45 shoulder pad sets were available for shipment out of the 75 that were ordered):

Quantity	Item Code	Description
25	BB-267	Goal and rim set
20	BB-358	Backboard
45	FB-027	Shoulder pad set
40	FB-225	Football helmet

Trans. No.	Dec.	
2	16	**Collect an account receivable and make a deposit:** Received an email notification from First American Bank and Trust of an ACH payment received from Branch College (Received from 408). The ACH payment of $1,622.88 was for payment in full of sales Invoice No. 730. The early payment discount taken by Branch College was $33.12. Select "e-CHECK" as the method of payment and type "ACH" in the Reference # box.

■ After recording the ACH payment receipt, record the receipt on the same day using the Make Deposits window (see pages 30 through 32 of the Reference book).

Trans. No.	Dec.	
3	16	**Prepare a purchase order:** Ordered the following inventory on account from Velocity Sporting Goods (Vendor 252) using Purchase Order No. 328. The goods will be received at the warehouse at a later date. The purchase order total is $25,335.

Item	Description	Quantity
BB-019	Basketball pole pad	115
BB-538	Basketball bag	125
BB-431	Whistle and lanyard - set of 6	75
BB-399	Basketball net	50
FB-027	Shoulder pad set (to cover back order and invetory restock)	100

Trans. No.	Dec.	
4	19	**Receive goods on a purchase order:** Received office supplies from Chicago Office Supply (Vendor 253) as listed on Purchase Order No. 327, which is shown as an open purchase order in *QuickBooks*. Chicago Office Supply's vendor Invoice No. 2378 was received with the goods, totaling $830.25 including sales tax of $47.00. All supplies ordered on Purchase Order No. 327 were received in good condition and taken to the office.

- Because Waren purchases similar items from Chicago Office Supply on a regular basis, each office supply item is kept track of in the inventory module as a non-inventory part. Office supplies expense is debited instead of inventory for these non-inventory parts.
- Remember to enter the sales tax portion of the invoice in the Expenses tab as a debit to the appropriate expense account (see step O in the Quick Reference Table).

Trans.	
No.	Dec.

5   19   **Receive a miscellaneous cash receipt:** Borrowed $90,000 from First American Bank and Trust (Received from 264) by issuing a two-year note payable. Received an email notification from the bank that the $90,000 proceeds were electronically deposited into Waren's checking account.

- The credit portion of the transaction should be posted to A/C #21100 (Notes Payable).
- Miscellaneous cash receipts are processed through the Banking Center Make Deposits window (see pages 42 and 43 of the Reference book).

6   20   **Purchase non-inventory items or services without a purchase order—payment made at time of purchase:** Received vendor Invoice No. 105963 for $1,710 from First Security Insurance (Pay to the Order of 260) for the fourth quarter's health insurance coverage for employees and immediately issued Check No. 1152 for payment in full.

7   20   **Change an employee record (employee maintenance):** Increased employee salary and wage rates, effective December 16. Recall that for hourly employees, overtime is paid at 1.5 times the regular hourly rate. There were no changes in filing status, dependents, or withholding allowances.

Employee	New Salary / Wage Rate
Ray Kramer	$3,650, semi-monthly (enter $87,600 Annual Rate)
Jim Adams	$21.80 per hour regular $32.70 per hour overtime
Nancy Ford	$18.30 per hour regular $27.45 per hour overtime

Trans. No.	Dec.	
8	20	**Receive goods on a purchase order:** Received merchandise from Velocity Sporting Goods (Vendor 252) as listed on Purchase Order No. 328, along with Invoice No. 34719. The payment terms on the invoice are 2/10, Net 30. All merchandise listed on the purchase order was delivered in good condition and in the quantities ordered, except that only 85 basketball pole pads (Item No. BB-019) were received. The total of the invoice is $22,515. The goods were placed immediately in the inventory warehouse.
9	21	**Make a credit sale:** Filled the backorder quantity of 30 shoulder pad sets (Item No. FB-027) for Rosemont University's Purchase Order # 53426. Approved Rosemont's credit and shipped the back ordered shoulder pad sets. Prepared Invoice No. 732 totaling $3,960 for the sale to Rosemont.
10	23	**Write off an uncollectible account receivable:** Received legal notification from Benson, Rosenbrook, and Martinson, P.C., attorneys at law, that Stevenson College (Received From 411) is unable to pay any of its outstanding debts to its suppliers. The $2,900 balance remaining on Invoice No. 719 should therefore be written off as uncollectible.

- Recall that Waren uses the allowance method for recording bad debt expense at year-end, but uses the direct write-off method during the year.
- Follow the instructions on pages 38 through 40 of the Reference book carefully so that you use the direct write-off method correctly (debit to bad debt expense, credit to accounts receivable). The allowance for uncollectible accounts and bad debt expense will be adjusted during the year-end procedures later in the chapter.

Trans. No.	Dec.	
11	23	**Process a sales return or allowance (credit memo):** Eastern Wisconsin University (Customer 410) returned 10 basketball pole pads (RET BB-019) and 8 scoreboard and timer sets (RET BB-113) that were originally purchased on Invoice No. 729. Waren previously authorized EWU by phone to return the goods for credit against their account balance. EWU's Return Request No. R8034 was received with the goods. Sales return document CM 42 was issued for $4,550 and applied to Invoice No. 729.

- Be sure to select the "RET" version of each inventory item when processing the sales return.
- When you select Save in the Create Credit Memos/Refunds window, the Available Credit window will appear. Make sure you select Apply to Invoice and then select the correct invoice for the credit memo.

Trans. No.	Dec.	
12	27	**Collect an account receivable and make a deposit:** Received and deposited Check No. 49326 for $12,000 from Eastern Wisconsin University (Received from 410) in partial payment of the remaining amount (after sales return) on Invoice No. 729.

- Be sure that the entry in the A/R Account box says "10200 Accounts Receivable."
- After recording the customer payment, record the deposit into the bank on the same day using the Make Deposits window (see pages 30 through 32 of the Reference book).

Trans. No.	Dec.	
13	27	**Make a cash sale and make a deposit:** Received and deposited Check No. 47852 for $5,835 from Hawkins College (CASHCUSTOMER) for a cash sale. The goods were shipped from the warehouse and the cash sale was processed and recorded (Invoice No. C-30 in the *SUA/ E-SUA*). All goods ordered were shipped as follows:

Item	Description	Quantity
BB-008	Basketball	30
FB-091	Hip, tail, arm pad set	45
FB-344	Football	75

- After recording the cash receipt, record the deposit into the bank on the same day using the Make Deposits window (see pages 30 through 32 of the Reference book).

Trans. No.	Dec.	
14	28	**Purchase non-inventory items or services without a purchase order—payment made at time of purchase:** Received vendor Invoice No. 72654 for $1,590 from the University Athletic News (Pay to the Order of 254) for advertisements Waren ran during the Christmas season and immediately issued Check No. 1153 for payment in full.
15	28	**Purchase non-inventory items or services without a purchase order—payment made at time of purchase:** Received Freight Bill No. 26245 for $738.15 from Interstate Motor Freight (Pay to the Order of 255) and immediately issued Check No. 1154 for payment in full. The freight bill is for the merchandise received from Purchase Order No. 328. The payment terms on the freight bill are Net 30.

Trans. No.	Dec.	
16	29	**Pay a vendor's outstanding invoice:** Issued an electronic payment (#E-53431) for $22,064.70 to Velocity Sporting Goods (Pay to the Order of 252) for payment in full of Invoice No. 34719. Recall that this invoice was for goods received December 20. The early payment discount taken by Waren was $450.30.

- The default method of payment of Check is correct for an electronic (ACH) payment.
- Be sure to select account #30700–Purchases Discounts—in the Discount Account box of the Discount and Credits window.
- If account #10100–Cash—is not already selected in the Account box, select it before clicking the Pay Selected Bills button.

Trans. No.	Dec.	
17	29	**Receive goods on a purchase order:** Received but did not pay for three standing workstations from Chicago Office Supply (Vendor 253) ordered on Waren's Purchase Order No. 325, which is shown as an open purchase order in *QuickBooks*. Also received vendor's Invoice No. 2423 from Chicago Office Supply, totaling $1,256.10 including sales tax of $71.10. The workstations were received in new and undamaged condition in the warehouse. After they were unpacked and inspected, they were taken directly to the office.

- You must enter A/C #10800 (Fixed Assets) in the Account column when entering sales tax in the Expenses tab because the default will be office supplies expense and the purchase should be debited to fixed assets.

Trans. No.	Dec.	
18	30	**Pay employees:** Finished the payroll for the semi-monthly pay period December 16–31, 2022, and issued Check Nos. 1155 through 1157. Regular and overtime hours for hourly employees were as follows:

Employee	Regular Hours	Overtime Hours
Jim Adams	88	9.3
Nancy Ford	88	6.7
Ray Kramer	N/A	N/A

- You do not need to enter anything for Ray Kramer's hours because he is a salaried employee.
- If you receive a message about payroll liabilities, click OK.

You should, but are not required to, perform backup procedures for Waren Sports Supply before proceeding, to reduce the potential for having to reenter the transactions. See E-Materials for backup procedures.

Perform December 2022 Month-end Procedures

Because many of Waren's month-end procedures are done automatically by *QuickBooks*, the only month-end procedures you will need to perform are:

- Prepare the December bank reconciliation.
- Print a customer monthly statement.

Check Figure for Your Cash Balance

Before starting the December bank reconciliation, be sure that your cash balance is correct by completing the following steps:

▶ *Click the Chart of Accounts icon and then double-click on the cash account (account #10100).*

Examine the ending balance in the cash account at 12/31/22. The balance should be $110,392.32. If the cash balance in your window differs significantly from this amount, return to the December 16–31 transactions to locate and correct any errors before starting the bank reconciliation. Because *QuickBooks* performs periodic automatic updates online, your cash balance may differ slightly (less than $15.00) due to changes in federal tax tables downloaded by the program. When your cash balance is correct, continue with the requirements that follow.

Bank Reconciliation Information, Process, and Printing

The following information is taken from the December bank statement and the November bank reconciliation, neither of which is included in these materials:

- The December 31, 2022, bank statement balance is $131,549.53.
- The following checks and ACH payments have not cleared the bank as of December 31:
  - Check Nos. 1118, 1142, 1152, 1153, 1154, 1155, 1156, and 1157
  - ACH #E-53431
- The December 27 deposits from Eastern Wisconsin University and Hawkins College have not cleared the bank as of December 31.
- ACH fees and service charges totaling $25.50 are included on the December bank statement. *Note:* These fees and charges should be posted to A/C #41000 (Other Operating Expense).

▷ *Prepare the December bank reconciliation. The cutoff date for the bank reconciliation is December 31, 2022.*

▷ *When the reconciliation is correct, click the Print button to print the bank reconciliation either in hard copy or in PDF format if you are submitting your work online. The Select Type of Reconciliation Report window will appear with the option to select Summary, Detail, or print Both reports; select Both.*

▷ *Review your printed reconciliation for accuracy and acceptability. You will submit these reports to your instructor along with year-end reports.*

Print a Customer Monthly Statement

At the end of each month, Waren sends monthly statements to all customers with an outstanding balance. For this section, you are to print the December monthly statement for Rosemont University.

▷ *Follow the instructions on pages 44 through 46 of the Reference book to print a December 2022 customer statement for Rosemont University either in hard copy or in PDF format if you are submitting your work online.*

> *In the Statement Date field select December 31, 2022, and check the Statement Period From and To field and enter the month of December date range.*

> *Click the Preview button to preview the statement. Click Print to print a copy to submit to your instructor with other chapter requirements.*

Print a General Ledger Trial Balance for Check Figures Prior to Year-end Adjusting Entries

The trial balance on page 9-23 shows the correct balances in all general ledger accounts after the December month-end procedures are completed. You will use the Memorized tab of the Report Center to access some reports that have been specifically set up for this project.

> *Click Report Center → Memorized tab (if not already opened) → Trial Balance to print a 12/31/22 trial balance to the screen.*

Compare the amounts on your printed trial balance with those on page 9-23. If any amounts are different, return to the December 16 – 31 transactions and the month-end procedures you processed in *QuickBooks* and make the necessary corrections using the procedures you learned in earlier chapters. When all errors are corrected, print a corrected trial balance either in hard copy or in PDF format if you are submitting your work online.

You can also compare the amounts on your printed trial balance with those included in the *SUA/E-SUA* year-end unadjusted trial balance (part of the year-end worksheet). All account balances should agree if your solution to the *SUA/E-SUA* was correct, except inventory-related accounts, bad debt expense, and the allowance for doubtful accounts. *Note:* Ignore any minor rounding differences in the cash and payroll-related accounts. Inventory-related account balances do not agree because of the use of different inventory methods. The balances in inventory-related accounts, bad debt expense, and the allowance account will agree after adjusting entries are completed. See the following page for a discussion of the inventory methods used in the *SUA/E-SUA* and in the *QuickBooks* project.

When your balances agree with those on page 9-23, go to the following section where you will record year-end adjusting entries.

Record 2022 Year-end Adjusting Entries

The next step at the end of an accounting year before printing output is to record year-end adjusting entries. The following are the types of year-end adjustments required for Waren:

- Inventory adjustment to the physical count
- Depreciation expense
- Accrued interest payable
- Bad debt expense and allowance
- Cost of goods sold for freight and sales discounts taken
- Federal income taxes

Each of the year-end adjustments is explained in a section that follows. Perform the procedures in the order listed.

Adjust Perpetual Inventory Records

Recall that in the *SUA/E-SUA* you were provided with the ending dollar balance in inventory and you adjusted to that total. That system was a periodic inventory system. *QuickBooks* uses a perpetual system, which provides a current inventory balance after each transaction. At year-end, the perpetual records are adjusted to a physical count to adjust for obsolescence, theft, or accounting errors.

The physical count was taken on December 31. A comparison of the physical count and the perpetual records showed a difference for certain items. Management is concerned about these inventory differences but knows that the physical count is accurate. Thus, the perpetual records must be adjusted as follows to agree with the physical count:

Item	Description	Quantity on Perpetual Records	Quantity per Physical Count
BB-019	Basketball pole pad	106 (96 regular, 10 returns)	109 (99 regular, 10 returns)
FB-027	Shoulder pad set	159 (all regular)	147 (all regular)
BA-158	Baseballs–12 balls	156 (all regular)	162 (all regular)

▶ *Record the inventory adjustments in QuickBooks following the guidance in the Reference book. Use Cost of Goods Sold as the Adjustment Account.*

After the inventory adjustments have been processed, record the remaining five year-end adjusting entries through the General Journal Entry window.

▶ *Use the information in the following five sections to record each of the remaining year-end adjusting entries by preparing a general journal entry in QuickBooks following the guidance in the Reference book pages 52 and 53.*

Depreciation Expense

Recall from the *SUA/E-SUA* that depreciation expense is calculated once at the end of each year. Depreciation is calculated using the straight-line method over the estimated useful lives of the assets (five or ten years for Waren's existing fixed assets). Waren's depreciation expense for Waren for 2022 totaled $34,779.31.

Accrued Interest Payable

Recall from Transaction No. 5 on page 9-10 that Waren has a $90,000 two-year note payable to First American Bank and Trust, dated December 19, 2022. The stated annual interest rate on the note is 5.5%. The terms of the note payable call for the following payments:

- $4,950 interest payments on 12/19/23 and 12/19/24
- $90,000 principal payment on 12/19/24

Recall from the *SUA/E-SUA* that interest accruals are calculated using a 365-day year with the day after the note was made counting as the first day. General ledger account numbers for the journal entry are: A/C #40800 (Interest Expense) and A/C #21000 (Interest Payable). Either enter the correct amount on the online grading portion of the Armond Dalton Resources website or show your calculation on the Chapter 9 homework pages available for download on the website (consult your instructor).

Bad Debt Expense and Allowance

Bad debt expense is estimated once annually at the end of each year as 1/2 of one percent (0.005) of net sales and is recorded in the general journal as of December 31. As explained in Chapter 7, Waren uses the direct write-off method during the year and then the allowance method at year-end. General ledger account numbers for the journal entry are: A/C #40900 (Bad Debt Expense) and A/C #10300 (Allowance for Doubtful Account). In order to balance out the Allowance for

Doubtful Account and Bad Debt Expense account due to the direct write-off to Bad Debt Expense, you must readjust the Bad Debt Expense account to equal the 1/2 of one percent (0.005) calculation of net sales. Either enter the correct amount on the online grading portion of the Armond Dalton Resources website or show your calculation on the Chapter 9 homework pages available for download on the website (consult your instructor).

- Determine the amount of net sales by examining the 2022 income statement on the screen. For your convenience, the 2022 income statement has been included in the Memorized tab of the Report Center.
- *QuickBooks* requires you to add a customer to the Name box. Type "write off" in the Name box and press Enter. If "write off" doesn't exist as a customer, select Quick Add and select the Customer category.

Cost of Goods Sold

QuickBooks automatically debits cost of goods sold and credits inventory for the product cost for each sale. The inventory account is also automatically updated for inventory purchases and purchases returns. Therefore, the *QuickBooks* data does not include the following accounts from the *SUA*/E-SUA: A/C #30500 (Purchases) and A/C #30600 (Purchase Returns and Allowance). Waren treats purchase discounts taken and freight-in as a part of cost of goods sold but records them in separate accounts during the accounting period. Therefore, these two accounts must be closed to A/C #30400 (Cost of Goods Sold): A/C #30700 (Purchases Discounts Taken) and A/C #30800 (Freight-In).

- Before preparing the general journal entry, determine the balance in each account being closed to cost of goods sold. Determine the balance in the accounts to be closed by examining the income statement.

Federal Income Taxes

Recall from the *SUA/E-SUA* that the corporate income tax rate is 21% for all regular corporations such as Waren. General ledger account numbers for the journal entry are: A/C #40700 (Federal Income Tax Expense) and A/C #20800 (Federal Income Taxes Payable). Either enter the correct amount on the online grading portion of the Armond Dalton Resources website or show your calculation on the Chapter 9 homework pages available for download on the website (consult your instructor).

- After all other adjusting entries are recorded, determine 2022 pre-tax income by examining the 2022 income statement from the Memorized tab in the Report Center.
- Do not be concerned if your amount is slightly different from the *SUA/E-SUA* amount for federal income taxes. The minor payroll differences will affect the calculation slightly.

Print a General Ledger Trial Balance for Check Figures After Year-end Adjusting Entries

The trial balance on page 9-24 shows the correct balances in all general ledger accounts after the year-end adjusting entries are recorded.

> ▶ *Open and use the general ledger trial balance for Waren to compare the amounts in your window to the correct balances. If there are differences, return to the year-end adjusting entries and make the necessary corrections. After you determine that your trial balance is correct, print the 12/31/22 trial balance either in hard copy or in PDF format if you are submitting your work online.* You will submit this report to your instructor along with year-end reports.

You can also compare the amounts on your printed trial balance with those included in the *SUA/E-SUA* year-end adjusted trial balance (part of the year-end worksheet). All account balances should agree if your *SUA/E-SUA* solution was correct, except for possible minor differences for cash, payroll-related accounts, and federal income tax expense because of the difference in the way payroll taxes are calculated in the *SUA/E-SUA* and *QuickBooks*.

When your balances agree with those on page 9-24, go to the following section where you will print financial statements and other reports. All entries have now been recorded.

Print Financial Statements and Other Reports

All of the following reports are to be submitted to your instructor either in hard copy or uploaded to the online grading page of Armond Dalton Resources (consult your instructor).

▶ *Print the following reports (print to PDF is best if submitting online). Each of these reports has already been set up in the Memorized tab of the Report Center.*

1. 12/31/22 balance sheet
2. 2022 income statement
3. General journal for December 2022
4. Accounts receivable aged trial balance as of 12/31/22
5. Accounts payable aged trial balance as of 12/31/22
6. Inventory valuation summary as of 12/31/22
7. Employee earnings register for December 2022
8. Sales journal for December 2022
9. Cash receipts journal for December 2022
10. Purchases journal for December 2022
11. Cash disbursements journal for December 2022
12. Payroll journal for December 2022

You can compare the reports printed using *QuickBooks* to the manual reports you prepared in the *SUA/E-SUA*.

Submit Reports and Answers to Assigned Questions

Submit the following to your course instructor either in hard copy or on the online grading page of the Armond Dalton Resources site (*consult your instructor*):

- All twelve reports just listed
- December 2022 bank reconciliation that you already printed
- Customer monthly statement for Rosemont University that you already printed
- Trial balance after year-end adjustments that you already printed
- Chapter 9 homework questions available on the Armond Dalton Resources website (calculations for accrued interest payable, bad debt expense, and federal income tax expense).

All procedures are now complete for this chapter. Now that you have completed Chapter 9, you should back up your data files for Waren Sports Supply following the instructions in the E-Materials.

Check Figures

Waren Sports Supply
Trial Balance
As of December 31, 2022

	Dec 31, 22	
	Debit	Credit
10100 · Cash	110,366.82	
10200 · Accounts Receivable	45,877.00	
10300 · Allowance for Doubtful Accts.		3,250.81
10400 · Inventory	203,454.00	
10600 · Marketable Securities	24,000.00	
12000 · Undeposited Funds	0.00	
10800 · Fixed Assets	329,288.10	
10900 · Accumulated Depreciation		81,559.50
20100 · Accounts Payable		5,736.35
20300 · Federal Income Tax Withheld		1,161.00
20400 · State Income Taxes Withheld		672.20
20500 · State Unemployment Taxes Pay.		117.89
20600 · Fed. Unemployment Taxes Pay.		19.92
20700 · FICA Taxes Payable		2,280.76
20800 · Federal Income Taxes Payable	0.00	
25500 · Sales Tax Payable	0.00	
21100 · Notes Payable		90,000.00
Opening Bal Equity	0.00	
26000 · Common Stock		225,000.00
29000 · *Retained Earnings		90,264.99
30100 · Sales		1,589,666.00
30200 · Sales Returns and Allowances	62,181.00	
30300 · Sales Discounts Taken	15,405.82	
31200 · Miscellaneous Revenue		825.00
30400 · Cost of Goods Sold	1,015,912.00	
30700 · Purchases Discounts Taken		16,733.90
30800 · Freight-in	24,897.84	
40100 · Rent Expense	57,600.00	
40200 · Advertising Expense	22,395.00	
40300 · Office Supplies Expense	5,892.55	
40500 · Wages and Salaries Expense	140,371.63	
40600 · Payroll Tax Expense	12,020.81	
40900 · Bad Debt Expense	4,400.00	
41000 · Other Operating Expense	33,225.75	
TOTAL	**2,107,288.32**	**2,107,288.32**

Waren Sports Supply
Trial Balance
As of December 31, 2022

	Dec 31, 22	
	Debit	Credit
10100 · Cash	110,366.82	
10200 · Accounts Receivable	45,877.00	
10300 · Allowance for Doubtful Accts.		6,411.21
10400 · Inventory	202,920.00	
10600 · Marketable Securities	24,000.00	
12000 · Undeposited Funds	0.00	
10800 · Fixed Assets	329,288.10	
10900 · Accumulated Depreciation		116,338.81
20100 · Accounts Payable		5,736.35
20300 · Federal Income Tax Withheld		1,161.00
20400 · State Income Taxes Withheld		672.20
20500 · State Unemployment Taxes Pay.		117.89
20600 · Fed. Unemployment Taxes Pay.		19.92
20700 · FICA Taxes Payable		2,280.76
20800 · Federal Income Taxes Payable		36,600.07
21000 · Interest Payable		162.74
25500 · Sales Tax Payable	0.00	
21100 · Notes Payable		90,000.00
Opening Bal Equity	0.00	
26000 · Common Stock		225,000.00
29000 · *Retained Earnings		90,264.99
30100 · Sales		1,589,666.00
30200 · Sales Returns and Allowances	62,181.00	
30300 · Sales Discounts Taken	15,405.82	
31200 · Miscellaneous Revenue		825.00
30400 · Cost of Goods Sold	1,024,609.94	
30700 · Purchases Discounts Taken	0.00	
30800 · Freight-in	0.00	
40100 · Rent Expense	57,600.00	
40200 · Advertising Expense	22,395.00	
40300 · Office Supplies Expense	5,892.55	
40400 · Depreciation Expense	34,779.31	
40500 · Wages and Salaries Expense	140,371.63	
40600 · Payroll Tax Expense	12,020.81	
40700 · Federal Income Tax Expense	36,600.07	
40800 · Interest Expense	162.74	
40900 · Bad Debt Expense	7,560.40	
41000 · Other Operating Expense	33,225.75	
TOTAL	2,165,256.94	2,165,256.94

Option B — Introduction

Waren Sports Supply Dataset

As described in the E-Materials, you should have downloaded an initial backup file for Waren Sports Supply to either your hard drive or to a USB flash drive after registering on the Armond Dalton Resources website (www. armonddaltonresources.com). If you correctly followed the instructions in the E-Materials, then Waren Sports Supply has been successfully restored into *QuickBooks*.

If you haven't yet completed these tasks from the E-Materials, complete the following step.

> ▶ *Follow the instructions in the E-Materials for downloading and restoring the Waren Sports Supply initial company backup file.*

Chapter Overview

In this chapter, you will record the same December 16–31, 2022, transactions for Waren Sports Supply that you did in the *Systems Understanding Aid*: either the 10th edition manual version (*SUA*) or the 1st edition electronic cloud version (*E-SUA*). You will also complete other activities commonly done with accounting software and print several items to submit to your instructor.

An important difference in this assignment compared to previous ones is the lack of detailed instructions for using *QuickBooks* to record transactions and perform other activities. You are expected to use the Reference book for guidance if you need any.

If, at any time, you decide that you want to start the chapter over, you may do so by restoring the Waren Sports Supply dataset using the initial backup you downloaded from the Armond Dalton Resources website (armonddaltonresources.com). If you have not downloaded this initial backup yet, take the time to do that now, following the instructions in the E-Materials. You may restore this backup at any time during your work on this chapter if you have made errors that are too difficult to correct or if you believe that you do not understand the material in this chapter.

In recording the transactions and performing the other activities for Waren Sports Supply, you will need several things:

1. **Optional Items from the SUA/E-SUA** (not required; all necessary information from the *SUA/E-SUA* has been incorporated into this chapter):

   - Instructions & Flowcharts book
   - Ledgers book
   - Journals book
   - All year-end financial statements and schedules you prepared for Waren Sports Supply in the *SUA/E-SUA*.

2. **Information in this chapter.** The material instructs you what to record or do.

3. **Reference Book Guide** (see inside front cover of Reference book). Use this to locate the appropriate pages in the Reference book for recording transactions or doing other activities.

4. **Reference book.** Open the Reference book to the appropriate pages for the transaction you are recording or other activity you are doing and follow the instructions. In some cases, you will not have practiced using a Reference book section. You should not be concerned about this lack of practice.

5. **Online Homework.** After you have completed the transactions and other requirements for Waren Sports Supply, you may access the questions for Chapter 9 online at the Armond Dalton Resources website. Either print a hard copy to complete and submit to your instructor or answer the questions online along with the other requirements of this chapter. Consult your instructor about which method to use.

6. *QuickBooks* **software and company data sets.**

7. **A printer connected to your computer and/or the ability to print reports to PDF format.**

When you have completed this chapter, you will also submit several reports to your instructor, along with the homework questions for Chapter 9 available on the Armond Dalton Resources website. Consult your instructor as to whether you should submit these items using the online grading page of the Armond Dalton Resources website or in hard copy.

Jim Adams has recorded all transactions for the year 2022 through December 15, 2022, using *QuickBooks*. This is consistent with the *SUA/E-SUA*. For this assignment, you will do the following using *QuickBooks*:

- Perform maintenance for inventory sales prices.
- Record December 16–31 transactions and perform related maintenance.
- Perform December 2022 month-end procedures.
- Record 2022 year-end adjusting entries.
- Print financial statements and other reports.

When you are finished, the financial statements and other results will be comparable to the correct solution for the *SUA/E-SUA*.

Perform Maintenance for Inventory Sales Prices

The price list on page 9-28, taken from the *SUA/E-SUA*, reflects the current selling prices for Waren's thirty products. In this section, you will compare the selling price of each product to the amount included in *QuickBooks* and update the software for any differences.

▶ *If you are not already working in QuickBooks, open the program and open Waren Sports Supply.*

▶ *Perform maintenance for inventory sales prices (Sales Information section in the Edit Item Window) for each inventory item, following the guidance on page 69 of the Reference book. Be sure to click the OK button after each inventory item is changed before proceeding to the next inventory item.*

Alternative Method

▶ *Perform maintenance for inventory sales prices for multiple inventory items by first highlighting any of the Inventory Part items in the Item List. Then, select the Add/Edit Multiple Items function from the Item drop-down list in the lower-left corner of the Item List. Edit the entries in the Sales Price column that need to be changed, using the directional buttons to move from item to item for editing. When you have finished editing your sales prices, make sure you select the Save Changes button in the lower-right corner of the Item List.*

PRICE LIST
As of December 15, 2022

Item No.	Description	Selling Price
BA-054 & RET BA-054	Premium aluminum bat	$198.00
BA-158 & RET BA-158	Baseballs–12 game balls	60.00
BA-199 & RET BA-199	Fielding glove	72.00
BA-281 & RET BA-281	60 lb. dry line marker	99.00
BA-445 & RET BA-445	Catcher's mask	67.00
BA-507 & RET BA-507	Baseball equipment bag	41.00
BA-667 & RET BA-667	Ball bucket with seat–set of 3	35.00
BA-694 & RET BA-694	Batting gloves–1 pair	38.00
BA-807 & RET BA-807	Pitching machine	260.00
BA-859 & RET BA-859	Set of bases	179.00
BB-008 & RET BB-008	Basketball	35.00
BB-019 & RET BB-019	Basketball pole pad	135.00
BB-113 & RET BB-113	Scoreboard and timer	400.00
BB-267 & RET BB-267	Goal and rim set	138.00
BB-358 & RET BB-358	Backboard	127.00
BB-399 & RET BB-399	Basketball net	15.00
BB-431 & RET BB-431	Whistle and lanyard–set of 6	35.00
BB-538 & RET BB-538	Basketball bag	39.00
BB-688 & RET BB-688	Portable inflation pump	102.00
BB-926 & RET BB-926	Trainer's first aid kit	43.00
FB-027 & RET FB-027	Shoulder pad set	132.00
FB-091 & RET FB-091	Hip, tail, arm pad set	58.00
FB-225 & RET FB-225	Football helmet	89.00
FB-344 & RET FB-344	Football	29.00
FB-513 & RET FB-513	Portable storage locker	209.00
FB-573 & RET FB-573	Kicking tees–set of 6	21.00
FB-650 & RET FB-650	Football post pad	149.00
FB-812 & RET FB-812	Collapsible cones–set of 8	37.00
FB-874 & RET FB-874	Sideline repair kit	127.00
FB-952 & RET FB-952	Portable hand warmer	38.00

As shown in the first column of the table above, be sure that you also adjust the 'RET' (Inventory Return Items) sales prices to the correct amounts as you just did for the regular inventory items. *QuickBooks* handles returns as separate inventory items for Waren, so if you have to change the sales price of an item, you will need to do it twice: once for the item and once for the 'RET' of that same item.

After you complete inventory sales price maintenance, the *QuickBooks* files will contain the correct default sales price for each inventory item. These sales prices are used for all sales of inventory between December 16 and December 31, 2022. You should recheck the amounts to make sure they are all correct before you proceed.

Record December 16-31 Transactions and Perform Related Maintenance

The transactions on pages 9-30 through 9-42 for December 16–31 are the same as the transactions you recorded in the *SUA/E-SUA*, except where noted. Events and information that are not necessary to process the transactions in *QuickBooks* have been removed. In addition, supplemental information from the *SUA/E-SUA* documents has been incorporated into the *QuickBooks* transactions list so that you do not need the transactions list or the documents from the *SUA/E-SUA* to complete this section. Deal with each transaction in the order listed. Some transactions must be recorded whereas others require only maintenance.

The information you have already learned about *QuickBooks* in Chapters 2 through 8 is used throughout the rest of this chapter. You should use the *QuickBooks* Reference book and information from prior chapters to the extent you need it. Also, if you want to check whether information was recorded and correctly included, use the Home Page buttons (for Centers), the Icon Bar, or the Company, Customer, Vendor, or Employee lists menu to view transactions, as you did in earlier chapters. You can also compare each transaction you record in *QuickBooks* to the result you obtained in the *SUA/E-SUA* journals book, although this is not required.

All default general ledger distribution accounts are correct for Waren's December 16–31 transactions unless otherwise noted on pages 9-30 through 9-42.

WAREN SPORTS SUPPLY TRANSACTIONS FOR DECEMBER 16–31, 2022

▶ *Record each of the following transactions (No. 1 through 29) using QuickBooks.*

■ Hints are provided in boxed areas like this.

Use care in recording each transaction. **You should follow each step in the Quick Reference Table for each transaction.** It may take slightly more time, but it will almost certainly help you avoid serious errors. Find the appropriate Quick Reference Table for each transaction or other activity by using the Reference Book Guide located on the inside front cover of the Reference book.

Trans. No.	Dec.	
1	16	**Make a credit sale:** Received customer Purchase Order No. 53426 in the mail from Rosemont University (Customer 406), approved their credit, prepared Invoice No. 731 totaling $15,490 and shipped the goods from the warehouse. The following goods were shipped (only 45 shoulder pad sets were available for shipment out of the 75 that were ordered):

Quantity	Item Code	Description
25	BB-267	Goal and rim set
20	BB-358	Backboard
45	FB-027	Shoulder pad set
40	FB-225	Football helmet

2	16	**Collect an account receivable and make a deposit:** Received an email notification from First American Bank and Trust of an ACH payment received from Branch College (Received from 408). The ACH payment of $1,622.88 was for payment in full of sales Invoice No. 730. The early payment discount taken by Branch College was $33.12. Select "e-CHECK" as the method of payment and type "ACH" in the Reference # box.

■ After recording the ACH payment receipt, record the receipt on the same day using the Make Deposits window (see pages 30 through 32 of the Reference book).

Trans. No.	Dec.	
3	16	**Prepare a purchase order:** Ordered the following inventory on account from Velocity Sporting Goods (Vendor 252) using Purchase Order No. 328. The goods will be received at the warehouse at a later date. The purchase order total is $25,335.

Item	Description	Quantity
BB-019	Basketball pole pad	115
BB-538	Basketball bag	125
BB-431	Whistle and lanyard - set of 6	75
BB-399	Basketball net	50
FB-027	Shoulder pad set (to cover back order and invetory restock)	100

4	19	**Receive goods on a purchase order:** Received office supplies from Chicago Office Supply (Vendor 253) as listed on Purchase Order No. 327, which is shown as an open purchase order in *QuickBooks*. Chicago Office Supply's vendor Invoice No. 2378 was received with the goods, totaling $830.25 including sales tax of $47.00. All supplies ordered on Purchase Order No. 327 were received in good condition and taken to the office.

- Because Waren purchases similar items from Chicago Office Supply on a regular basis, each office supply item is kept track of in the inventory module as a non-inventory part. Office supplies expense is debited instead of inventory for these non-inventory parts.
- Remember to enter the sales tax portion of the invoice in the Expenses tab as a debit to the appropriate expense account (see step O in the Quick Reference Table).

Trans. No.	Dec.	
5	19	**Receive a miscellaneous cash receipt:** Borrowed $90,000 from First American Bank and Trust (Received from 264) by issuing a two-year note payable. Received an email notification from the bank that the $90,000 proceeds were electronically deposited into Waren's checking account.

- The credit portion of the transaction should be posted to A/C #21100 (Notes Payable).
- Miscellaneous cash receipts are processed through the Banking Center Make Deposits window (see pages 42 and 43 of the Reference book).

6	20	**Purchase non-inventory items or services without a purchase order—payment made at time of purchase:** Received vendor Invoice No. 105963 for $1,710 from First Security Insurance (Pay to the Order of 260) for the fourth quarter's health insurance coverage for employees and immediately issued Check No. 1152 for payment in full.
7	20	**Change an employee record (employee maintenance):** Increased employee salary and wage rates, effective December 16. Recall that for hourly employees, overtime is paid at 1.5 times the regular hourly rate. There were no changes in filing status, dependents, or withholding allowances.

Employee	New Salary / Wage Rate
Ray Kramer	$3,650, semi-monthly (enter $87,600 Annual Rate)
Jim Adams	$21.80 per hour regular $32.70 per hour overtime
Nancy Ford	$18.30 per hour regular $27.45 per hour overtime

Trans. No.	Dec.	
8	20	**Receive goods on a purchase order:** Received merchandise from Velocity Sporting Goods (Vendor 252) as listed on Purchase Order No. 328, along with Invoice No. 34719. The payment terms on the invoice are 2/10, Net 30. All merchandise listed on the purchase order was delivered in good condition and in the quantities ordered, except that only 85 basketball pole pads (Item No. BB-019) were received. The total of the invoice is $22,515. The goods were placed immediately in the inventory warehouse.
9	21	**Make a credit sale:** Filled the backorder quantity of 30 shoulder pad sets (Item No. FB-027) for Rosemont University's Purchase Order # 53426. Approved Rosemont's credit and shipped the back ordered shoulder pad sets. Prepared Invoice No. 732 totaling $3,960 for the sale to Rosemont.
10	23	**Write off an uncollectible account receivable:** Received legal notification from Benson, Rosenbrook, and Martinson, P.C., attorneys at law, that Stevenson College (Received From 411) is unable to pay any of its outstanding debts to its suppliers. The $2,900 balance remaining on Invoice No. 719 should therefore be written off as uncollectible.

- Recall that Waren uses the allowance method for recording bad debt expense at year-end, but uses the direct write-off method during the year.
- Follow the instructions on pages 38 through 40 of the Reference book carefully so that you use the direct write-off method correctly (debit to bad debt expense, credit to accounts receivable). The allowance for uncollectible accounts and bad debt expense will be adjusted during the year-end procedures later in the chapter.

Trans. No.	Dec.	
11	23	**Process a sales return or allowance (credit memo):** Eastern Wisconsin University (Customer 410) returned 10 basketball pole pads (RET BB-019) and 8 scoreboard and timer sets (RET BB-113) that were originally purchased on Invoice No. 729. Waren previously authorized EWU by phone to return the goods for credit against their account balance. EWU's Return Request No. R8034 was received with the goods. Sales return document CM 42 was issued for $4,550 and applied to Invoice No. 729.

- Be sure to select the "RET" version of each inventory item when processing the sales return.
- When you select Save in the Create Credit Memos/Refunds window, the Available Credit window will appear. Make sure you select Apply to Invoice and then select the correct invoice for the credit memo.

Trans. No.	Dec.	
12	27	**Collect an account receivable and make a deposit:** Received and deposited Check No. 49326 for $12,000 from Eastern Wisconsin University (Received from 410) in partial payment of the remaining amount (after sales return) on Invoice No. 729.

- Be sure that the entry in the A/R Account box says "10200 Accounts Receivable."
- After recording the customer payment, record the deposit into the bank on the same day using the Make Deposits window (see pages 30 through 32 of the Reference book).

Trans.	
No.	Dec.

13   27   **Make a cash sale and make a deposit:** Received and deposited Check No. 47852 for $5,835 from Hawkins College (CASHCUSTOMER) for a cash sale. The goods were shipped from the warehouse and the cash sale was processed and recorded (Invoice No. C-30 in the *SUA/ E-SUA*). All goods ordered were shipped as follows:

Item	Description	Quantity
BB-008	Basketball	30
FB-091	Hip, tail, arm pad set	45
FB-344	Football	75

- After recording the cash receipt, record the deposit into the bank on the same day using the Make Deposits window (see pages 30 through 32 of the Reference book).

14   28   **Purchase non-inventory items or services without a purchase order—payment made at time of purchase:** Received vendor Invoice No. 72654 for $1,590 from the University Athletic News (Pay to the Order of 254) for advertisements Waren ran during the Christmas season and immediately issued Check No. 1153 for payment in full.

15   28   **Purchase non-inventory items or services without a purchase order—payment made at time of purchase:** Received Freight Bill No. 26245 for $738.15 from Interstate Motor Freight (Pay to the Order of 255) and immediately issued Check No. 1154 for payment in full. The freight bill is for the merchandise received from Purchase Order No. 328. The payment terms on the freight bill are Net 30.

Trans. No.	Dec.	
16	28	**Make a credit sale:** Made a special promotional sale on account to University of Southern Iowa (USI, Customer 409), using Invoice No. 733, totaling $12,064.50. For the promotion, Waren agreed to a 10% reduction in the selling prices of the items sold. USI did not submit a purchase order for the sale. The following goods were shipped from the warehouse for this sale:

Units	Item No.	Description
45	BA-281	60 lb. dry line marker
50	BA-859	Set of bases

Trans. No.	Dec.	
17	29	**Pay a vendor's outstanding invoice:** Issued an electronic payment using ACH Payment Authorization No. E-53431 for $22,064.70 to Velocity Sporting Goods (Pay to the Order of 252) for payment in full of Invoice No. 34719. Recall that this invoice was for goods received December 20. The early payment discount taken by Waren was $450.30.

- The default method of payment of Check is correct for an electronic (ACH) payment.
- Be sure to select account #30700–Purchases Discounts—in the Discount Account box of the Discount and Credits window.
- If account #10100–Cash—is not already selected in the Account box, select it before clicking the Pay Selected Bills button.

Trans. No.	Dec.	
18	29	**Receive goods on a purchase order:** Received but did not pay for three standing workstations from Chicago Office Supply (Vendor 253) ordered on Waren's Purchase Order No. 325, which is shown as an open purchase order in *QuickBooks*. Also received vendor's Invoice No. 2423 from Chicago Office Supply, totaling $1,256.10 including sales tax of $71.10. The workstations were received in new and undamaged condition in the warehouse. After they were unpacked and inspected, they were taken directly to the office.

- You must enter A/C #10800 (Fixed Assets) in the Account column when entering sales tax in the Expenses tab because the default will be office supplies expense and the purchase should be debited to fixed assets.

19	29	**Prepare a general journal entry to sell a fixed asset:** Sold two bookshelves to an employee, Nancy Ford, for $275. Nancy will pay this amount to Waren in January of 2023. The bookshelves were purchased for a cost of $925 on September 30, 2016. The bookshelves were fully depreciated at the end of 2021.

- The receivable from Nancy Ford should be posted to A/C #10210 (Accounts Receivable from Employees) and the gain/loss on the sale should be posted to A/C #30900 (Gain/Loss on Sale of Fixed Assets).
- Type Ford in the Name box on the line for account 10210 and press Enter. Use Quick Add to add Ford in the Customer category when prompted. *QuickBooks* will not allow posting to an account receivable account without a corresponding customer record.

Trans. No.	Dec.	
20	30	**Collect an account receivable and make a deposit:** Received an email notification from First American Bank and Trust for an ACH payment of $11,823.21 from University of Southern Iowa (Received From 409) in payment of Invoice No. 733 (see Transaction No. 16 on page 9-36 for the original sale transaction). The early payment discount taken by USI was $241.29.

- Be sure that the entry in the A/R Account box says "10200 Accounts Receivable."
- After recording the customer payment, record the deposit into the bank on the same day using the Make Deposits window (see pages 30 through 32 of the Reference book).

21	30	**Pay employees:** Finished the payroll for the semi-monthly pay period December 16–31, 2022, and issued Check Nos. 1155 through 1157. Regular and overtime hours for hourly employees were as follows:

Employee	Regular Hours	Overtime Hours
Jim Adams	88	9.3
Nancy Ford	88	6.7
Ray Kramer	N/A	N/A

- You do not need to enter anything for Ray Kramer's hours because he is a salaried employee.
- If you receive a message about payroll liabilities, click OK.

Trans. No.	Dec.	
22	30	**Receive a miscellaneous cash receipt:** Received an email notification from First American Bank and Trust for $1,500 of dividend income received from Central Brokerage (Received from 262). The dividends were earned on various common stocks in the marketable securities general ledger account.

- The credit portion of the transaction should be posted to A/C #31100 (Interest Dividend Income).
- Miscellaneous cash receipts are processed through the Banking Center Make Deposits window (see pages 42 and 43 of the Reference book).

Trans. No.	Dec.	
23	30	**Receive a miscellaneous cash receipt:** Sold 200 shares of Lucas Corporation common stock for $27.00 per share. The shares were originally purchased on July 11, 2022, for $23.00 per share plus a commission of $115. Central Brokerage retained a commission of $135 on the sale and sent the net proceeds of $5,265 via ACH payment to Waren. Received an email notification from First American Bank and Trust for this ACH cash receipt. Either recompute the amounts for this transaction now or obtain the correct amounts from the *SUA* cash receipts journal.

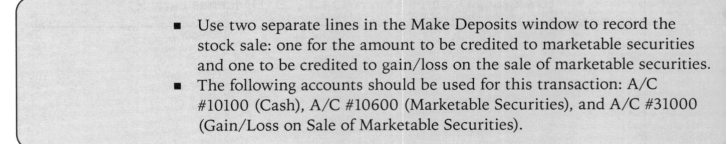

- Use two separate lines in the Make Deposits window to record the stock sale: one for the amount to be credited to marketable securities and one to be credited to gain/loss on the sale of marketable securities.
- The following accounts should be used for this transaction: A/C #10100 (Cash), A/C #10600 (Marketable Securities), and A/C #31000 (Gain/Loss on Sale of Marketable Securities).

Trans. No.	Dec.	
24	30	**Purchase non-inventory items or services without a purchase order–payment made at time of purchase:** Purchased 150 shares of Henry Corporation (Pay to the Order of 262) common stock for $30.00 per share plus commission of $120. Immediately issued an electronic payment to Central Brokerage using ACH Payment Authorization No. E-53432. Either recompute the amounts for this transaction now, or obtain the correct information from the *SUA* general journal.

- The debit portion of the transaction should be posted to A/C #10600 (Marketable Securities).

25	30	**Prepare a general journal entry:** The Board of Directors declared a $3.00 per share dividend on the 3,000 shares of $75 par value common stock outstanding. The dividends will be payable on January 31, 2023, to all stockholders of record as of January 25, 2023. Either recompute the amounts for this transaction now, or obtain the correct information from the *SUA* general journal.

- Use the following accounts for the general journal entry: A/C #29010 (Dividends Declared) and A/C #20900 (Dividends Payable).

Trans. No.	Dec.	
26	30	**Purchase non-inventory items or services without a purchase order—payment made at time of purchase:** Issued a $15,000 ACH payment to First American Bank and Trust (Pay to the Order of 264) for partial payment on the bank note, which included no payment for interest. ACH Payment Authorization No. E-53433 was used to initiate the ACH payment. The terms on the back of the bank note stipulate that prepayments such as this one can be made without early payment penalty. For purposes of your year-end adjusting journal entry for interest, note that this payment will not reach the bank until January 3, 2023.

- The debit portion of the transaction should be posted to A/C #21100 (Notes Payable).

27	30	**Purchase non-inventory items or services without a purchase order—payment made at time of purchase:** Issued Check No. 1158 for $3,600 to First Security Insurance (Pay to the Order of 260) for the premium on Waren's six-month liability insurance policy. The policy period runs from December 1, 2022, to June 1, 2023. First Security's invoice number was 106742.

- The expense portion of the transaction should be posted to A/C #41000 (Other Operating Expenses), while the prepaid portion of the transaction should be posted to A/C #10500 (Prepaid Expenses).

Trans. No.	Dec.	
28	30	**Receive a miscellaneous cash receipt:** The company signed an agreement to sublease an office in its building to Leverett & Associates at a monthly rental rate of $2,200. In connection with the sublease, Waren received a $6,600 ACH payment from Leverett & Associates covering rent for the first quarter of 2023.

- Type Leverett & Associates in the Received From box of the Make Deposits window and press Enter. Then use Quick Add to add Leverett & Associates as an "Other" name type.
- The credit portion of the transaction should be posted to A/C #21200 (Unearned Revenue).

Trans. No.	Dec.	
29	30	**Collect an account receivable and make a deposit:** Received check No. 34982 for $1,000 from Stevenson College. The check was received along with notification from Stevenson's attorneys, Benson, Rosenbrook, and Martinson, P.C., stating that Stevenson was able to pay $1,000 of the $2,900 balance due from the charge invoice No. 719 prior to Stevenson's final bankruptcy filing. Recall that the full $2,900 balance due from the invoice was written off as uncollectible on December 23, 2022.

- In addition to recording this customer cash receipt and bank deposit, you will need to record a general journal entry for the reversal of part of the account receivable write-off transaction.

You should, but are not required to, perform backup procedures for Waren Sports Supply before proceeding, to reduce the potential for having to reenter the transactions. See E-Materials for backup procedures.

Perform December 2022 Month-end Procedures

Because many of Waren's month-end procedures are done automatically by *QuickBooks*, the only month-end procedures you will need to perform are:

- Prepare the December bank reconciliation.
- Print a customer monthly statement.

Check Figure for Your Cash Balance

Before starting the December bank reconciliation, be sure that your cash balance is correct by completing the following steps:

▶ *Click the Chart of Accounts icon and then double-click on the cash account (account #10100).*

Examine the ending balance in the cash account at 12/31/22. The balance should be $113,360.53. If the cash balance in your window differs significantly from this amount, return to the December 16–31 transactions to locate and correct any errors before starting the bank reconciliation. Because *QuickBooks* performs periodic automatic updates online, your cash balance may differ slightly (less than $15.00) due to changes in federal tax tables downloaded by the program. When your cash balance is correct, continue with the requirements that follow.

Bank Reconciliation Information, Process, and Printing

The following information is taken from the December bank statement and the November bank reconciliation, neither of which is included in these materials:

- The December 31, 2022, bank statement balance is $131,549.53.
- The following checks and ACH payments have not cleared the bank as of December 31:
  - Check Nos. 1118, 1142, 1152, 1153, 1154, 1155, 1156, 1157, and 1158
  - ACH #E-53431, #E-53432, and #E-53433
- The following deposits have not cleared the bank as of December 31, 2022:
  1. The December 27 account receivable collection from Eastern Wisconsin University.
  2. The December 27 cash sale proceeds from Hawkins College.
  3. The December 30 account receivable collection from University of Southern Iowa.
  4. The December 30 receipt of dividend income (see top of next page for more deposits in transit).

5. The December 30 deposit from the Henry Corporation stock sale.
6. The December 30 deposit of rent from Leverett & Associates.
7. The December 30 account receivable collection from Stevenson College

- ACH fees and service charges totaling $25.50 are included on the December bank statement. *Note:* These fees and charges should be posted to A/C #41000 (Other Operating Expense).

▶ *Prepare the December bank reconciliation. The cutoff date for the bank reconciliation is December 31, 2022.*

▶ *When the reconciliation is correct, click the Print button to print the bank reconciliation either in hard copy or in PDF format if you are submitting your work online. The Select Type of Reconciliation Report window will appear with the option to select Summary, Detail, or print Both reports; select Both.*

▶ *Review your printed reconciliation for accuracy and acceptability. You will submit these reports to your instructor along with year-end reports.*

Print a Customer Monthly Statement

At the end of each month, Waren sends monthly statements to all customers with an outstanding balance. For this section, you are to print the December monthly statement for Rosemont University.

▶ *Follow the instructions on pages 44 through 46 of the Reference book to print a December 2022 customer statement for Rosemont University either in hard copy or in PDF format if you are submitting your work online.*

▶ *In the Statement Date field select December 31, 2022, and check the Statement Period From and To field and enter the month of December date range.*

▶ *Click the Preview button to preview the statement. Click Print to print a copy to submit to your instructor with other chapter requirements.*

Print a General Ledger Trial Balance for Check Figures Prior to Year-end Adjusting Entries

The trial balance on page 9-51 shows the correct balances in all general ledger accounts after the December month-end procedures are completed. You will use the Memorized tab of the Report Center to access some reports that have been specifically set up for this project.

▶ *Click Report Center → Memorized tab (if not already opened) → Trial Balance to print a 12/31/22 trial balance to the screen.*

Compare the amounts on your printed trial balance with those on page 9-51. If any amounts are different, return to the December 16–31 transactions and the month-end procedures you processed in *QuickBooks* and make the necessary corrections using the procedures you learned in earlier chapters. When all errors are corrected, print a corrected trial balance either in hard copy or in PDF format if you are submitting your work online.

You can also compare the amounts on your printed trial balance with those included in the *SUA/E-SUA* year-end unadjusted trial balance (part of the year-end worksheet). All account balances should agree if your solution to the *SUA/E-SUA* was correct, except inventory-related accounts, bad debt expense, and the allowance for doubtful accounts. *Note:* Ignore any minor rounding differences in the cash and payroll-related accounts. Inventory-related account balances do not agree because of the use of different inventory methods. The balances in inventory-related accounts, bad debt expense, and the allowance account will agree after adjusting entries are completed. See the following page for a discussion of the inventory methods used in the *SUA/E-SUA* and in the *QuickBooks* project.

When your balances agree with those on page 9-51, go to the following section where you will record year-end adjusting entries.

Record 2022 Year-end Adjusting Entries

The next step at the end of an accounting year before printing output is to record year-end adjusting entries. The following are the types of year-end adjustments required for Waren:

- Inventory adjustment to the physical count
- Depreciation expense
- Accrued interest payable
- Bad debt expense and allowance
- Cost of goods sold for freight and sales discounts taken
- Federal income taxes

Each of the year-end adjustments is explained in a section that follows. Perform the procedures in the order listed.

Adjust Perpetual Inventory Records

Recall that in the *SUA/E-SUA* you were provided with the ending dollar balance in inventory and you adjusted to that total. That system was a periodic inventory system. *QuickBooks* uses a perpetual system, which provides a current inventory balance after each transaction. At year-end, the perpetual records are adjusted to a physical count to adjust for obsolescence, theft, or accounting errors.

The physical count was taken on December 31. A comparison of the physical count and the perpetual records showed a difference for certain items. Management is concerned about these inventory differences but knows that the physical count is accurate. Thus, the perpetual records must be adjusted as follows to agree with the physical count:

Item	Description	Quantity on Perpetual Records	Quantity per Physical Count
BB-019	Basketball pole pad	106 (96 regular, 10 returns)	109 (99 regular, 10 returns)
FB-027	Shoulder pad set	159 (all regular)	147 (all regular)
BA-158	Baseballs–12 balls	156 (all regular)	162 (all regular)

▶ *Record the inventory adjustments in QuickBooks following the guidance in the Reference book. Use Cost of Goods Sold as the Adjustment Account.*

After the inventory adjustments have been processed, record the remaining five year-end adjusting entries through the General Journal Entry window.

▶ *Use the information in the following five sections to record each of the remaining year-end adjusting entries by preparing a general journal entry in QuickBooks following the guidance in the Reference book pages 52 and 53.*

Depreciation Expense

Recall from the *SUA/E-SUA* that depreciation expense is calculated once at the end of each year. Depreciation is calculated using the straight-line method over the estimated useful lives of the assets (five or ten years for Waren's existing fixed assets). Waren's depreciation expense for Waren for 2022 totaled $34,779.31.

Accrued Interest Payable

Recall from Transaction No. 5 on page 9-32 that Waren has a $90,000 two-year note payable to First American Bank and Trust, dated December 19, 2022. The stated annual interest rate on the note is 5.5%. The terms of the note payable call for the following payments:

- $4,950 interest payments on 12/19/23 and 12/19/24
- $90,000 principal payment on 12/19/24

Recall from the *SUA/E-SUA* that interest accruals are calculated using a 365-day year with the day after the note was made counting as the first day. General ledger account numbers for the journal entry are: A/C #40800 (Interest Expense) and A/C #21000 (Interest Payable). Either enter the correct amount on the online grading portion of the Armond Dalton Resources website or show your calculation on the Chapter 9 homework pages available for download on the website (consult your instructor).

Bad Debt Expense and Allowance

Bad debt expense is estimated once annually at the end of each year as 1/2 of one percent (0.005) of net sales and is recorded in the general journal as of December 31. As explained in Chapter 7, Waren uses the direct write-off method during the year and then the allowance method at year-end. General ledger account numbers for the journal entry are: A/C #40900 (Bad Debt Expense) and A/C #10300 (Allowance for Doubtful Account). In order to balance out the Allowance for Doubtful Account and Bad Debt Expense account due to the direct write-off to Bad Debt Expense, you must readjust the Bad Debt Expense account to equal the 1/2 of one percent (0.005) calculation of net sales. Either enter the correct amount on the online grading portion of the Armond Dalton Resources website or show your calculation on the Chapter 9 homework pages available for download on the website (consult your instructor).

- Determine the amount of net sales by examining the 2022 income statement on the screen. For your convenience, the 2022 income statement has been included in the Memorized tab of the Report Center.
- *QuickBooks* requires you to add a customer to the Name box. Type "write off" in the Name box and press Enter. If "write off" doesn't exist as a customer, select Quick Add and select the Customer category.

Cost of Goods Sold

QuickBooks automatically debits cost of goods sold and credits inventory for the product cost for each sale. The inventory account is also automatically updated for inventory purchases and purchases returns. Therefore, the *QuickBooks* data does not include the following accounts from the *SUA*/E-SUA: A/C #30500 (Purchases) and A/C #30600 (Purchase Returns and Allowance). Waren treats purchase discounts taken and freight-in as a part of cost of goods sold but records them in separate accounts during the accounting period. Therefore, these two accounts must be closed to A/C #30400 (Cost of Goods Sold): A/C #30700 (Purchases Discounts Taken) and A/C #30800 (Freight-In).

- Before preparing the general journal entry, determine the balance in each account being closed to cost of goods sold. Determine the balance in the accounts to be closed by examining the income statement.

Federal Income Taxes

Recall from the *SUA/E-SUA* that the corporate income tax rate is 21% for all regular corporations such as Waren. General ledger account numbers for the journal entry are: A/C #40700 (Federal Income Tax Expense) and A/C #20800 (Federal Income Taxes Payable). Either enter the correct amount on the online grading portion of the Armond Dalton Resources website or show your calculation on the Chapter 9 homework pages available for download on the website (consult your instructor).

- After all other adjusting entries are recorded, determine 2022 pre-tax income by examining the 2022 income statement from the Memorized tab in the Report Center.
- Do not be concerned if your amount is slightly different from the *SUA/ E-SUA* amount for federal income taxes. The minor payroll differences will affect the calculation slightly.

Print a General Ledger Trial Balance for Check Figures After Year-end Adjusting Entries

The trial balance on page 9-52 shows the correct balances in all general ledger accounts after the year-end adjusting entries are recorded.

> ▶ *Open and use the general ledger trial balance for Waren to compare the amounts in your window to the correct balances. If there are differences, return to the year-end adjusting entries and make the necessary corrections. After you determine that your trial balance is correct, print the 12/31/22 trial balance either in hard copy or in PDF format if you are submitting your work online.* You will submit this report to your instructor along with year-end reports.

You can also compare the amounts on your printed trial balance with those included in the *SUA/E-SUA* year-end adjusted trial balance (part of the year-end worksheet). All account balances should agree if your *SUA/E-SUA* solution was correct, except for possible minor differences for cash, payroll-related accounts, and federal income tax expense because of the difference in the way payroll taxes are calculated in the *SUA/E-SUA* and *QuickBooks*.

When your balances agree with those on page 9-52, go to the following section where you will print financial statements and other reports. All entries have now been recorded.

Print Financial Statements and Other Reports

All of the following reports are to be submitted to your instructor either in hard copy or uploaded to the online grading page of Armond Dalton Resources (consult your instructor).

> ▶ *Print the following reports (print to PDF is best if submitting online). Each of these reports has already been set up in the Memorized tab of the Report Center.*

1. 12/31/22 balance sheet
2. 2022 income statement
3. General journal for December 2022
4. Accounts receivable aged trial balance as of 12/31/22
5. Accounts payable aged trial balance as of 12/31/22
6. Inventory valuation summary as of 12/31/22
7. Employee earnings register for December 2022
8. Sales journal for December 2022
9. Cash receipts journal for December 2022

10. Purchases journal for December 2022
11. Cash disbursements journal for December 2022
12. Payroll journal for December 2022

You can compare the reports printed using *QuickBooks* to the manual reports you prepared in the *SUA/E-SUA*.

Submit Reports and Answers to Assigned Questions

Submit the following to your course instructor either in hard copy or on the online grading page of the Armond Dalton Resources site *(consult your instructor)*:

- All twelve reports just listed
- December 2022 bank reconciliation that you already printed
- Customer monthly statement for Rosemont University that you already printed
- Trial balance after year-end adjustments that you already printed
- Chapter 9 homework questions available on the Armond Dalton Resources website (calculations for accrued interest payable, bad debt expense, and federal income tax expense).

All procedures are now complete for this chapter. Now that you have completed Chapter 9, you should back up your data files for Waren Sports Supply following the instructions in the E-Materials.

Check Figures

Waren Sports Supply
Trial Balance
As of December 31, 2022

	Dec 31, 22	
	Debit	Credit
10100 · Cash	113,335.03	
10100 o · Checking	0.00	
10200 · Accounts Receivable	45,877.00	
10210 · Accounts Rec from Employees	275.00	
10300 · Allow for Doubtful Accounts		4,250.81
10400 · Inventory	194,979.00	
10500 · Prepaid Expenses	3,000.00	
10600 · Marketable Securities	23,905.00	
12000 · Undeposited Funds	0.00	
10800 · Fixed Assets	328,363.10	
10900 · Accumulated Depreciation		80,634.50
20100 · Accounts Payable		5,736.35
20300 · Federal Income Tax Withheld		1,161.00
20400 · State Income Taxes Withheld		672.20
20500 · State Unemployment Taxes Pay.		117.89
20600 · Fed. Unemployment Taxes Pay.		19.92
20700 · FICA Taxes Payable		2,280.76
20800 · Federal Income Taxes Payable	0.00	
20900 · Dividends Payable		9,000.00
21200 · Unearned Revenue		6,600.00
25500 · Sales Tax Payable	0.00	
21100 · Notes Payable		75,000.00
Opening Bal Equity	0.00	
26000 · Common Stock		225,000.00
29000 · *Retained Earnings		90,264.99
29010 · Dividends Declared	9,000.00	
30100 · Sales		1,601,730.50
30200 · Sales Returns and Allowances	62,181.00	
30300 · Sales Discounts Taken	15,647.11	
30900 · G/L on Sale of Fixed Assets		275.00
31000 · G/L on Sale of Mkt. Securities		550.00
31100 · Interest/Dividend Income		1,500.00
31200 · Miscellaneous Revenue		825.00
30400 · Cost of Goods Sold	1,024,387.00	
30700 · Purchases Discounts Taken		16,733.90
30800 · Freight-in	24,897.84	
40100 · Rent Expense	57,600.00	
40200 · Advertising Expense	22,395.00	
40300 · Office Supplies Expense	5,892.55	
40500 · Wages and Salaries Expense	140,371.63	
40600 · Payroll Tax Expense	12,020.81	
40800 · Interest Expense	0.00	
40900 · Bad Debt Expense	4,400.00	
41000 · Other Operating Expense	33,825.75	
TOTAL	**2,122,352.82**	**2,122,352.82**

Waren Sports Supply
Trial Balance
As of December 31, 2022

	Dec 31, 22	
	Debit	Credit
10100 · Cash	113,335.03	
10100 o · Checking	0.00	
10200 · Accounts Receivable	45,877.00	
10210 · Accounts Rec from Employees	275.00	
10300 · Allow for Doubtful Accounts		7,470.32
10400 · Inventory	194,445.00	
10500 · Prepaid Expenses	3,000.00	
10600 · Marketable Securities	23,905.00	
12000 · Undeposited Funds	0.00	
10800 · Fixed Assets	328,363.10	
10900 · Accumulated Depreciation		115,413.81
20100 · Accounts Payable		5,736.35
20300 · Federal Income Tax Withheld		1,161.00
20400 · State Income Taxes Withheld		672.20
20500 · State Unemployment Taxes Pay.		117.89
20600 · Fed. Unemployment Taxes Pay.		19.92
20700 · FICA Taxes Payable		2,280.76
20800 · Federal Income Taxes Payable		37,653.03
20900 · Dividends Payable		9,000.00
21000 · Interest Payable		162.74
21200 · Unearned Revenue		6,600.00
25500 · Sales Tax Payable	0.00	
21100 · Notes Payable		75,000.00
Opening Bal Equity	0.00	
26000 · Common Stock		225,000.00
29000 · *Retained Earnings		90,264.99
29010 · Dividends Declared	9,000.00	
30100 · Sales		1,601,730.50
30200 · Sales Returns and Allowances	62,181.00	
30300 · Sales Discounts Taken	15,647.11	
30900 · G/L on Sale of Fixed Assets		275.00
31000 · G/L on Sale of Mkt. Securities		550.00
31100 · Interest/Dividend Income		1,500.00
31200 · Miscellaneous Revenue		825.00
30400 · Cost of Goods Sold	1,033,084.94	
30700 · Purchases Discounts Taken	0.00	
30800 · Freight-in	0.00	
40100 · Rent Expense	57,600.00	
40200 · Advertising Expense	22,395.00	
40300 · Office Supplies Expense	5,892.55	
40400 · Depreciation Expense	34,779.31	
40500 · Wages and Salaries Expense	140,371.63	
40600 · Payroll Tax Expense	12,020.81	
40700 · Federal Income Tax Expense	37,653.03	
40800 · Interest Expense	162.74	
40900 · Bad Debt Expense	7,619.51	
41000 · Other Operating Expense	33,825.75	
TOTAL	**2,181,433.51**	**2,181,433.51**

Option C — Introduction

Waren Sports Supply Dataset

As described in the E-Materials, you should have downloaded an initial backup file for Waren Sports Supply to either your hard drive or to a USB flash drive after registering on the Armond Dalton Resources website (www. armonddaltonresources.com). If you correctly followed the instructions in the E-Materials, then Waren Sports Supply has been successfully restored into *QuickBooks*.

If you haven't yet completed these tasks from the E-Materials, complete the following step.

> ▶ *Follow the instructions in the E-Materials for downloading and restoring the Waren Sports Supply initial company backup file.*

Chapter Overview

In this chapter, you will record transactions for an existing company, Waren Sports Supply, for December 16–31, 2022. You will also complete other activities commonly done with accounting software and print several items to submit to your instructor.

An important difference in this assignment compared to previous ones is the lack of detailed instructions for using *QuickBooks* to record transactions and perform other activities. You are expected to use the Reference book for guidance if you need any.

If, at any time, you decide that you want to start the chapter over, you may do so by restoring the Waren Sports Supply dataset using the initial backup you downloaded from the Armond Dalton Resources website (armonddaltonresources.com). If you have not downloaded this initial backup yet, take the time to do that now, following the instructions in the E-Materials. You may restore this backup at any time during your work on this chapter if you have made errors that are too difficult to correct or if you believe that you do not understand the material in this chapter.

In recording the transactions and performing the other activities for Waren Sports Supply, you will need several things:

1. **Information in this chapter.** The material instructs you what to record or do.
2. **Reference Book Guide** (see inside front cover of Reference book). Use this to locate the appropriate pages in the Reference book for recording transactions or doing other activities.
3. **Reference book.** Open the Reference book to the appropriate pages for the transaction you are recording or other activity you are doing and follow the instructions. In some cases, you will not have practiced using a Reference book section. You should not be concerned about this lack of practice.
4. **Online Homework.** After you have completed the transactions and other requirements for Waren Sports Supply, you may access the questions for Chapter 9 online at the Armond Dalton Resources website. Either print a hard copy to complete and submit to your instructor or answer the questions online along with the other requirements of this chapter. Consult your instructor about which method to use.
5. *QuickBooks* **software and company data sets.**
6. **A printer connected to your computer and/or the ability to print reports to PDF format.**

When you have completed this chapter, you will also submit several reports to your instructor, along with the homework questions for Chapter 9 available on the Armond Dalton Resources website. Consult your instructor as to whether you should submit these items using the online grading page of the Armond Dalton Resources website or in hard copy.

Waren Sports Supply is a distributor of sporting goods to colleges and universities in the Midwest. Waren's accountant has recorded all transactions for the year 2022 through December 15, 2022, using *QuickBooks*. For this assignment, you will do the following using *QuickBooks*:

- Perform maintenance for inventory sales prices.
- Record December 16–31 transactions and perform related maintenance.
- Perform December 2022 month-end procedures.
- Record 2022 year-end adjusting entries.
- Print financial statements and other reports.

Perform Maintenance for Inventory Sales Prices

The price list on page 9-56 reflects the current selling prices for Waren's thirty products. Waren purchases all products for resale from one vendor, Velocity Sporting Goods. Waren sells each inventory item at the same price to all customers. A new price list is prepared each time there is a change in an item's cost or selling price. In this section, you will compare the selling price of each product to the amount included in *QuickBooks* and update the software for any differences.

> *If you are not already working in QuickBooks, open the program and open Waren Sports Supply.*

> *Perform maintenance for inventory sales prices (Sales Information section in the Edit Item Window) for each inventory item, following the guidance on page 69 of the Reference book. Be sure to click the OK button after each inventory item is changed before proceeding to the next inventory item.*

Alternative Method

> *Perform maintenance for inventory sales prices for multiple inventory items by first highlighting any of the Inventory Part items in the Item List. Then, select the Add/Edit Multiple Items function from the Item drop-down list in the lower-left corner of the Item List. Edit the entries in the Sales Price column that need to be changed, using the directional buttons to move from item to item for editing. When you have finished editing your sales prices, make sure you select the Save Changes button in the lower-right corner of the Item List.*

PRICE LIST
As of December 15, 2022

Item No.	Description	Selling Price
BA-054 & RET BA-054	Premium aluminum bat	$198.00
BA-158 & RET BA-158	Baseballs–12 game balls	60.00
BA-199 & RET BA-199	Fielding glove	72.00
BA-281 & RET BA-281	60 lb. dry line marker	99.00
BA-445 & RET BA-445	Catcher's mask	67.00
BA-507 & RET BA-507	Baseball equipment bag	41.00
BA-667 & RET BA-667	Ball bucket with seat–set of 3	35.00
BA-694 & RET BA-694	Batting gloves–1 pair	38.00
BA-807 & RET BA-807	Pitching machine	260.00
BA-859 & RET BA-859	Set of bases	179.00
BB-008 & RET BB-008	Basketball	35.00
BB-019 & RET BB-019	Basketball pole pad	135.00
BB-113 & RET BB-113	Scoreboard and timer	400.00
BB-267 & RET BB-267	Goal and rim set	138.00
BB-358 & RET BB-358	Backboard	127.00
BB-399 & RET BB-399	Basketball net	15.00
BB-431 & RET BB-431	Whistle and lanyard–set of 6	35.00
BB-538 & RET BB-538	Basketball bag	39.00
BB-688 & RET BB-688	Portable inflation pump	102.00
BB-926 & RET BB-926	Trainer's first aid kit	43.00
FB-027 & RET FB-027	Shoulder pad set	132.00
FB-091 & RET FB-091	Hip, tail, arm pad set	58.00
FB-225 & RET FB-225	Football helmet	89.00
FB-344 & RET FB-344	Football	29.00
FB-513 & RET FB-513	Portable storage locker	209.00
FB-573 & RET FB-573	Kicking tees–set of 6	21.00
FB-650 & RET FB-650	Football post pad	149.00
FB-812 & RET FB-812	Collapsible cones–set of 8	37.00
FB-874 & RET FB-874	Sideline repair kit	127.00
FB-952 & RET FB-952	Portable hand warmer	38.00

As shown in the first column of the table above, be sure that you also adjust the 'RET' (Inventory Return Items) sales prices to the correct amounts as you just did for the regular inventory items. *QuickBooks* handles returns as separate inventory items for Waren, so if you have to change the sales price of an item, you will need to do it twice: once for the item and once for the 'RET' of that same item.

After you complete inventory sales price maintenance, the *QuickBooks* files will contain the correct default sales price for each inventory item. These sales prices are used for all sales of inventory between December 16 and December 31, 2022. You should recheck the amounts to make sure they are all correct before you proceed.

Record December 16-31 Transactions and Perform Related Maintenance

The transactions on pages 9-59 through 9-66 for December 16 – 31 should be dealt with in the order listed. Some transactions must be recorded whereas others require only maintenance.

The information you have already learned about *QuickBooks* in Chapters 2 through 8 is used throughout the rest of this chapter. You should use the *QuickBooks* Reference book and information from prior chapters to the extent you need it. Also, if you want to check whether information was recorded and correctly included, use the Home Page buttons (for Centers), the Icon Bar, or the Company, Customer, Vendor, or Employee lists menu to view transactions, as you did in earlier chapters.

All default general ledger distribution accounts are correct for Waren's December 16 – 31 transactions unless otherwise noted on pages 9-59 through 9-66.

The following is background information that you will need to record Waren's December 16–31 transactions.

Bank

Waren uses only one bank, First American Bank and Trust, for all deposits, checks, and ACH payments, including payroll.

Credit Terms for Waren Sports Supply

Waren requires most of its customers to prepay for goods ordered. For these cash sales, the customer sends a check or electronic payment with its purchase order and Waren ships the merchandise. All trade discounts are already factored into the price list. Only a few favored customers with long-standing relationships with Waren and those who buy larger quantities are granted credit. These favored customers receive the following cash discount for early payment: 2/10, Net 30.

Waren receives a similar cash discount from its main inventory supplier, Velocity Sporting Goods (2/10, Net 30). No cash discount is offered by Chicago Office Supply, whose invoices are payable upon receipt. All discount terms have already been included as default information in *QuickBooks*.

Sales Tax for Waren Sports Supply

Waren Sports Supply makes only wholesale sales, which are exempt from state sales tax. Because Waren purchases all of its inventory items for resale, there is also no sales tax on its inventory purchases. Sales tax of 6% applies to office supplies and fixed asset purchases.

Inventory Method

Waren uses the perpetual inventory method. All purchases of inventory are debited directly to the inventory account. Cost of goods sold for each sale is calculated automatically by *QuickBooks*. Waren conducts a year-end physical inventory count and adjusts the perpetual inventory records as necessary. You will make those adjustments later.

WAREN SPORTS SUPPLY TRANSACTIONS FOR DECEMBER 16–31, 2022

▶ *Record each of the following transactions (No. 1 through 18) using QuickBooks.*

- Hints are provided in boxed areas like this.

Use care in recording each transaction. **You should follow each step in the Quick Reference Table for each transaction.** It may take slightly more time, but it will almost certainly help you avoid serious errors. Find the appropriate Quick Reference Table for each transaction or other activity by using the Reference Book Guide located on the inside front cover of the Reference book.

Trans. No.	Dec.	
1	16	**Make a credit sale:** Received customer Purchase Order No. 53426 in the mail from Rosemont University (Customer 406), approved their credit, prepared Invoice No. 731 totaling $15,490 and shipped the goods from the warehouse. All goods ordered were shipped as follows:

Quantity	Item Code	Description
25	BB-267	Goal and rim set
20	BB-358	Backboard
45	FB-027	Shoulder pad set
40	FB-225	Football helmet

Trans. No.	Dec.	
2	16	**Collect an account receivable and make a deposit:** Received an email notification from First American Bank and Trust of an ACH payment received from Branch College (Received from 408). The ACH payment of $1,622.88 was for payment in full of sales Invoice No. 730. The early payment discount taken by Branch College was $33.12. Select "e-CHECK" as the method of payment and type "ACH" in the Reference # box.

- After recording the ACH payment receipt, record the receipt on the same day using the Make Deposits window (see pages 30 through 32 of the Reference book).

Trans. No.	Dec.	
3	16	**Prepare a purchase order:** Ordered the following inventory on account from Velocity Sporting Goods (Vendor 252) using Purchase Order No. 328. The goods will be received at the warehouse at a later date. The purchase order total is $25,335.

Item	Description	Quantity
BB-019	Basketball pole pad	115
BB-538	Basketball bag	125
BB-431	Whistle and lanyard - set of 6	75
BB-399	Basketball net	50
FB-027	Shoulder pad set (to cover back order and invetory restock)	100

Trans. No.	Dec.	
4	19	**Receive goods on a purchase order:** Received office supplies from Chicago Office Supply (Vendor 253) as listed on Purchase Order No. 327, which is shown as an open purchase order in *QuickBooks*. Chicago Office Supply's vendor Invoice No. 2378 was received with the goods, totaling $830.25 including sales tax of $47.00. All supplies ordered on Purchase Order No. 327 were received in good condition and taken to the office.

- Because Waren purchases similar items from Chicago Office Supply on a regular basis, each office supply item is kept track of in the inventory module as a non-inventory part. Office supplies expense is debited instead of inventory for these non-inventory parts.
- Remember to enter the sales tax portion of the invoice in the Expenses tab as a debit to the appropriate expense account (see step O in the Quick Reference Table).

Trans. No.	Dec.	
5	19	**Receive a miscellaneous cash receipt:** Borrowed $90,000 from First American Bank and Trust (Received from 264) by issuing a two-year note payable. Received an email notification from the bank that the $90,000 proceeds were electronically deposited into Waren's checking account.

- The credit portion of the transaction should be posted to A/C #21100 (Notes Payable).
- Miscellaneous cash receipts are processed through the Banking Center Make Deposits window (see pages 42 and 43 of the Reference book).

6	20	**Purchase non-inventory items or services without a purchase order—payment made at time of purchase:** Received vendor Invoice No. 105963 for $1,710 from First Security Insurance (Pay to the Order of 260) for the fourth quarter's health insurance coverage for employees and immediately issued Check No. 1152 for payment in full.
7	20	**Change an employee record (employee maintenance):** Increased employee salary and wage rates, effective December 16. For hourly employees, overtime is paid at 1.5 times the regular hourly rate. There were no changes in filing status, dependents, or withholding allowances.

Employee	New Salary / Wage Rate
Ray Kramer	$3,650, semi-monthly (enter $87,600 Annual Rate)
Jim Adams	$21.80 per hour regular $32.70 per hour overtime
Nancy Ford	$18.30 per hour regular $27.45 per hour overtime

Trans. No.	Dec.	
8	20	**Receive goods on a purchase order:** Received merchandise from Velocity Sporting Goods (Vendor 252) as listed on Purchase Order No. 328, along with Invoice No. 34719. The payment terms on the invoice are 2/10, Net 30. All merchandise listed on the purchase order was delivered in good condition and in the quantities ordered, except that only 85 basketball pole pads (Item No. BB-019) were received. The total of the invoice is $22,515. The goods were placed immediately in the inventory warehouse.
9	21	**Make a credit sale:** Filled the backorder quantity of 30 shoulder pad sets (Item No. FB-027) for Rosemont University's Purchase Order # 53426. Approved Rosemont's credit and shipped the back ordered shoulder pad sets. Prepared Invoice No. 732 totaling $3,960 for the sale to Rosemont.
10	23	**Write off an uncollectible account receivable:** Received legal notification from Benson, Rosenbrook, and Martinson, P.C., attorneys at law, that Stevenson College (Received From 411) is unable to pay any of its outstanding debts to its suppliers. The $2,900 balance remaining on Invoice No. 719 should therefore be written off as uncollectible.

- Recall that Waren uses the allowance method for recording bad debt expense at year-end, but uses the direct write-off method during the year.
- Follow the instructions on pages 38 through 40 of the Reference book carefully so that you use the direct write-off method correctly (debit to bad debt expense, credit to accounts receivable). The allowance for uncollectible accounts and bad debt expense will be adjusted during the year-end procedures later in the chapter.

Trans. No.	Dec.	
11	23	**Process a sales return or allowance (credit memo):** Eastern Wisconsin University (Customer 410) returned 10 basketball pole pads (RET BB-019) and 8 scoreboard and timer sets (RET BB-113) that were originally purchased on Invoice No. 729. Waren previously authorized EWU by phone to return the goods for credit against their account balance. EWU's Return Request No. R8034 was received with the goods. Sales return document CM 42 was issued for $4,550 and applied to Invoice No. 729.

- Be sure to select the "RET" version of each inventory item when processing the sales return.
- When you select Save in the Create Credit Memos/Refunds window, the Available Credit window will appear. Make sure you select Apply to Invoice and then select the correct invoice for the credit memo.

12	27	**Collect an account receivable and make a deposit:** Received and deposited Check No. 49326 for $12,000 from Eastern Wisconsin University (Received from 410) in partial payment of the remaining amount (after sales return) on Invoice No. 729.

- Be sure that the entry in the A/R Account box says "10200 Accounts Receivable."
- After recording the customer payment, record the deposit into the bank on the same day using the Make Deposits window (see pages 30 through 32 of the Reference book).

Trans. No.	Dec.	
13	27	**Make a cash sale and make a deposit:** Received and deposited Check No. 47852 for $5,835 from Hawkins College (CASHCUSTOMER) for a cash sale. The goods were shipped from the warehouse and the cash sale was processed and recorded (Invoice No. C-30. All goods ordered were shipped as follows:

Item	Description	Quantity
BB-008	Basketball	30
FB-091	Hip, tail, arm pad set	45
FB-344	Football	75

- After recording the cash receipt, record the deposit into the bank on the same day using the Make Deposits window (see pages 30 through 32 of the Reference book).

14	28	**Purchase non-inventory items or services without a purchase order—payment made at time of purchase:** Received vendor Invoice No. 72654 for $1,590 from the University Athletic News (Pay to the Order of 254) for advertisements Waren ran during the Christmas season and immediately issued Check No. 1153 for payment in full.
15	28	**Purchase non-inventory items or services without a purchase order—payment made at time of purchase:** Received Freight Bill No. 26245 for $738.15 from Interstate Motor Freight (Pay to the Order of 255) and immediately issued Check No. 1154 for payment in full. The freight bill is for the merchandise received from Purchase Order No. 328. The payment terms on the freight bill are Net 30.

Trans.	
No.	Dec.

16   29   **Pay a vendor's outstanding invoice:** Issued an electronic payment (#E-53431) for $22,064.70 to Velocity Sporting Goods (Pay to the Order of 252) for payment in full of Invoice No. 34719. Recall that this invoice was for goods received December 20. The early payment discount taken by Waren was $450.30.

- The default method of payment of Check is correct for an electronic (ACH) payment.
- Be sure to select account #30700–Purchases Discounts—in the Discount Account box of the Discount and Credits window.
- If account #10100–Cash—is not already selected in the Account box, select it before clicking the Pay Selected Bills button.

17   29   **Receive goods on a purchase order:** Received but did not pay for three standing workstations from Chicago Office Supply (Vendor 253) ordered on Waren's Purchase Order No. 325, which is shown as an open purchase order in *QuickBooks*. Also received vendor's Invoice No. 2423 from Chicago Office Supply, totaling $1,256.10 including sales tax of $71.10. The workstations were received in new and undamaged condition in the warehouse. After they were unpacked and inspected, they were taken directly to the office.

- You must enter A/C #10800 (Fixed Assets) in the Account column when entering sales tax in the Expenses tab because the default will be office supplies expense and the purchase should be debited to fixed assets.

Trans. No.	Dec.	
18	30	**Pay employees:** Finished the payroll for the semi-monthly pay period December 16–31, 2022, and issued Check Nos. 1155 through 1157. Regular and overtime hours for hourly employees were as follows:

Employee	Regular Hours	Overtime Hours
Jim Adams	88	9.3
Nancy Ford	88	6.7
Ray Kramer	N/A	N/A

- You do not need to enter anything for Ray Kramer's hours because he is a salaried employee.
- If you receive a message about payroll liabilities, click OK.

You should, but are not required to, perform backup procedures for Waren Sports Supply before proceeding, to reduce the potential for having to reenter the transactions. See E-Materials for backup procedures.

Perform December 2022 Month-end Procedures

Because many of Waren's month-end procedures are done automatically by *QuickBooks,* the only month-end procedures you will need to perform are:

- Prepare the December bank reconciliation.
- Print a customer monthly statement.

Check Figure for Your Cash Balance

Before starting the December bank reconciliation, be sure that your cash balance is correct by completing the following steps:

▶ *Click the Chart of Accounts icon and then double-click on the cash account (account #10100).*

Examine the ending balance in the cash account at 12/31/22. The balance should be $110,392.32. If the cash balance in your window differs significantly from this amount, return to the December 16–31 transactions to locate and correct any errors before starting the bank reconciliation. Because *QuickBooks* performs periodic automatic updates online, your cash balance may differ slightly (less than $15.00) due to changes in federal tax tables downloaded by the program. When your cash balance is correct, continue with the requirements that follow.

Bank Reconciliation Information, Process, and Printing

The following information is taken from the December bank statement and the November bank reconciliation, neither of which is included in these materials:

- The December 31, 2022, bank statement balance is $131,549.53.
- The following checks and ACH payments have not cleared the bank as of December 31:
  - Check Nos. 1118, 1142, 1152, 1153, 1154, 1155, 1156, and 1157
  - ACH #E-53431
- The December 27 deposits from Eastern Wisconsin University and Hawkins College have not cleared the bank as of December 31.
- ACH fees and service charges totaling $25.50 are included on the December bank statement. *Note:* These fees and charges should be posted to A/C #41000 (Other Operating Expense).

▷ *Prepare the December bank reconciliation. The cutoff date for the bank reconciliation is December 31, 2022.*

▷ *When the reconciliation is correct, click the Print button to print the bank reconciliation either in hard copy or in PDF format if you are submitting your work online. The Select Type of Reconciliation Report window will appear with the option to select Summary, Detail, or print Both reports; select Both.*

▷ *Review your printed reconciliation for accuracy and acceptability. You will submit these reports to your instructor along with year-end reports.*

Print a Customer Monthly Statement

At the end of each month, Waren sends monthly statements to all customers with an outstanding balance. For this section, you are to print the December monthly statement for Rosemont University.

▷ *Follow the instructions on pages 44 through 46 of the Reference book to print a December 2022 customer statement for Rosemont University either in hard copy or in PDF format if you are submitting your work online.*

> ▶ *In the Statement Date field select December 31, 2022, and check the Statement Period From and To field and enter the month of December date range.*

> ▶ *Click the Preview button to preview the statement. Click Print to print a copy to submit to your instructor with other chapter requirements.*

Print a General Ledger Trial Balance for Check Figures Prior to Year-end Adjusting Entries

The trial balance on page 9-73 shows the correct balances in all general ledger accounts after the December month-end procedures are completed. You will use the Memorized tab of the Report Center to access some reports that have been specifically set up for this project.

> ▶ *Click Report Center → Memorized tab (if not already opened) → Trial Balance to print a 12/31/22 trial balance to the screen.*

Compare the amounts on your printed trial balance with those on page 9-73. If any amounts are different, return to the December 16 – 31 transactions and the month-end procedures you processed in *QuickBooks* and make the necessary corrections using the procedures you learned in earlier chapters. When all errors are corrected, print a corrected trial balance either in hard copy or in PDF format if you are submitting your work online.

When your balances agree with those on page 9-73, go to the following section where you will record year-end adjusting entries.

Record 2022 Year-end Adjusting Entries

The next step at the end of an accounting year before printing output is to record year-end adjusting entries. The following are the types of year-end adjustments required for Waren:

- Inventory adjustment to the physical count
- Depreciation expense
- Accrued interest payable
- Bad debt expense and allowance
- Cost of goods sold for freight and sales discounts taken
- Federal income taxes

Each of the year-end adjustments is explained in a section that follows. Perform the procedures in the order listed.

Adjust Perpetual Inventory Records

The physical count was taken on December 31. A comparison of the physical count and the perpetual records showed a difference for certain items. Management is concerned about these inventory differences but knows that the physical count is accurate. Thus, the perpetual records must be adjusted as follows to agree with the physical count:

Item	Description	Quantity on Perpetual Records	Quantity per Physical Count
BB-019	Basketball pole pad	106 (96 regular, 10 returns)	109 (99 regular, 10 returns)
FB-027	Shoulder pad set	159 (all regular)	147 (all regular)
BA-158	Baseballs–12 balls	156 (all regular)	162 (all regular)

▶ *Record the inventory adjustments in QuickBooks following the guidance in the Reference book. Use Cost of Goods Sold as the Adjustment Account.*

After the inventory adjustments have been processed, record the remaining five year-end adjusting entries through the General Journal Entry window.

▶ *Use the information in the following five sections to record each of the remaining year-end adjusting entries by preparing a general journal entry in QuickBooks following the guidance in the Reference book pages 52 and 53.*

Depreciation Expense

Depreciation expense is calculated once at the end of each year. Depreciation is calculated using the straight-line method over the estimated useful lives of the assets (five or ten years for Waren's existing fixed assets). Waren's depreciation expense for Waren for 2022 totaled $34,779.31.

Accrued Interest Payable

Recall from Transaction No. 5 on page 9-61 that Waren has a $90,000 two-year note payable to First American Bank and Trust, dated December 19, 2022. The stated annual interest rate on the note is 5.5%. The terms of the note payable call for the following payments:

- $4,950 interest payments on 12/19/23 and 12/19/24
- $90,000 principal payment on 12/19/24

Interest accruals are calculated using a 365-day year with the day after the note was made counting as the first day. General ledger account numbers for the journal entry are: A/C #40800 (Interest Expense) and A/C #21000 (Interest Payable). Either enter the correct amount on the online grading portion of the Armond Dalton Resources website or show your calculation on the Chapter 9 homework pages available for download on the website (consult your instructor).

Bad Debt Expense and Allowance

Bad debt expense is estimated once annually at the end of each year as 1/2 of one percent (0.005) of net sales and is recorded in the general journal as of December 31. As explained in Chapter 7, Waren uses the direct write-off method during the year and then the allowance method at year-end. General ledger account numbers for the journal entry are: A/C #40900 (Bad Debt Expense) and A/C #10300 (Allowance for Doubtful Account). In order to balance out the Allowance for Doubtful Account and Bad Debt Expense account due to the direct write-off to Bad Debt Expense, you must readjust the Bad Debt Expense account to equal the 1/2 of one percent (0.005) calculation of net sales. Either enter the correct amount on the online grading portion of the Armond Dalton Resources website or show your calculation on the Chapter 9 homework pages available for download on the website (consult your instructor).

- Determine the amount of net sales by examining the 2022 income statement on the screen. For your convenience, the 2022 income statement has been included in the Memorized tab of the Report Center.
- *QuickBooks* requires you to add a customer to the Name box. Type "write off" in the Name box and press Enter. If "write off" doesn't exist as a customer, select Quick Add and select the Customer category.

Cost of Goods Sold

QuickBooks automatically debits cost of goods sold and credits inventory for the product cost for each sale. The inventory account is also automatically updated for inventory purchases and purchases returns. Waren treats purchase discounts taken and freight-in as a part of cost of goods sold but records them in separate accounts during the accounting period. Therefore, these two accounts must be closed to A/C #30400 (Cost of Goods Sold): A/C #30700 (Purchases Discounts Taken) and A/C #30800 (Freight-In).

- Before preparing the general journal entry, determine the balance in each account being closed to cost of goods sold. Determine the balance in the accounts to be closed by examining the income statement.

Federal Income Taxes

Assume that the corporate income tax rate is 21% for all regular corporations such as Waren. General ledger account numbers for the journal entry are: A/C #40700 (Federal Income Tax Expense) and A/C #20800 (Federal Income Taxes Payable). Either enter the correct amount on the online grading portion of the Armond Dalton Resources website or show your calculation on the Chapter 9 homework pages available for download on the website (consult your instructor).

- After all other adjusting entries are recorded, determine 2022 pre-tax income by examining the 2022 income statement from the Memorized tab in the Report Center.

Print a General Ledger Trial Balance for Check Figures After Year-end Adjusting Entries

The trial balance on page 9-74 shows the correct balances in all general ledger accounts after the year-end adjusting entries are recorded.

▶ *Open and use the general ledger trial balance for Waren to compare the amounts in your window to the correct balances. If there are differences, return to the year-end adjusting entries and make the necessary corrections. After you determine that your trial balance is correct, print the 12/31/22 trial balance.* You will submit this report to your instructor along with year-end reports.

When your balances agree with those on page 9-74, go to the following section where you will print financial statements and other reports. All entries have now been recorded.

Print Financial Statements and Other Reports

All of the following reports are to be submitted to your instructor either in hard copy or uploaded to the online grading page of Armond Dalton Resources (consult your instructor).

▶ *Print the following reports (print to PDF is best if submitting online). Each of these reports has already been set up in the Memorized tab of the Report Center.*

1. 12/31/22 balance sheet
2. 2022 income statement
3. General journal for December 2022
4. Accounts receivable aged trial balance as of 12/31/22
5. Accounts payable aged trial balance as of 12/31/22
6. Inventory valuation summary as of 12/31/22
7. Employee earnings register for December 2022
8. Sales journal for December 2022
9. Cash receipts journal for December 2022
10. Purchases journal for December 2022
11. Cash disbursements journal for December 2022
12. Payroll journal for December 2022

Submit Reports and Answers to Assigned Questions

Submit the following to your course instructor either in hard copy or on the online grading page of the Armond Dalton Resources site (*consult your instructor*):

- All twelve reports just listed
- December 2022 bank reconciliation that you already printed
- Customer monthly statement for Rosemont University that you already printed
- Trial balance after year-end adjustments that you already printed
- Chapter 9 homework questions available on the Armond Dalton Resources website (calculations for accrued interest payable, bad debt expense, and federal income tax expense).

All procedures are now complete for this chapter. Now that you have completed Chapter 9, you should back up your data files for Waren Sports Supply following the instructions in the E-Materials.

Check Figures

Waren Sports Supply
Trial Balance
As of December 31, 2022

	Dec 31, 22	
	Debit	Credit
10100 · Cash	110,366.82	
10200 · Accounts Receivable	45,877.00	
10300 · Allowance for Doubtful Accts.		3,250.81
10400 · Inventory	203,454.00	
10600 · Marketable Securities	24,000.00	
12000 · Undeposited Funds	0.00	
10800 · Fixed Assets	329,288.10	
10900 · Accumulated Depreciation		81,559.50
20100 · Accounts Payable		5,736.35
20300 · Federal Income Tax Withheld		1,161.00
20400 · State Income Taxes Withheld		672.20
20500 · State Unemployment Taxes Pay.		117.89
20600 · Fed. Unemployment Taxes Pay.		19.92
20700 · FICA Taxes Payable		2,280.76
20800 · Federal Income Taxes Payable	0.00	
25500 · Sales Tax Payable	0.00	
21100 · Notes Payable		90,000.00
Opening Bal Equity	0.00	
26000 · Common Stock		225,000.00
29000 · *Retained Earnings		90,264.99
30100 · Sales		1,589,666.00
30200 · Sales Returns and Allowances	62,181.00	
30300 · Sales Discounts Taken	15,405.82	
31200 · Miscellaneous Revenue		825.00
30400 · Cost of Goods Sold	1,015,912.00	
30700 · Purchases Discounts Taken		16,733.90
30800 · Freight-in	24,897.84	
40100 · Rent Expense	57,600.00	
40200 · Advertising Expense	22,395.00	
40300 · Office Supplies Expense	5,892.55	
40500 · Wages and Salaries Expense	140,371.63	
40600 · Payroll Tax Expense	12,020.81	
40900 · Bad Debt Expense	4,400.00	
41000 · Other Operating Expense	33,225.75	
TOTAL	**2,107,288.32**	**2,107,288.32**

Waren Sports Supply
Trial Balance
As of December 31, 2022

	Dec 31, 22	
	Debit	Credit
10100 · Cash	110,366.82	
10200 · Accounts Receivable	45,877.00	
10300 · Allowance for Doubtful Accts.		6,411.21
10400 · Inventory	202,920.00	
10600 · Marketable Securities	24,000.00	
12000 · Undeposited Funds	0.00	
10800 · Fixed Assets	329,288.10	
10900 · Accumulated Depreciation		116,338.81
20100 · Accounts Payable		5,736.35
20300 · Federal Income Tax Withheld		1,161.00
20400 · State Income Taxes Withheld		672.20
20500 · State Unemployment Taxes Pay.		117.89
20600 · Fed. Unemployment Taxes Pay.		19.92
20700 · FICA Taxes Payable		2,280.76
20800 · Federal Income Taxes Payable		36,600.07
21000 · Interest Payable		162.74
25500 · Sales Tax Payable	0.00	
21100 · Notes Payable		90,000.00
Opening Bal Equity	0.00	
26000 · Common Stock		225,000.00
29000 · *Retained Earnings		90,264.99
30100 · Sales		1,589,666.00
30200 · Sales Returns and Allowances	62,181.00	
30300 · Sales Discounts Taken	15,405.82	
31200 · Miscellaneous Revenue		825.00
30400 · Cost of Goods Sold	1,024,609.94	
30700 · Purchases Discounts Taken	0.00	
30800 · Freight-in	0.00	
40100 · Rent Expense	57,600.00	
40200 · Advertising Expense	22,395.00	
40300 · Office Supplies Expense	5,892.55	
40400 · Depreciation Expense	34,779.31	
40500 · Wages and Salaries Expense	140,371.63	
40600 · Payroll Tax Expense	12,020.81	
40700 · Federal Income Tax Expense	36,600.07	
40800 · Interest Expense	162.74	
40900 · Bad Debt Expense	7,560.40	
41000 · Other Operating Expense	33,225.75	
TOTAL	2,165,256.94	2,165,256.94

NEW COMPANY SETUP

Introduction

When a company uses *QuickBooks* for the first time, considerable maintenance is sometimes required before transactions can be entered. When the company has used an earlier version of *QuickBooks* the software imports the data easily, including maintenance information and transactions that were previously recorded. Similarly, *QuickBooks* imports maintenance and transactions from other accounting software such as *Sage 50*. However, when a company is converting from a manual system to *QuickBooks*, such importing cannot be done. The initial setup in this case usually requires considerable time, especially for larger companies.

In this chapter you will set up a new company in *QuickBooks*. Super Office Furniture Plus is a furniture retailer that has been in operation for five years. The company has maintained a manual accounting system since its inception. The company's management has decided to change to a computerized system using *QuickBooks* as of January 1, 2021. To learn setup, yet keep the amount of setup time minimized, an extremely small company is used.

If, at any time, you decide that you want to start the chapter over, you may do so by restoring the Super Office Furniture Plus dataset following the instructions in the E-Materials, which you should have already downloaded from the Armond Dalton Resources website (www.armonddaltonresources.com).

Create a New Company

The first step in new company setup is to create a new company in *QuickBooks*. In this case, you are converting from a manual system.

The authors have created a shell company for you to start with in order to save time for you to perform other setup procedures for vendors, customers, inventory, etc. In the real world, there are preliminary steps that you would go through to create the shell company, including selecting the industry, the type of entity, the fiscal year, and other information. For purposes of this project, Super Office Furniture Plus has been created as a retail shop, a regular corporation, and has a January fiscal year start. You will now enter other details for the company.

> ▶ *Open Super Office Furniture Plus. When you receive a password prompt, enter Admin1111 and click OK.* Note that you will need to enter this password each time you open the company in *QuickBooks*.
> ▶ *Click Company → My Company to open the My Company window.*
> ▶ *Click the Edit button [✎] in the top-right corner of the Company Information section of the window to open the Company Information window.*

The following illustrations show the completed windows for the first four tabs of the Company Information window. You will not use the fifth tab. Only some of the basic information has already been entered in these tabs when you first open them.

▶ *Enter any remaining items until your windows look like the ones that follow. Click OK when you are done entering information and then close the My Company window.*

▶ *If a window opens at any time asking if you want to add this file to your payroll subscription, click Skip.*

Company Information Window—Contact Information Tab

Company Information Window—Legal Information Tab

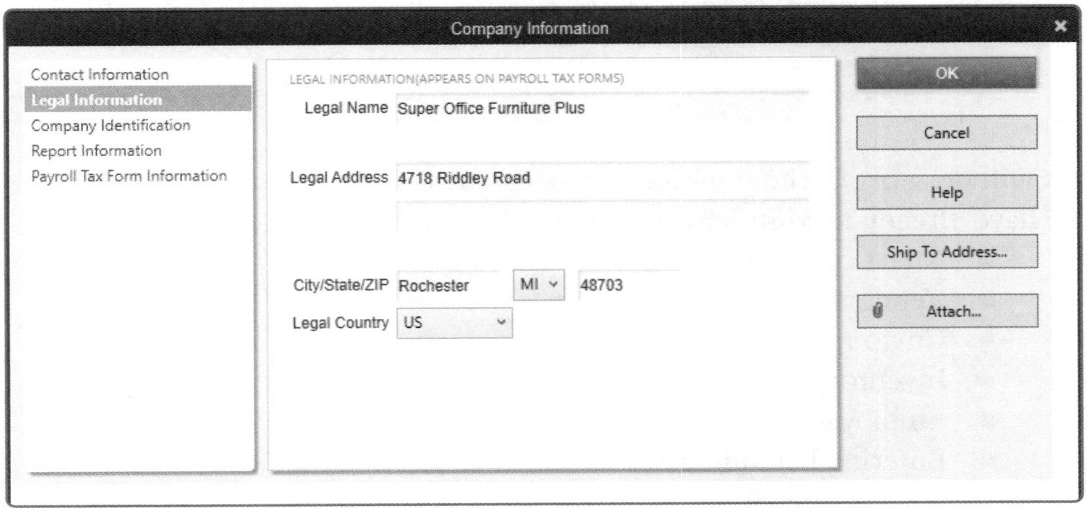

Company Information Window—Company Identification Tab

Company Information Window—Report Information Tab

You will do most of the remainder of setup by using the maintenance windows that you have already used in previous chapters in the order listed below:

- Chart of accounts
- Vendors
- Customers
- Inventory
- Employees
- Entering beginning account balances

Observe that all of these except the last item are maintenance items you dealt with previously. You can access any of these at any time starting with the Home Page.

Change the Default Chart of Accounts

When setting up a new company in *QuickBooks*, a user can either enter the company's chart of accounts manually or choose a default chart of accounts from a list provided by *QuickBooks*.

Recall that Super Office Furniture Plus was originally set up as a retail store operating as a corporation. The default accounts have already been included as part of the general system setup. You will change the default chart of accounts to match the one used in the company's manual accounting system.

> ▶ *Click the Home Page icon for Super Office Furniture Plus (if it is not already open) → Chart of Accounts (in the Company section) to access the default chart of accounts for a retail store.* Observe that the chart of accounts includes account number, account name, and Type. The entries in the Type column are used to format financial statements. There are no balances included yet, but you will enter those later.
>
> ▶ *Use the scroll bar and the up and down scroll arrows to review the company's default chart of accounts.*

To match the chart of accounts Super Office Furniture Plus uses in its manual accounting system, you need to make some changes. Information necessary to edit the default chart of accounts to match the company's current chart of accounts is included in the boxes on the following page. Later you will be entering beginning balances. Before you make any changes to the default chart of accounts, the following describes how to make each change.

> ▶ *Perform general ledger account maintenance following the instructions on pages 82 through 85 of the Reference book.* The boxes on the following page show the information to be added, deleted, and edited.

Note: Click No if you receive a message to "Set Up Bank Feed."

ACCOUNTS TO BE ADDED

Account Type	Number	Account Name and Description
Bank	10200	Savings Account
Accounts Receivable	11500	Allowance for Doubtful Accounts
Other Current Asset	13000	Inventory
Other Current Asset	14000	Prepaid Expenses
Accounts Payable	20000	Trade Accounts Payable
Other Current Liability	25000	Income Taxes Payable
Long-Term Liability	27000	Notes Payable

ACCOUNT NAMES TO BE REVISED

Account Type	Number	Existing Acct. Name and Desc.
Fixed Asset	15000	Furniture and Equipment
Income	46000	Merchandise Sales
Cost of Goods Sold	51800	Merchant Account Fees

Account Type	Number	Revised Acct. Name and Desc.
Fixed Asset	15000	Equipment
Income	46000	Sales
Cost of Goods Sold	51800	Cost of Goods Sold

ACCOUNTS TO BE DELETED

Number	Account Name
18700	Security Deposits Asset
30200	Dividends Paid
68500	Uniforms
80000	Ask My Accountant
90000	Estimates
90100	Purchase Orders

▶ *Click the Reports icon (or the Reports menu) → Accountant & Taxes → Account Listing to access the revised account listing.*

▶ *Click the Customize Report button.*

▶ *Remove the check marks next to "Balance Total" and "Tax Line" to remove those columns from the display.*

> ▶ *Choose Account in the "Sort by" box, click the "Ascending order" radio button if not already selected, then click OK.*

> ▶ *Compare the accounts, account numbers, and types of accounts to the ones in the report shown below. If there are differences, change them now using the information you learned in this section.*

Super Office Furniture Plus
Account Listing
December 15, 2021

Account	Type	Description	Accnt. #
10100 · Checking Account	Bank		10100
10200 · Savings Account	Bank	Savings Account	10200
11000 · Accounts Receivable	Accounts Receivable	Unpaid or unapplied customer invoices and credits	11000
11500 · Allowance for Doubtful ...	Accounts Receivable	Allowance for Doubtful Accounts	11500
12000 · Undeposited Funds	Other Current Asset	Funds received, but not yet deposited to a bank acco...	12000
13000 · Inventory	Other Current Asset	Inventory	13000
14000 · Prepaid Expenses	Other Current Asset	Prepaid Expenses	14000
15000 · Equipment	Fixed Asset	Equipment	15000
17000 · Accumulated Depreciati...	Fixed Asset	Accumulated depreciation on equipment, buildings a...	17000
20000 · Trade Accounts Payable	Accounts Payable	Trade Accounts Payable	20000
24000 · Payroll Liabilities	Other Current Liability	Payroll Liabilities	24000
24000 · Payroll Liabilities:24010 ...	Other Current Liability		24010
24000 · Payroll Liabilities:24020 ...	Other Current Liability		24020
24000 · Payroll Liabilities:24040 ...	Other Current Liability		24040
24000 · Payroll Liabilities:24050 ...	Other Current Liability		24050
24000 · Payroll Liabilities:24060 ...	Other Current Liability		24060
25000 · Income Taxes Payable	Other Current Liability	Income Taxes Payable	25000
25500 · Sales Tax Payable	Other Current Liability	Sales Tax Payable	25500
27000 · Notes Payable	Long Term Liability	Notes Payable	27000
30000 · Opening Balance Equity	Equity	Opening balances during setup post to this account. ...	30000
30100 · Capital Stock	Equity	Value of corporate stock	30100
32000 · Retained Earnings	Equity	Undistributed earnings of the corporation	32000
46000 · Sales	Income	Sales	46000
48300 · Sales Discounts	Income	Discounts given to customers	48300
51800 · Cost of Goods Sold	Cost of Goods Sold	Cost of Goods Sold	51800
60000 · Advertising and Promoti...	Expense	Advertising, marketing, graphic design, and other pro...	60000
60200 · Automobile Expense	Expense	Fuel, oil, repairs, and other automobile maintenance ...	60200
60400 · Bank Service Charges	Expense	Bank account service fees, bad check charges and o...	60400
61700 · Computer and Internet ...	Expense	Computer supplies, off-the-shelf software, online fee...	61700
62100 · Insurance	Expense	Insurance	62100
62100 · Insurance:62130 · Work...	Expense	Workman's Compensation	62130
62400 · Depreciation Expense	Expense	Depreciation on equipment, buildings and improvem...	62400
63400 · Interest Expense	Expense	Interest payments on business loans, credit card bal...	63400
63500 · Janitorial Expense	Expense	Janitorial expenses and cleaning supplies	63500
64300 · Meals and Entertainment	Expense	Meals and Entertainment	64300
64900 · Office Supplies	Expense	Office supplies expense	64900
66000 · Payroll Expenses	Expense		66000
66000 · Payroll Expenses:62710...	Expense		62710
66000 · Payroll Expenses:62720...	Expense		62720
66000 · Payroll Expenses:62730...	Expense		62730
66000 · Payroll Expenses:62740...	Expense		62740
66700 · Professional Fees	Expense	Payments to accounting professionals and attorneys ...	66700
67100 · Rent Expense	Expense	Rent paid for company offices or other structures use...	67100
67200 · Repairs and Maintenance	Expense	Incidental repairs and maintenance of business asse...	67200
68100 · Telephone Expense	Expense	Telephone and long distance charges, faxing, and ot...	68100
68600 · Utilities	Expense	Water, electricity, garbage, and other basic utilities e...	68600

Add Vendor Records

Entering vendor records for a new company can be a time-consuming process if there are a lot of vendors. You will set up only three vendors. Vendors are added through the Vendors Center.

> ▶ *Make sure you are in the Super Office Furniture Plus Home Page.*

You will enter information in the New Vendor window for each new vendor using the instructions on pages 64 through 67 of the Reference book. You have used this window several times in earlier chapters. Complete only those boxes for each vendor where information that follows is provided. You will enter the Beginning balances later when you enter historical data.

> ▶ *Use the information in the following box to complete the window for the first new vendor.* If no information for a box is provided, leave the box blank. If there is default information already included, do not change it unless new information is provided.

FIRST VENDOR

- **Vendor Name:** OAK
- **Opening Balance:** (leave blank)
- **As of:** 01/01/2021

Address Info tab

- **Company Name:** The Oak Factory
- **Main Phone:** 810-555-1200
- **Main Email:** oak@oakfactory.com
- **Website:** www.oakfactory.com
- **Fax:** 810-555-5227
- **Address Details (Billed From and Shipped From):** The Oak Factory
  566 Chilson Ave.
  Romeo, MI 48605

Payment Settings tab

- **Account Number:** 54678
- **Payment Terms:** 2% 10, Net 30

Account Settings tab

- **General Ledger Account:** 13000 (Inventory)

▶ *Save the new record after you have entered the information for the first vendor. Then enter the information for the second and third vendors using the following information.*

SECOND VENDOR

- **Vendor Name:**   GAR
- **Opening Balance:**   (leave blank)
- **As of:**   01/01/2021

Address Info tab

- **Company Name:**   Garner Properties
- **Main Phone:**   616-555-5784
- **Fax:**   616-555-5910
- **Address Details (Billed From and Shipped From):**   Garner Properties
  15700 W. Huron St.
  Otsego, MI 49078

Payment Settings tab

- **Account Number:**   15445
- **Payment Terms:**   Net 15

Account Settings tab

- **General Ledger Account:**   67100 (Rent Expense)

THIRD VENDOR

- **Vendor Name:**   TAX
- **Opening Balance:**   (leave blank)
- **As of:**   01/01/2021

Address Info tab

- **Company Name:**   Michigan Department of Taxation
- **Main Phone:**   517-412-1672
- **Website:**   www.mitax.org
- **Fax:**   517-412-1770
- **Address Details (Billed From and Shipped From):**   Michigan Department of Taxation
  6478 Capital Ave.
  Lansing, MI 48826

Payment Settings tab

- **Account Number:**   37211
- **Payment Terms:**   Net 30

Account Settings tab

- **General Ledger Account:**   25500 (Sales Tax Payable)

> *After entering and saving the information for the last two vendors, Click OK. You are now in the Vendors Center window, which should show all three vendors each with no balance total. Don't be concerned if you see other default-type vendors included. Those are typically included in shell companies.*

> *Click GAR. Observe that the maintenance window shows the information that you just entered.*

> *Make sure the information for each of the three vendors is consistent with the information provided. If it isn't, make corrections before closing the Vendor Center and proceeding to the following section.*

Assign Vendor for State Withholding and Unemployment Tax Payments

After adding the Michigan Department of Taxation (TAX) as a vendor, you need to designate this as the vendor for state withholding and state unemployment taxes.

> *Click Employees → Manage Payroll Items → View/Edit Payroll Item List.*

> *Double-click on MI-Withholding to open the Edit payroll Item window for the state withholding.*

> *Click Next.*

> *Select TAX in the first drop-down list.*

> *Type 37211 in the 2nd box, which asks for "the number that identifies you to agency."*

> *Click Next and then click Finish.*

> *After returning to the Payroll Item List window, double-click on MI-Unemployment Company to open the Edit payroll item window for this tax.*

> *Select TAX in the first drop-down list.*

> *Type 37211 in the 2nd box, which asks for "the number that identifies you to agency."*

> *Click Next and then click Finish.*

> *After both payroll items have been updated properly, close the Payroll Item List window to return to the Home Page.*

Add Sales Tax Preferences

You will add customers and inventory later in the chapter. Before doing so, you need to add sales tax preferences to enable *QuickBooks* to automatically charge customers for sales tax. In this case all sales are taxable to customers at a 6% rate.

▶ *Click the Edit menu → Preferences → Sales Tax in the Preferences window (fifth item from the bottom) → Company Preferences tab.*

▶ *Click the "Yes" radio button in the "Do you charge sales tax?" line.* Your screen should now look like the following illustration.

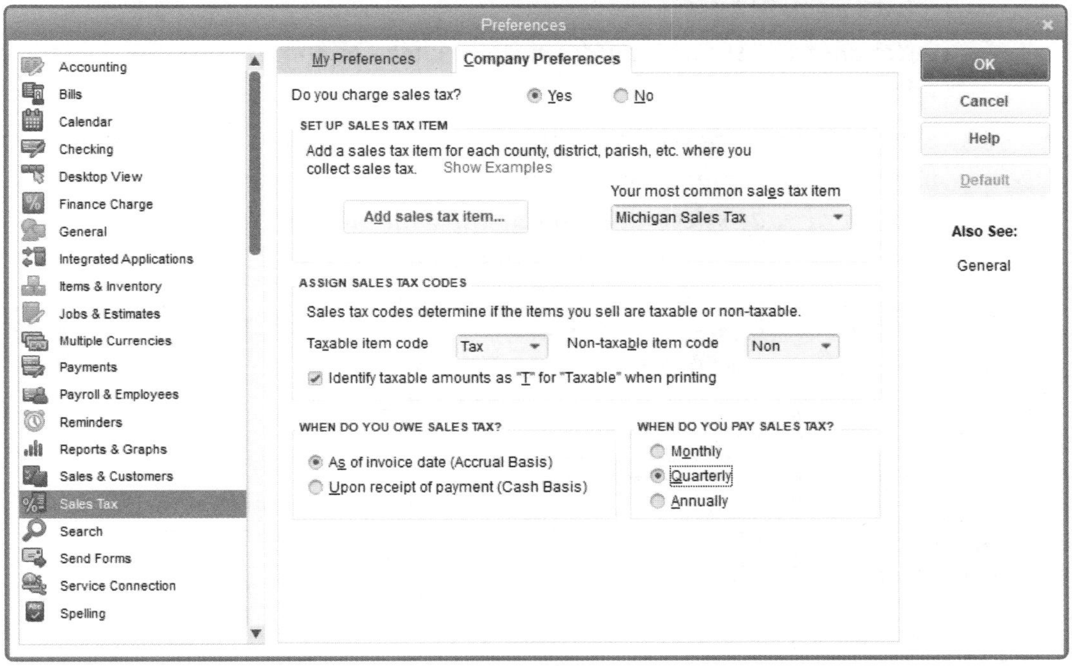

▶ *Click the "Add sales tax item" button to open the New Item window shown below.*

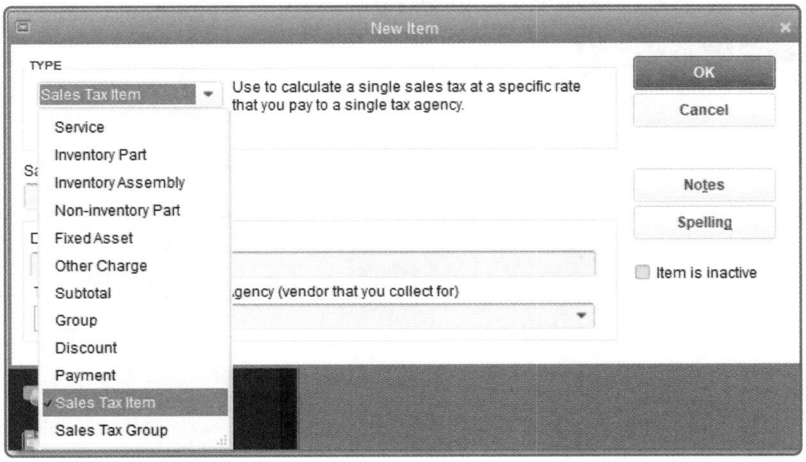

▶ *Press Tab to accept Sales Tax Item, which is the default selection.*

▶ *Enter or select the following information.*

- **Sales Tax Name:**   Michigan Sales Tax
- **Description:**   Sales Tax
- **Tax Rate (%):**   6
- **Tax Agency**
  (vendor that you collect for):   Select TAX (the vendor you
                                  entered earlier)

▶ *After entering the above information, click OK to return to the Preferences window.*

▶ *Select Michigan Sales Tax in the "Your most common sales tax item" drop-down box. Click the Quarterly radio button on the bottom of the Preference window if it is not already selected. Examine the window to make sure it includes the same information as the following window. Make changes if necessary.*

▶ *Click OK. If additional windows open relating to the sales tax you just created, click OK in each window.*

▶ *If the Updating Sales Tax window opens, click OK.*

Add Customer Records

Recall that instructions for adding customer records are included on pages 60 through 63 of the Reference book.

▶ *Use the Reference book instructions and the information in the following boxes to add two customers for the company. Save each new record.*

FIRST CUSTOMER

- **Customer Name:** LEVERETT
- **Opening Balance:** (leave blank)
- **As of:** 01/01/2021

Address Info tab

- **Company Name:** Leverett Enterprises
- **Main Phone:** 616-555-7800
- **Fax:** 616-555-8889
- **Address Details
  (Invoice/Bill To and Ship To):** Leverett Enterprises
  600 Columbia, Suite 602
  Holland, MI 49024

Payment Settings tab

- **Account No.:** 63699
- **Credit Limit:** $10,000
- **Payment Terms:** 2% 10, Net 30
- **Preferred Delivery Method:** Mail
- **Preferred Payment Method:** Check

Sales Tax Settings tab

- **Tax Code:** Tax
- **Tax Item:** Michigan Sales Tax default is correct (This is a result of the sales tax preference work you just completed.)

SECOND CUSTOMER

- **Customer Name:** THURGOOD
- **Opening Balance:** (leave blank)
- **As of:** 01/01/2021

Address Info tab

- **Company Name:** Thurgood Insurance Company
- **Main Phone:** 616-555-0002
- **Main Email:** daphne@thurgood.com
- **Fax:** 616-555-5231
- **Address Details**
  (Invoice/Bill To and Ship To): Thurgood Insurance Company
  8900 Wellston Blvd.
  Grand Haven, MI 49417

Payment Settings tab

- **Account No.:** 68319
- **Credit Limit:** $20,000
- **Payment Terms:** Net 30
- **Preferred Delivery Method:** Mail
- **Preferred Payment Method:** Check

Sales Tax Settings tab

- **Tax Code:** Tax
- **Tax Item:** Michigan Sales Tax default is correct
  (This is a result of the sales tax
  preference work you just completed.)

▶ *Close the Customer Center after adding and saving both customers.*

Add Inventory Items and Beginning Inventory Balances

The process of adding inventory items, their beginning quantities, and unit costs is similar to what you have already done for customers and vendors. Instructions for adding inventory items are included on pages 68 through 72 of the Reference book.

▶ *Add three inventory items using the Reference book instructions and the information that follows. As you did for previous maintenance items, leave a box blank and default information unchanged unless new or different information is provided. Click OK after you have entered all information for each inventory item. If you receive a message about a transaction being more than 30 days in the future, click Yes.*

FIRST INVENTORY ITEM

- **Type:** Inventory Part
- **Item Name/Number:** Basic Desk
- **Description on Purchases and Sales Transactions:** Basic Desk
- **Cost:** 236.00
- **COGS Account:** 51800 Cost of Goods Sold
  (you will need to change the default)
- **Preferred Vendor:** OAK (The Oak Factory)
- **Sales Price:** 350.00
- **Income Account:** 46000 Sales
- **Asset Account:** 13000 Inventory
  (you will need to change the default)
- **Reorder Point:** 30
- **On Hand:** 172
- **As of:** 01/01/2021

SECOND INVENTORY ITEM

- **Type:** Inventory Part
- **Item Name/Number:** Office Chair
- **Description on Purchases and Sales Transactions:** Office Chair
- **Cost:** 122.00

(continued on the following page)

SECOND INVENTORY ITEM
(continued from previous page)

- **COGS Account:** 51800 Cost of Goods Sold
  (change default if necessary)
- **Preferred Vendor:** OAK (The Oak Factory)
- **Sales Price:** 175.00
- **Income Account:** 46000 Sales
- **Asset Account:** 13000 Inventory
  (change default if necessary)
- **Reorder Point:** 50
- **On Hand:** 225
- **As of:** 01/01/2021

THIRD INVENTORY ITEM

- **Type:** Inventory Part
- **Item Name/Number:** Bookshelf
- **Description on Purchases and Sales Transactions:** Bookshelf
- **Cost:** 142.00
- **COGS Account:** 51800 Cost of Goods Sold
  (change default if necessary)
- **Preferred Vendor:** OAK (The Oak Factory)
- **Sales Price:** 225.00
- **Income Account:** 46000 Sales
- **Asset Account:** 12000 Inventory
  (change default if necessary)
- **Reorder Point:** 10
- **On Hand:** 52
- **As of:** 01/01/2021

▶ *Close the New Item window after entering the last item to return to the Home Page.*

Add Employees

Adding employees is similar to what you have already done for chart of accounts, vendors, customers, and inventory except there are more windows to complete. You will add two employees through the New Employee maintenance window.

Before adding the new employees, you first need to make sure that the payroll preference is set to full payroll.

> ▶ *Click the Edit menu → Preferences → Payroll & Employees → Company Preferences tab. If the Full radio button is not selected, select it and click OK to close the window.*

Instructions for adding employees are included on pages 74 through 80 of the Reference book.

> ▶ *Use the Reference book instructions and the information in the boxes that follow to complete the New Employee window for the two employees.* There are multiple steps for payroll, so extra guidance is provided. *As done with previous maintenance items, leave a box blank, a tab unopened, and default information unchanged unless new or different information is provided.*

> ▶ *Enter the following information in the Personal, Address & Contact, Additional Info, and Employment Info tabs of the New Employee window.*

FIRST EMPLOYEE–HOURLY

Personal tab
- First Name: Regina
- Last Name: Rexrode
- Social Security Number: 549-56-3982
- Gender: Female
- Date of Birth: 05/16/1976

Address & Contact tab
- Address: 462 Sibley Lane
- City: Southfield
- State: MI
- Zip: 47349
- Main Phone: 810-555-8888

Additional Info tab
- Account No.:   REX

Employment Info tab
- Hire Date: 04/03/2015

* Note: Do not save the record yet; there are other steps detailed on the next page.

▶ *Change tabs to the Payroll Info tab and enter the pay frequency and pay rates information listed in the box that follows.*

> **Payroll Info tab**
> - **Pay Frequency:** Biweekly (default setting)
> - **Earnings:**
>   - **Item Name (drop-down arrow):** Regular Pay
>   - **Hourly/Annual Rate (regular):** 16.00
>   - **Item Name (drop-down arrow):** Overtime
>   - **Hourly/Annual Rate (overtime):** 24.00

▶ *Click the Taxes button in the top-right corner of the Payroll Info tab window to enter the "Taxes for Regina Rexrode" window. Enter the information below:*

> **Federal tab**
> - **Form W-4:** 2020 and Later
> - **Filing Status:** Married filing jointly
> - **Dependents:** 3
>
> **State tab**
> - **State Worked:** MI
> - **State Subject to Withholding:** MI
> - **Allowances:** 3

▶ *When you are asked about city taxes and the Michigan Obligation Assessment, click OK and then indicate there are no such taxes by deleting each item when the appropriate window opens. Click OK and click No if asked whether the employee is subject to the taxes you just deleted. Also do not set up vacation pay if you are asked if you want vacation/sick/personal pay set up.*

▶ *Before proceeding to set up the second employee, click Regina Rexrode in the Employees tab and make sure you correctly entered the information for each tab.*

▶ *Set up the payroll information for the second employee following the same procedures as you did for Regina Rexrode.*

SECOND EMPLOYEE–SALARIED

Personal tab
- First Name: Uma
- Last Name: Jenkins
- Social Security Number: 642-55-1342
- Gender: Female
- Date of Birth: 02/18/1980

Address & Contact tab
- Address: 185 Post Ave.
- City: Mt. Clemens
- State: MI
- Zip: 46329
- Main Phone: 810-555-0052

Additional Info tab
- Account No.: JEN

Employment Info tab
- Hire Date: 01/19/2011

Payroll Info tab
- Pay Frequency: Biweekly
- Earnings:
  - Item Name (drop-down arrow): Salary
  - Hourly/Annual Rate (regular): 65,000.00

Taxes button - Federal tab
- Filing Status: Single or Married filing separately
- Dependents: 0

Taxes button - State tab
- State Worked: MI
- State Subject to Withholding: MI
- Allowances: 1

▶ *Click OK to close the New Employee window. Open the Employees window again for Uma Jenkins and make sure the information is correct in all windows.*

Enter Chart of Accounts (General Ledger) Beginning Balances

Entering Beginning Balances In Accounts

When another system is converted to *QuickBooks*, it is almost always done at the beginning of a fiscal year, which means that only balance sheet accounts are carried forward from the previous system into the beginning trial balance. There is a distinction between the two types of balance sheet accounts:

- Accounts with subsidiary records, where the dates of the transactions that affected the account balance are important, must be set up through the subsidiary accounting modules. The three accounts for Super Office Furniture Plus with subsidiary accounts are accounts receivable, accounts payable, and inventory. The beginning balance for the inventory account was set up earlier when you entered the cost and quantities on hand of each item. Accounts receivable is set up next using transactions prior to the beginning balance sheet date.
- Accounts with no subsidiary balances, which are all other balance sheet accounts with beginning balances, are set up with a general journal entry.

Setting Up Accounts Receivable

Only Thurgood Insurance Company has a beginning balance, which is $14,840. It resulted from a sale in December of 2020, but you will enter it on 12/31/2020. The invoice number is 1207.

> ▶ *Click the Home Page icon → Create Invoices icon to open the Create Invoices window.*

> ▶ *Type Thurgood Insurance Company (don't select THURGOOD) in the Customer: Job window. Click [Tab] to open the following window.*

➤ *Click the Quick Add button.*

➤ *Select "Intuit Product Invoice" in the Template box.*

➤ *Add the Date (use 12/31/2020) and Invoice # (1207) in the appropriate boxes at the top of the window → click [Tab].* **Note:** *If accounts receivable—a/c #11000—is not selected in the Account box, do that now.*

➤ *Type Historical Transaction in the Item Code box → click [Tab] to open the window shown below.*

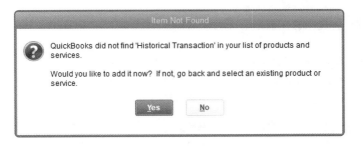

➤ *Click Yes to include Historical Transaction in the Item List and to open the window shown below.*

➤ *Enter Service for Type and 46000 in the Account box → click OK to return to the Create Invoices window.*

➤ *Type 14840 in the Amount box and select "none" in the Tax box. Click Save & Close.* Do not be concerned that the transaction is old or the credit limit for Thurgood has been exceeded. *Click Yes if you receive any such prompts.*

➤ *If the Information Changed window opens, click No.*

Setting Up Accounts Payable

▶ *Set up accounts payable the same way as you just did for accounts receivable (use QuickAdd again), but use the Enter Bills window. The Oak Factory is the only vendor with a beginning balance. Invoice No. R2263 (Ref. No. box) for $2,000.00 is dated 12/29/2020. Use 12/31/2020 as the date, however, as you did for the opening account receivable balance. Select 51800 as the Account and enter $2,000.00 in the Amount box within the Expenses tab. Click Save & Close.*

Setting Up the Remaining Balance Sheet Account Balances

▶ *Click the Reports icon (or the Reports menu) → Accountant & Taxes → Trial Balance. Change the To and From dates to 01/01/2021 → Refresh to open the trial balance. It should include the following trial balance.*

		Trial Balance									_ □ ×
Customize Report	Comment on Report	Share Template	Memorize	Print ▼	E-mail ▼	Excel ▼	Hide Header	Collapse Rows		Refresh	

Dates Custom ▼ From 01/01/2021 📅 To 01/01/2021 📅 Sort By Default ▼

Report Basis: ● Accrual ○ Cash   Show Filters

9:17 AM
12/15/21
Accrual Basis

Super Office Furniture Plus
Trial Balance
As of January 1, 2021

	Jan 1, 21	
	Debit	Credit
11000 · Accounts Receivable	14,840.00 ◀	
13000 · Inventory	75,426.00	
20000 · Trade Accounts Payable		2,000.00
25500 · Sales Tax Payable	0.00	
30000 · Opening Balance Equity		75,426.00
32000 · Retained Earnings		12,840.00
TOTAL	90,266.00	90,266.00

QuickBooks automatically records the effects of the inventory beginning balance to the account called Opening Balance Equity. Notice that the two other opening balance entries—for accounts payable and accounts receivable—were posted to Retained Earnings. You will reclassify things appropriately when you enter all other beginning balances shortly.

▶ *Use a journal entry to reclassify the amount in the Opening Balance Equity account to Retained Earnings ($75,426.00) as of 01/01/2021. Click OK when you receive a warning about posting to Retained Earnings.* Normally it is inappropriate to record transactions directly to retained earnings, but in this case the reclassification is acceptable.

▶ *Prepare, but do not print, a trial balance at 01/01/2021.* The trial balance should now include four accounts with balances as follows:

Accounts Receivable	14,840	Debit	
Inventory	75,426	Debit	
Accounts Payable	2,000	Credit	
Retained Earnings	88,266	Credit	

▶ *If the balances are different from those, make corrections until they are the same. Otherwise, proceed with the next step.*

The table below shows what will the beginning trial balance will eventually look like for the company at 01/01/21. Your next task will be to prepare a general journal entry to record the beginning balances for all accounts other than accounts receivable, accounts payable, and inventory. Recall that these three accounts (shaded gray in the box below) already have beginning balances as a result of transactions you recorded earlier.

Super Office Furniture Plus
Beginning Trial Balance as of 01/01/2021

Number	Account Name	Balance Dr.	Balance (Cr.)
10100	Checking Account	$ 16,875.42	
10200	Savings Account	7,852.50	
11000	Accounts Receivable	14,840.00	
12000	Inventory	75,426.00	
14000	Prepaid Expenses	6,200.00	
15000	Equipment	36,980.00	
17000	Accumulated Depreciation		$ 14,409.48
20000	Accounts Payable		2,000.00
24010	Payroll Liabilities - Federal Withholding		224.98
25000	Income Taxes Payable		1,248.76
27000	Notes Payable		33,000.00
30100	Capital Stock		50,000.00
32000	Retained Earnings		57,290.70
		$158,173.92	$158,173.92

Note: You do not need to enter anything for the shaded accounts because their beginning balances were already entered during previous setup procedures.

▶ *Prepare a journal entry as of 01/01/21 to adjust all other accounts so that they agree with the balances in the table on the previous page.* **Because you already entered beginning balances for Accounts Receivable, Inventory, and Accounts Payable through earlier work in this chapter, you do not need to include these three accounts in your beginning balance journal entry.** The debit or credit to retained earnings will be used to balance the general journal entry. It is again appropriate to adjust retained earnings as part of the journal entry. *If you receive a message about not posting to the payroll liabilities account, click Yes to continue. If you also receive another warning message about posting to Retained Earnings, click OK.*

Print a Beginning Trial Balance

▶ *Prepare a trial balance at 01/01/2021 and view it on your screen.* The trial balance should now include all accounts with a balance that are the same as the ones in the previous table. *If the balances are different from those, make corrections until they are the same.*

▶ *Print the trial balance.*

This completes Setup. Go to the following section where you will record a sample set of transactions for Super Office Furniture Plus.

Process Transactions and Do Other Activities for the New Company

In this section, you will process transactions and do other activities for Super Office Furniture Plus for the first week of January 2021 using *QuickBooks*.

In processing these transactions or doing other activities, you should first find the appropriate reference pages and then use the Reference book to guide you.

Transaction #1

▶ *Record the following transaction using QuickBooks.*

On January 4, 2021, the company sold merchandise on account to Leverett Enterprises. Other details of the credit sale follow.

■ **Customer Job:**   LEVERETT
■ **Date:**   January 2, 2021
■ **Invoice No.:**   1208
■ **Customer PO No.:**   89458
■ **Items sold:**

Qty.	Item Code	Unit Price
15	Office Chair	$175.00
3	Bookshelf	225.00

■ **General Ledger Account Information:**   All default account numbers are correct
■ **Invoice Total (check figure):** $3,498.00, including tax

Transaction #2

▶ *Record the following transaction using QuickBooks.*

On January 5, 2021, the company received a check from Thurgood Insurance Company (the one you set up via QuickAdd, not the THURGOOD customer) in full payment of an accounts receivable for Invoice No. 1207. Other details of the collection follow.

■ **Amount:** $14,840.00 (no discount; terms were Net 30)
■ **Customer's Check No.:** 10053
■ **General Ledger Account Information:**   All default accounts numbers are correct

Notes: (1) Do not forget to make a bank deposit for this receipt.
(2) Make sure to select the Quick Add version of Thurgood, not the regular one.

Transaction #3

▶ *Process the following purchase order using QuickBooks.*

On January 7, 2021, the company ordered inventory from The Oak Factory (OAK). The inventory was not received on January 7. Other details of the purchase order follow.

- ■ **Vendor:** OAK
- ■ **Date:** January 7, 2021
- ■ **PO No.:** 1407
- ■ **Inventory items ordered:**

Item	Qty.	Unit Price
Basic Desk	35	$236.00
Office Chair	40	122.00

- ■ **Purchase order total (check figure):** $13,140.00

Transaction #4

▶ *Record the following receipt of goods in QuickBooks.*

On January 11, 2021, Super Office Furniture Plus received the inventory merchandise from The Oak Factory for Purchase Order No. 1407 along with Invoice No. 56781. Other details of the purchase follow.

- ■ **Select PO (PO No.):** 1407
- ■ **Vendor:** OAK
- ■ **Date goods were received:** January 11, 2021
- ■ **Ref. No. (Invoice No.):** 56781
- ■ **Goods shipped/invoiced:** All goods ordered were received no trade discount, freight, miscellaneous charges, or taxes
- ■ **Payment terms:** Net 30 (change default but do not save the setting for future bills when prompted)
- ■ **General ledger account information:** All default information is correct
- ■ **Invoice total (check figure):** $13,140.00

Transaction #5

▶ *Record the following cash disbursement transaction.*

On January 15, 2021, the company issued a check to The Oak Factory in full payment of Invoice No. 56781. Other details of the cash disbursement follow.

- **Vendor:** OAK
- **Check No.:** 124307 (click the Assign check number radio button in the Pay Bills window if it is not already selected)
- **Check amount:** $13,140 (no discount; terms were Net 30)
- **Invoice paid:** 56781
- **Account:** 10100 Checking Account
  (Edit if necessary. Account 10100 must be selected in the Account box)
- **General ledger Account Information:** All default information is correct

Transaction #6

▶ *Record the biweekly payroll for Super Office Furniture Plus's two employees in QuickBooks. If you receive a Workers Comp Not Set Up window, click the Turn Off Workers Comp button.* Information necessary to process the biweekly payroll follows.

- **Pay End Date:** Jan 15, 2021
- **Check Date:** Jan 15, 2021
- **First Check #:** 124308

Hourly employee's info (you do not have to enter hours for the salaried employee)

- **Employee ID:** REX
- **Employee Name:** Regina Rexrode
- **Regular pay (in hours):** 88
- **Overtime rate (in hours):** 11.5

Other Activity

▶ *Print a hard copy of the general ledger trial for Super Office Furniture Plus as of January 31, 2021.* Notice that the January 2021 transactions you recorded are reflected in this trial balance.

Compare the balances on your printed trial balance with those in the table on page 10-29. Because *QuickBooks* payroll tables update periodically, depending on when you downloaded the software, there may be minor differences in payroll withholdings and cash. You can ignore those differences. If there are any differences other than payroll withholdings and the cash effect of those withholding differences, make necessary corrections as you have learned in previous chapters. When your balances agree with those on page 10-29, print a corrected trial balance and hand it in to your instructor.

Chapter Summary

After completing Chapter 10, you have now learned:

- ✔ how to set up a new company in the software.
- ✔ how to add records and account balances for vendors, customers, inventory, and the chart of accounts.
- ✔ how to add employee records.

You should now save your work by making a periodic backup of Super Office Furniture Plus using the instructions in the E-Materials you downloaded from the Armond Dalton Resources website. Then proceed to the Chapter 10 homework assigned by your instructor either, which is available on the Armond Dalton Resources website at www.armonddaltonresources.com.

Check Figures

Super Office Furniture Plus
Trial Balance as of 01/31/2021

Number	Account Name	Balance Dr.	(Cr.)
10100	Checking Account	$ 15,302.55	
10200	Savings Account	7,852.50	
11000	Accounts Receivable	3,498.00	
12000	Undeposited Funds	0.00	
13000	Inventory	86,310.00	
14000	Prepaid Expenses	6,200.00	
15000	Equipment	36,980.00	
17000	Accumulated Depreciation		$ 14,409.48
20000	Accounts Payable		2,000.00
24000	Payroll Liabilities	0.00	
24000	Payroll Liabilities:24010 - Federal Withholding		666.98
24000	Payroll Liabilities:24020 - FICA Payable		640.16
24000	Payroll Liabilities:24040 - FUTA Payable		25.10
24000	Payroll Liabilities:24050 - State Withholding		149.05
24000	Payroll Liabilities:24060 - SUTA Payable		112.97
25000	Income Taxes Payable		1,248.76
25500	Sales Tax Payable		198.00
27000	Notes Payable		33,000.00
30000	Opening Balance Equity	0.00	
30100	Capital Stock		50,000.00
32000	Retained Earnings		57,290.70
46000	Sales		3,300.00
51800	Cost of Goods Sold	2,256.00	
62710	Gross Wages	4,184.00	
66000	Payroll Expenses:62720 - Employer FICA Expense	320.08	
66000	Payroll Expenses:62730 - FUTA Expense	25.10	
66000	Payroll Expenses:62740 - SUTA Expense	112.97	
		$163,041.20	$163,041.20

Notes

Notes

Notes

Notes

Notes

Notes

Notes

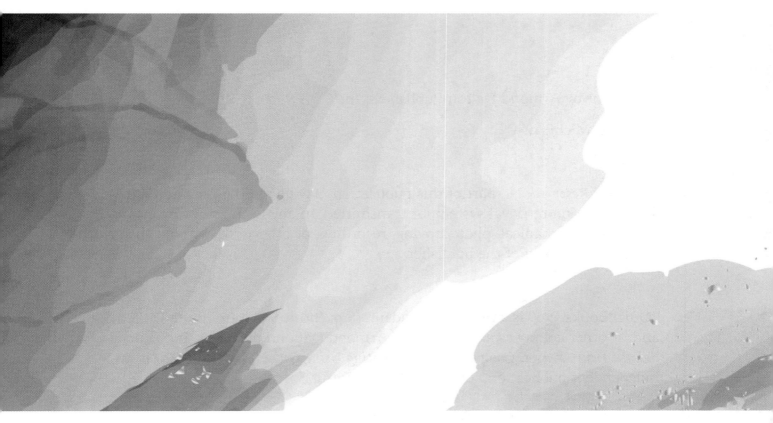

Computerized Accounting
using QuickBooks Pro 2020
Sixth Edition

Alvin A. Arens ~ D. Dewey Ward ~ Carol Borsum Sohn

Reference ~ Book 2 of 2

© 2020

Copyright by Armond Dalton Publishers, Inc.

Okemos, Michigan

ISBN 978-0-912503-79-0

Printed in the United States of America

TABLE OF CONTENTS

Introduction

Purchases and Cash Disbursements Cycle Activities

TABLE OF CONTENTS (CONTINUED)

Sales and Cash Receipts Cycle Activities

Payroll Cycle and Other Activities

Introduction

Overview

The *QuickBooks* software is intended primarily for a wide variety of small and medium-size businesses and is therefore designed to accommodate many different circumstances. As a result, the software has dozens of windows and hundreds of boxes in which to enter or accept information.

To help students learn to use *QuickBooks*, the Reference book is a useful guide to correctly process transactions and do other activities. Based on experience with many students learning to use the software, those who follow the Reference book for each transaction or other activity perform better than those who do not. You will begin using the Reference book in Chapter 5 of the Instructions book.

The Reference book contains 25 sections, one for each transaction or other activity included in the *Computerized Accounting Using QuickBooks Pro 2020* project. See the table of contents on pages 1 and 2 for a list of the transactions and activities covered.

Contents of Reference Book

There are four parts to the Reference book:

1. **Inside Front Cover Listing of Transactions and Other Activities** — This listing can be used to help you locate the appropriate pages in the Reference book for recording transactions or doing other activities.

2. **Transaction or Other Activity Overview** — The brief overview describes what happens in *QuickBooks* for the transaction or other activity. The overview for each section is located above the Quick Reference Table.

3. **Quick Reference Table** — The Quick Reference Table is a guide to help you open the correct window(s) and enter or accept the correct information in each box.

4. **Window(s) on the Page Facing the Quick Reference Table** — You will be using these windows to process the transaction or other activity that you are dealing with. The circled letters on the window(s) match the steps on the Quick Reference Table. The letters will not appear on your screen.

Suggested Way To Use the Reference Book

The information in the Instructions book in Chapters 5 through 8 will direct you to the relevant Reference book pages. For each transaction or other activity you should first read the brief overview at the top of the page to help you understand what is happening in the *QuickBooks* software. Then follow the step-by-step instructions in the Quick Reference Table and related window or windows to process the transaction or complete the other activity.

For Chapters 9 and 10, you will not be told which pages include the relevant Quick Reference Table and related window or windows. For those transactions or other activities the following are suggestions to help you effectively use the Reference book:

- Determine the type of transaction or other activity you are to process. You will be able to make the determination using the information provided in the Instructions book and the knowledge gained in earlier chapters.

- Determine the applicable Reference book page numbers. You can locate the transaction or other activity on the inside front cover of the Reference book and determine the applicable page number.

- Open the Reference book to the pages for the transaction or other activity that you will be processing. Read the information in the brief overview at the top of the page to help you understand what is happening in the *QuickBooks* software

- Follow the step-by-step instructions in the Quick Reference Table and related window or windows to process the transaction or complete the other activity.

As you become proficient with *QuickBooks*, you may decide to process the transactions and other activities using the windows as guidance and refer to the Reference book only if you forget which window to use or the appropriate steps to follow. If you make an error, it is usually easy to correct it by either accessing the window again and correcting the information or deleting and reentering the transaction. Even if you follow that approach you will often find it useful to refer to the inside front cover of the Reference book to make sure you are processing the transaction or other activity in the correct window. You may also decide to follow the guidance in the Reference book for all transactions and other activities to minimize the likelihood of making errors.

This page is intentionally blank.

Prepare a Purchase Order

The purchase order window is used to prepare purchase orders for inventory. No accounting entry is made to any journal, subsidiary record, or general ledger after a purchase order is saved because a liability does not yet exist.

Quick Reference Table

Step	Box or Other Location	Procedure
A	Home Page	Click the Purchase Orders icon under Vendors.
B	Vendor	Select Vendor from drop-down list or add new. For a new vendor addition, refer to maintenance tasks in Chapter 5.
C	Date	Verify the date posted or enter new date.
D	P.O. No.	Accept the purchase order number or change.
E	Ship To	Accept the shipping address or change by typing in a different name and / or address.
F	Item	Select an item from drop-down list or add new item.
G	Description	Accept the default description or change.
H	Qty.	Enter the quantity to be ordered.
I	Rate	Accept the default rate or change.
J	Amount	Accept the total amount of the items ordered. Changing the amount column will recalculate the Rate.
K	Various	Repeat steps F – J for each inventory item to be ordered.
L	Create Purchase Orders window	Review the information to verify that it is correct.
M	Print button	Click the Print button, select the printer, and print the purchase order, if desired.
N	Save & Close / Save & New buttons	Click Save & Close or Save & New to save the purchase order.

Prepare a Purchase Order
QuickBooks windows

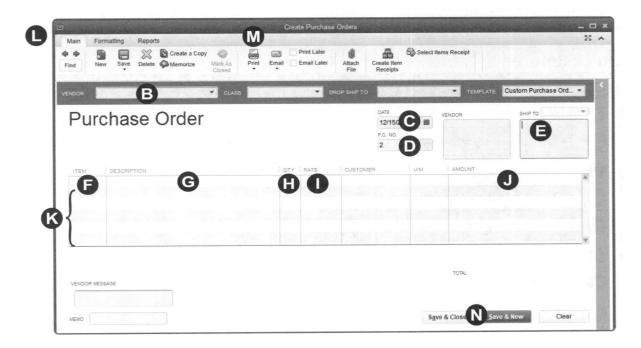

Receive Goods On a Purchase Order

The Enter Bills window is used to process and record the receipt of goods from an open purchase order. After the Enter Bills window is saved the following occurs:

Transactions	DR	CR	Subsidiary Records Updated	General Ledger Updated
Inventory, Fixed Assets, or Expenses	$		✓ (inventory and fixed assets)	✓
Accounts Payable		$	✓	✓

Quick Reference Table

Step	Box or Other Location	Procedure
A	Home Page	Click the Receive Inventory drop-down button under Vendors.
B	Receive Inventory drop-down list	Select "Receive Inventory with Bill" to open the Enter Bills window.
C	Vendor	Select a vendor from the drop-down list.
D	Open POs Exist window *(not shown)*	Click Yes.
E	Open Purchase Orders window	Select which purchase order is being received by placing a check mark on its line and click OK to return to Enter Bills window.
F	Date	Accept default date or change.
G	Ref No.	Type the vendor's invoice number.
H	Amount Due	Accept listed amount due or change. *(Not possible to verify unless the information is provided.)*
I	Terms	Accept the default terms or select from the drop-down list.
J	Items tab	Click to open the Items tab if it is not open.
K	Item	For each item, accept the items ordered or change using the drop-down list.
L	Description	Accept the default description or edit.
M	Qty.	For each item type received, accept the quantity ordered or change to the quantity that was received.
N	Cost	For each item received, accept default cost or change.
O	Expenses tab *(content not shown)*	Click the Expenses tab. Verify that correct general ledger account is in Account Box. Verify that correct general ledger account is in Account Box. If applicable, type the sales tax amount in the Amount Box, then type "Sales Tax" in the Memo box.
P	Enter Bills window	Review the information to verify that it is correct.
Q	Save & Close / Save & New buttons	Click Save & Close or Save & New button.

Receive Goods On a Purchase Order
QuickBooks windows

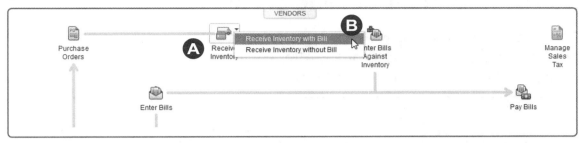

VENDORS

Purchase Orders

A Receive Inventory

B Receive Inventory with Bill
Receive Inventory without Bill

Enter Bills Against Inventory

Manage Sales Tax

Enter Bills

Pay Bills

P Enter Bills

Main	Reports

Find | New | Save | Delete | Create a Copy | Memorize | Print | Attach File | Select PO | Enter Time | Clear Splits | Recalculate | Pay Bill

○ Bill   ○ Credit   ☑ Bill Received

Bill

VENDOR **C**

ADDRESS

TERMS **I**

MEMO

DATE 12/15/2 **F**

REF. NO. **G**

AMOUNT DUE 0.00 **H**

BILL DUE 12/25/2021

Expenses **O** $0.00   Items **J** $0.00

ITEM	DESCRI...	QTY	U/M	COST	AMOUNT	CUSTOMER:JOB	BILLA...	CLASS
K	**L**	**M**		**N**				

Receive All   Show PO

Save & Close **Q** Save & New   Clear

E Open Purchase Orders

Vendor American Linen Supply

Select a Purchase Order to receive

✓	DATE	PO NO.	MEMO
	12/15/2021	1	

OK
Cancel
Help

Purchase Inventory Without a Purchase Order— No Payment Made at Time of Purchase

The Enter Bills window is used to process and record the receipt of goods purchased without a purchase order. After entering information and saving the completed Enter Bills window, the following has occurred:

Transactions	DR	CR	Subsidiary Records Updated	General Ledger Updated
Inventory	$		✓	✓
Accounts Payable		$	✓	✓

Quick Reference Table

Step	Box or Other Location	Procedure
A	Home Page	Click the Receive Inventory icon under Vendors.
B	Receive Inventory drop-down list	Select Receive Inventory with Bill (not shown) to open the Enter Bills window.
C	Vendor	Select a vendor from the drop-down list or add new.
D	Open POs Exist window (not shown)	If there are open POs for this vendor, this window will open. Click No.
E	Date	Accept default date or change.
F	Ref No.	Type the vendor's invoice number.
G	Amount Due	Leave blank. Information is automatically entered when steps J–M are entered.
H	Terms	Accept the default payment terms or select from the drop-down list.
I	Items tab	Click to open the Items tab if it is not open.
J	Item	For each item, select the items received from the drop-down list or add new.
K	Description	For each item, accept the default description or edit.
L	Qty.	For each item, enter the quantity of items received.
M	Cost	For each item received, accept default cost or change.
N	Amount	Verify the total is correct. (Not possible to verify unless the information is provided.)
O	Enter Bills window	Review the information to verify that it is correct.
P	Save & Close / Save & New buttons	Click the Save & Close or Save & New button.

Purchase Inventory Without a Purchase Order—
No Payment Made At Time of Purchase

QuickBooks windows

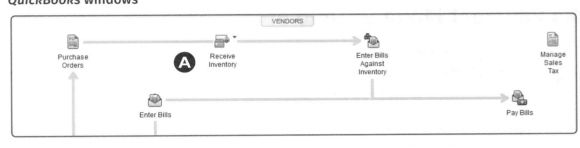

Purchase Non-Inventory Items or Services Without a Purchase Order— No Payment Made at Time of Purchase

The Enter Bills window is used to process and record the receipt of non-inventory items or services purchased without a purchase order. After entering information and saving the completed Enter Bills window, the following has occurred:

Transactions	DR	CR	Subsidiary Records Updated	General Ledger Updated
Expense and Non-Inv. Asset Accounts	$		✓ (fixed assets)	✓
Accounts Payable		$	✓	✓

Quick Reference Table

Step	Box or Other Location	Procedure
A	Home Page	Click the Enter Bills icon under Vendors.
B	Vendor	Select a vendor from the drop-down list or add new.
C	Open POs Exist window *(not shown)*	If there are open POs for this vendor, this window will open. Click No.
D	Date	Accept default date or change.
E	Ref No.	Type the vendor's invoice number.
F	Terms	Accept the default payment terms or select from the drop-down list.
G	Expenses tab	Click to open the Expenses tab if it is not open.
H	Account	Select account from drop-down list or add new.
I	Amount	Enter the amount of the purchase that is associated with the account.
J	Memo	Type a description of the amount that is being charged to the account (legal services, for example).
K	Various	Repeat steps H – J for any other accounts that are applicable to the purchase.
L	Amount Due	Verify that the amount due is correct. *(Not possible to verify unless the information is provided.)*
M	Enter Bills window	Review the information to verify that it is correct.
N	Save & Close / Save & New buttons	Click the Save & Close or Save & New button.

Purchase Non-Inventory Items or Services Without a Purchase Order—No Payment Made At Time of Purchase

QuickBooks windows

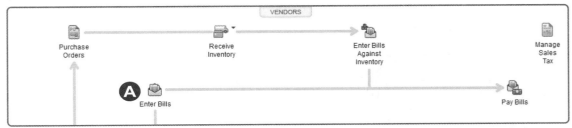

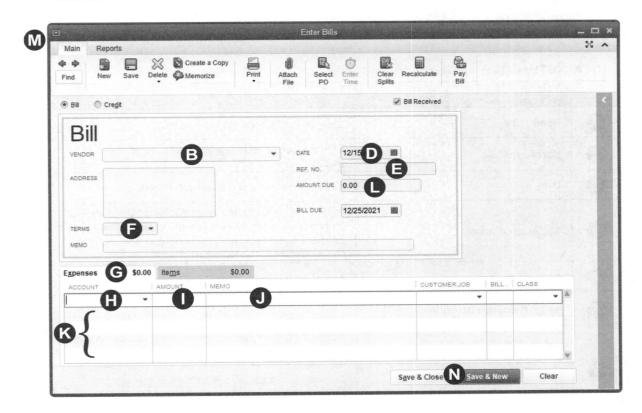

Pay a Vendor's Outstanding Invoice

The Pay Bills window is used to record and process a payment for a vendor's existing invoice. After selecting a bill to be paid and saving the transaction, the following has occurred:

Transactions	DR	CR	Subsidiary Records Updated	General Ledger Updated
Accounts Payable	$		✓	✓
Cash		$		✓
Discount/Credit		$		✓

Quick Reference Table

Step	Box or Other Location	Procedure
A	Home Page	Click the Pay Bills icon under Vendors.
B	List of open bills	Click to place a checkmark and select the bill or bills to be paid.
C	Date	Accept default date or click calendar icon to change.
D	Set Discount button	Click the Set Discount button to display the Discount and Credits window (not shown). Accept the Amount of Discount and the Discount Account or edit. Note: Discounts are not normally given for partial payments. Click Done.
E	Amt. To Pay	Accept default amount or change for a partial payment.
F	Assign check number button	Select the Assign check number radio button if it is not already selected.
G	Method	Accept the default payment method or change from the drop-down list. Note: For ACH payments, use Check as the default method. In order to set up ACH payments for a company, QuickBooks requires online linking with the company's bank, which you cannot do with a fictitious company.
H	Pay Bills window	Review the information to verify that it is correct.
I	Pay Selected Bills button	Click the Pay Selected Bills button.
J	Check No. box (Assign Check Numbers window)	Type check number or ACH payment number and click the OK button.
K	Payment Summary window	Review the information to verify that it is correct.
L	Done button (Payment Summary window)	Click the Done button to exit to the Home Page.

Pay a Vendor's Outstanding Invoice

QuickBooks windows

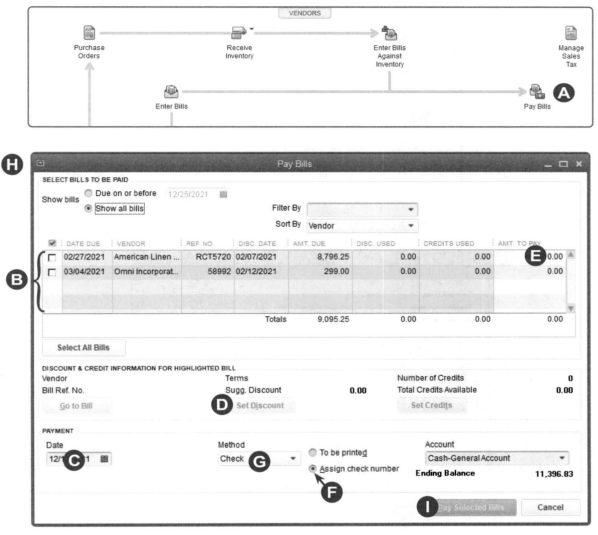

(windows continued on the following page)

Pay a Vendor's Outstanding Invoice

QuickBooks windows *(continued)*

Assign Check Numbers

Payment Account   **10100 · Cash-General Account**

How do you want to assign check numbers?

○ Let QuickBooks assign check numbers.

◉ Let me assign the check numbers below.

CHECK NO.	DATE	PAYEE	AMOUNT
J	02/10/20... 🔲	Omni Incorporated	293.02

[OK]   [Cancel]   [Help]

K — Payment Summary

PAYMENT DETAILS

Payment Date	02/10/2021
Payment Account	10100 · Cash-General Account
Payment Method	Check

Payment has been successfully recorded for the following bill:

CHECK NO	DATE DUE	VENDOR	AMOUNT PAID
513	03/04/2021	Omni Incorporated	293.02
		Total	293.02

How do I find and change a bill payment?

[Pay More Bills]   [Done] **L**

This page is intentionally blank.

Purchase Inventory Without a Purchase Order—Payment Made at Time of Purchase

The Write Checks window is used to process and record purchases without a recorded purchase order that are paid at the time of the purchase. After the Write Checks window is saved, the following has occurred:

Transactions	DR	CR	Subsidiary Records Updated	General Ledger Updated
Inventory	$		✓	✓
Checking Account		$		✓

Quick Reference Table

Step	Box or Other Location	Procedure
A	Home Page	Click the Write Checks icon under Banking.
B	No.	Accept default or enter the correct check number.
C	Date	Accept default date or change.
D	Pay to the Order of	Click the drop-down list arrow and select vendor or add new.
E	Open POs Exist window *(not shown)*	If there are open POs for this vendor, this window will open. Click No.
F	"Write your check" button (Open Bills Exist window - *not shown*)	If there are open bills for this vendor, the Open Bills Exist window will open. Click the "Write your check" button to return to the Write Checks window.
G	Memo	Enter the vendor invoice number.
H	Items tab	Click the Items tab if it is not already open.
I	Item	Select the first item from drop-down list or add new.
J	Description	Accept default description or edit.
K	Qty.	Enter the quantity purchased.
L	Cost	Accept the default cost or edit.
M	Various	Repeat steps I – L for each inventory item purchased.
N	$	Verify the total amount of the check. *(Not possible to verify unless the information is provided.)*
O	Write Checks window	Review the information to verify that it is correct.
P	Save & Close / Save & New buttons	Click the Save & Close or Save & New button.

Purchase Inventory Without a Purchase Order—Payment Made At Time of Purchase

QuickBooks windows

Purchase Non-Inventory Items or Services Without a Purchase Order— Payment Made at Time of Purchase

The Write Checks window is used to process and record purchases without a recorded purchase order that are paid at the time of the purchase. After the Write Checks window is saved, the following has occurred:

Transactions	DR	CR	Subsidiary Records Updated	General Ledger Updated
Various Exp. or Non-Inv. Asset Accounts	$		✓ (fixed assets)	✓
Checking Account		$		✓

Quick Reference Table

Step	Box or Other Location	Procedure
A	Home Page	Click the Write Checks icon under Banking.
B	No.	Accept default or enter the correct check number.
C	Date	Accept default date or click the calendar icon to change.
D	Pay to the Order of	Click the drop-down list arrow and select vendor or add new.
E	Open POs Exist window (not shown)	If there are open POs for this vendor, this window will open. Click No.
F	"Write your check" button (Open Bills Exist window - not shown)	If there are open bills for this vendor, the Open Bills Exist window will open. Click the "Write your check" button to return to the Write Checks window.
G	Memo	Enter the vendor invoice number.
H	Expenses tab	Click the Expenses tab if it is not already open.
I	Account	Select account from the drop-down list or add new.
J	Amount	Enter the amount of the purchase that is associated with the account.
K	Memo	Type a description of the amount that is being charged to the account.
L	Various	Repeat steps I–K for any other accounts applicable to the purchase.
M	$	Verify the total amount of the check. (Not possible to verify unless the information is provided.)
N	Write Checks window	Review the information to verify that it is correct.
O	Save & Close / Save & New buttons	Click the Save & Close or Save & New button.

Purchase Non-Inventory Items or Services Without a Purchase Order—Payment Made At Time of Purchase

QuickBooks windows

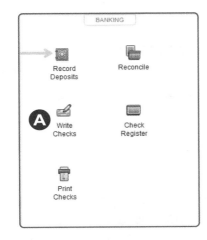

Return Inventory From a Purchase

The Enter Bills window is used to record and process returns made from purchases. After entering the credit information and saving, the following has occurred:

Transactions	DR	CR	Subsidiary Records Updated	General Ledger Updated
Accounts Payable	$		✓	✓
Inventory		$	✓	✓

Quick Reference Table

Step	Box or Other Location	Procedure
A	Home Page	Click the Enter Bills icon under Vendors.
B	Credit button	Select the Credit button at the top of window.
C	Vendor	Select a vendor from the drop-down list or add new.
D	Date	Accept default date or change.
E	Ref. No.	Type the debit memo number.
F	Memo	Type the invoice number related to the return.
G	Items tab	Click the Items tab if it is not already open.
H	Item	For each item, select items being returned from drop-down list.
I	Description	For each returned item, accept the default description or edit.
J	Qty.	For each item, enter the quantity being returned.
K	Cost	Accept the default cost for each item or edit.
L	Various	Repeat steps H – K for each item returned
M	Credit Amount	Verify that the listed amount is correct. *(Not possible to verify unless information is provided.)*
N	Enter Bills window	Review the information to verify that it is correct.
O	Save & Close / Save & New buttons	Click the Save & Close or Save & New button.

Return Inventory From a Purchase

QuickBooks windows

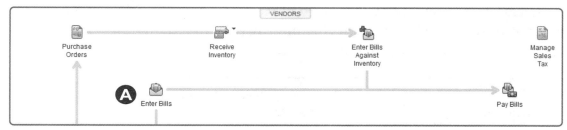

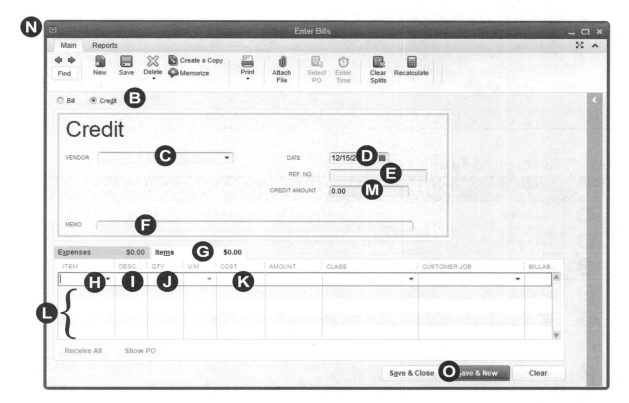

Make a Credit Sale

The Create Invoices window is used to process and record a sale when payment is expected in the future. After entering information and saving the completed Create Invoices window, the following has occurred:

Transactions	DR	CR	Subsidiary Records Updated	General Ledger Updated
Accounts Receivable	$		✓	✓
Cost of Goods Sold*	$			✓*
Sales Revenue		$		✓
Inventory*		$	✓*	✓*
Sales Taxes Payable		$		✓

Applies only to sales of inventory, not services.

Quick Reference Table

Step	Box or Other Location	Procedure
A	Home Page	Click the Create Invoices icon under Customers.
B	Customer: Job	Select a customer from the drop-down list or add new.
C	Date	Accept default date or edit.
D	Invoice #	Accept default number or edit.
E	Bill To	Verify that the correct customer information is displayed or edit.
F	P.O. Number	Enter the customer purchase order number.
G	Terms	Accept the default terms or select different terms from the drop-down list.
H	Quantity	Enter the quantity ordered for the first item sold. (Note that the item code will be entered next.)
I	Item Code	For the first item sold, select the item from the drop-down list or add new.
J	Description	Accept the default description or edit.
K	Price Each	Accept the default price or edit.
L	Various	Repeat steps H – K for each inventory item sold.
M	Balance Due	Verify that the balance due is correct. (Not possible to verify unless information is provided.)
N	Create Invoices – Accounts Receivable window	Review the information to verify that it is correct.
O	Print button	Select the print button at the top of the window only if the invoice is to be printed.
P	Save & Close / Save & New buttons	Click the Save & Close or Save & New button.

Make a Credit Sale
QuickBooks windows

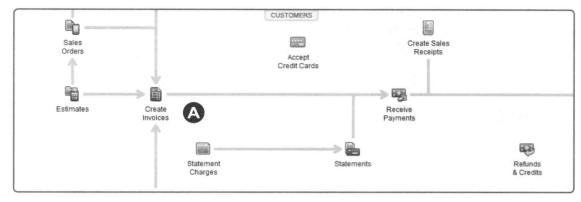

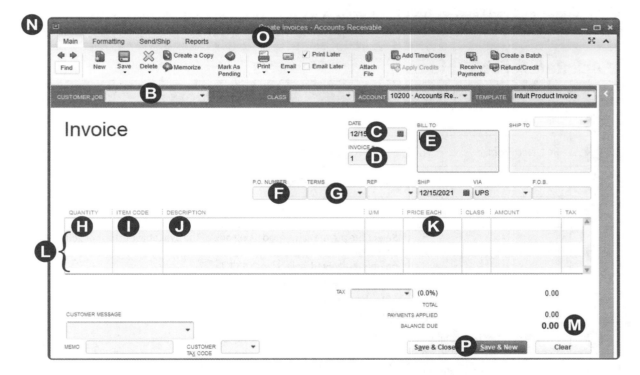

Collect an Account Receivable

The Receive Payments window is used to process and record the collection of an account receivable. After entering information and saving the completed Receive Payments window, the following has occurred:

Transactions	DR	CR	Subsidiary Records Updated	General Ledger Updated
Undeposited Funds	$			✓
Accounts Receivable		$	✓	✓

QuickBooks keeps track of money received in the Undeposited Funds Account. Money is kept in the fund until it is deposited into the bank.

Quick Reference Table

Step	Box or Other Location	Procedure
A	Home Page	Click the Receive Payments icon under Customers.
B	Received From	Select a customer from the drop-down list.
C	Payment Amount	Enter the amount of collection.
D	Date	Accept default date or change.
E	Payment Method buttons	Select the payment method using one of the available buttons or select an alternative using the More drop-down list. For an electronic (ACH) payment received, select "e-CHECK."
F	Reference # / Check #	For a check, enter the check #. For an electronic (ACH) payment, type ACH. If there is a specific number for the ACH payment, you can add that too.
G	Invoice number being paid	Click the check box next to the invoice(s) being paid.
H	Discount and Credits button	Click the Discount and Credits button to display the Discount and Credits window, then click the Discount tab if it is not already open.
I	Discount and Credits window	Verify that the applicable discount (amount and account) is correct or change and click the Done button to return to the Receive Payments window, then click the Discount tab if it is not already open.
J	Receive Payments window	Review the information to verify that it is correct.
K	Print button	Select the Print button at the top of the window if the receipt is to be printed.
L	Save & Close / Save & New buttons	Click the Save & Close or Save & New button.

Collect an Account Receivable

QuickBooks windows

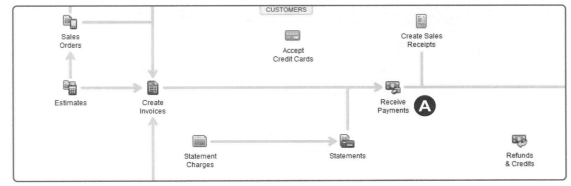

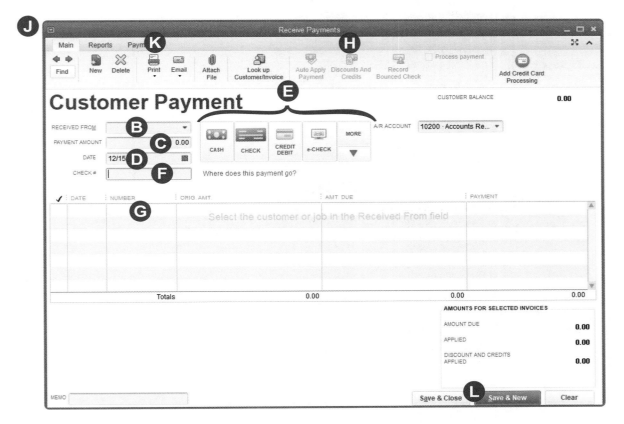

(windows continued on the following page)

Collect an Account Receivable

QuickBooks windows *(continued)*

I

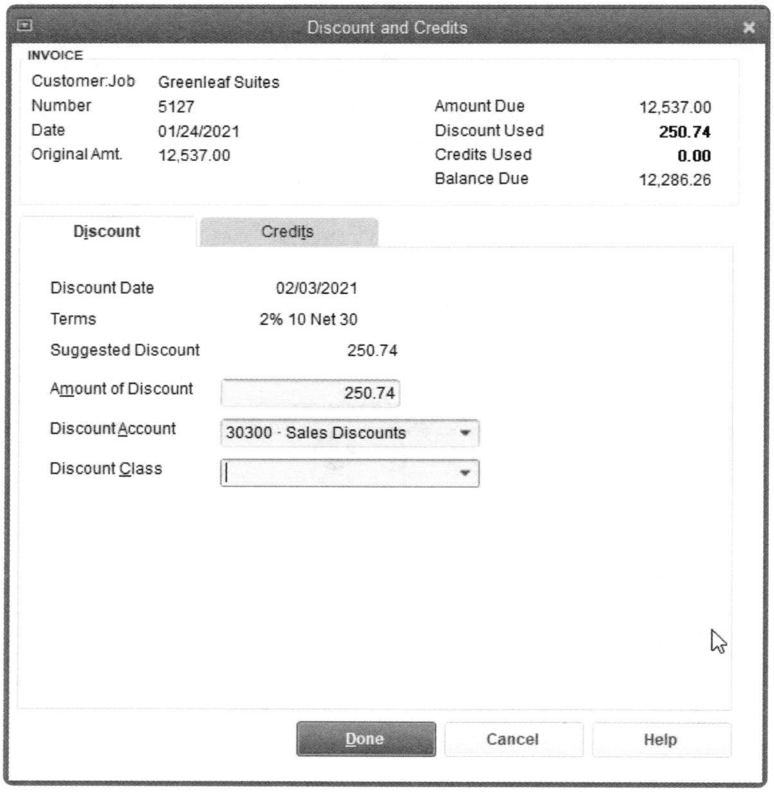

Discount and Credits	

INVOICE

Customer:Job	Greenleaf Suites		
Number	5127	Amount Due	12,537.00
Date	01/24/2021	Discount Used	**250.74**
Original Amt.	12,537.00	Credits Used	**0.00**
		Balance Due	12,286.26

Discount | Credits

Discount Date	02/03/2021
Terms	2% 10 Net 30
Suggested Discount	250.74
Amount of Discount	250.74
Discount Account	30300 · Sales Discounts
Discount Class	

Done Cancel Help

This page is intentionally blank.

Make a Deposit

The Record Deposits window is used to record deposits into one of the company's bank accounts. After the payment information has been updated and saved, the following had occurred:

Transactions	DR	CR	Subsidiary Records Updated	General Ledger Updated
Checking Account	$			✓
Undeposited Funds		$		✓

Quick Reference Table

Step	Box or Other Location	Procedure
A	Home Page	Click the Record Deposits icon under Banking.
B	Payments to Deposit window	Click anywhere on the line to mark each payment to be deposited and click the OK button to open the Make Deposits window.
C	Date	Accept the default date or enter the correct date of the deposit.
D	Make Deposits window	Review the information to verify that it is correct.
E	Print button	Select the Print button at the top of the window if the deposit is to be printed.
F	Save & Close / Save & New buttons	Click the Save & Close or Save & New button.

Make a Deposit
QuickBooks windows

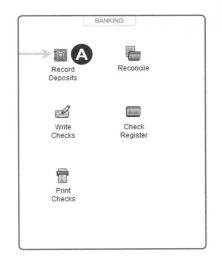

(windows continued on the following page)

Make a Deposit

QuickBooks windows *(continued)*

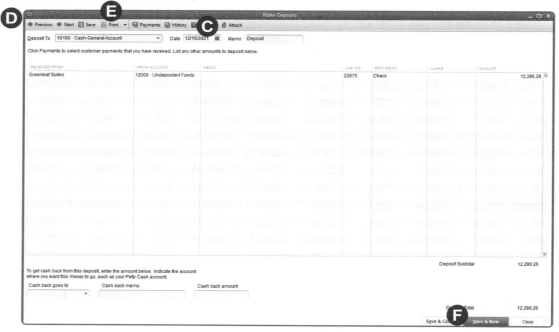

This page is intentionally blank.

Make a Cash Sale

The Create Sales Receipts window is used to process and record receipts of cash sales to customers. After the sales receipt information has been updated and saved, the following has occurred:

Transactions	DR	CR	Subsidiary Records Updated	General Ledger Updated
Undeposited Funds	$			✓
Cost of Goods Sold*	$			✓*
Sales Revenue		$		✓
Inventory*		$	✓*	✓*
Sales Taxes Payable		$		✓

Applies only to sales of inventory, not services.

QuickBooks keeps track of money received in the Undeposited Funds Account. Money is kept in the fund until it is deposited into the bank.

Quick Reference Table

Step	Box or Other Location	Procedure
A	Home Page	Click the Create Sales Receipts icon under Customers.
B	Customer: Job	Select a customer from the drop-down list or add new. For cash customers not in AR subsidiary records, select customer ID for cash customer.
C	Payment Method buttons	Select the payment method using one of the available buttons or select an alternative using the More drop-down list.
D	Date	Accept default date or edit.
E	Sale No.	Accept the default number or enter the cash sale invoice number.
F	Sold To	Verify the customer information is correct or edit. For cash customers not in AR subsidiary records, type customer information.
G	Check No.	Enter the customer's check number.
H	Item	For the first item sold, select the item from the drop-down list or add new.
I	Description	Accept the default description or edit.
J	Qty.	Enter the quantity sold.
K	Rate	Accept the default rate or enter the correct rate.
L	Amount	Accept the default amount or edit.

(table continued on the following page)

Quick Reference Table *(continued)*

Step	Box or Other Location	Procedure
M	Various	Repeat steps H – L for each inventory item sold.
N	Total	Verify that the amount is correct. *(Not possible to verify unless information is provided).*
O	Enter Sales Receipts window	Review the information to verify that it is correct.
P	Print button	Select the print button at the top of the window if the invoice is to be printed.
Q	Save & Close / Save & New buttons	Click the Save & Close or Save & New button. If you receive a message about changing the billing address for cash customers, click No.

Make a Cash Sale

QuickBooks windows

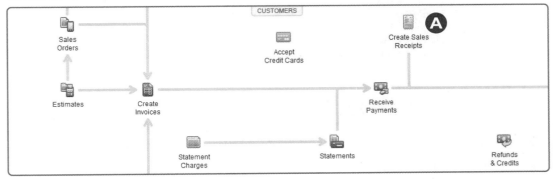

Process a Sales Return or Allowance (Credit Memo)

The Create Credit Memos/Refunds window is used to process credit memos for returns and allowances to customers. After the sales receipt information has been updated and saved, the following has occurred:

Transactions	DR	CR	Subsidiary Records Updated	General Ledger Updated
Sales Returns & Allowance	$			✓
Inventory*	$		✓*	✓*
Sales Taxes Payable	$			✓
Accounts Receivable		$	✓	✓
Cost of Goods Sold*		$		✓*

*Applies only to returns, not allowances.

Quick Reference Table

Step	Box or Other Location	Procedure
A	Home Page	Click the Refunds & Credits icon under Customers.
B	Customer: Job	Select a customer from the drop-down list or add new.
C	Date	Accept default date or edit.
D	Credit No.	Accept the default credit memo number or edit.
E	Customer	Verify that the customer information is correct or edit.
F	P.O. No.	Enter the sales invoice number of the sale related to the sales return or allowance.
G	Item	Select the first inventory item returned or given an allowance.
H	Description	Accept the default description or edit
I	Qty.	Enter the quantity returned. For allowances, leave blank.
J	Rate	Accept the default rate or edit. For allowances, enter the amount of the allowance.
K	Various	Repeat steps G–J for each inventory item returned.
L	Create Memos/Refunds window	Review the information to verify that it is correct.
M	Print button	Select the print button to print a receipt.
N	Save & Close / Save & New buttons	Click the Save & Close or Save & New button.
O	Available Credit message (not shown)	When the customer has an Accounts Receivable balance, the Available Credit message opens. Select the appropriate radio button. Click OK. For Apply to an invoice, the Apply Credit to Invoices window opens.
P	Apply Credit to Invoices window (not shown)	Highlight anywhere on the relevant invoice number line. Click Done.

Process a Sales Return or Allowance (Credit Memo)
QuickBooks windows

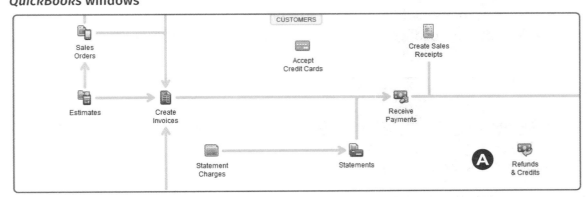

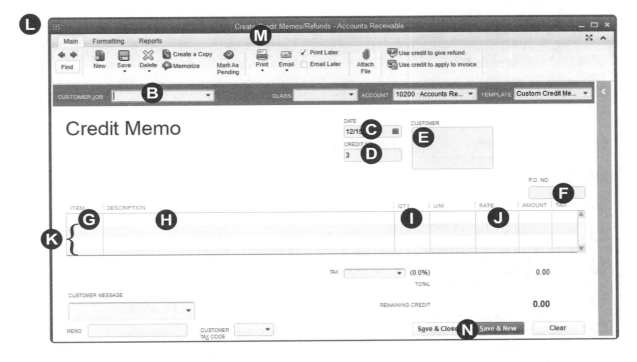

Write Off an Uncollectible Account Receivable

The Receive Payments window is used to process and record write off of accounts receivable that are uncollectible. After the write-off information has been updated and saved, the following has occurred:

Transactions	DR	CR	Subsidiary Records Updated	General Ledger Updated
Bad Debt Expense	$			✓
Accounts Receivable		$	✓	✓

Quick Reference Table

Step	Box or Other Location	Procedure
A	Home Page	Click the Receive Payments icon under Customers.
B	Received From	Select a customer from the drop-down list.
C	Payment Amount	Accept the "0.00" default.
D	Date	Accept the default date or edit.
E	Payment Method buttons	Select the Cash button.
F	Reference #	Type "write off."
G	Invoice number line being written off	Highlight anywhere on the relevant invoice number line. *(Skip this step if it is the only item or top item on the list.)*
H	Discount and Credits button	Click the Discount and Credits button to open the Discounts and Credits window, then click the Discount tab if it is not already open.
I	Amount of Discount	Enter the amount to be written off.
J	Discount Account	Select the Bad Debt Expense account from the drop-down list.
K	Discount and Credits window	Verify that the information entered is correct and click the Done button to return to the Receive Payments window.
L	Receive Payments window	Review the information to verify that it is correct.
M	Print button	Select the Print button to print the receipt.
N	Save & Close / Save & New buttons	Click the Save & Close or Save & New button.

Write Off an Uncollectible Account Receivable

QuickBooks windows

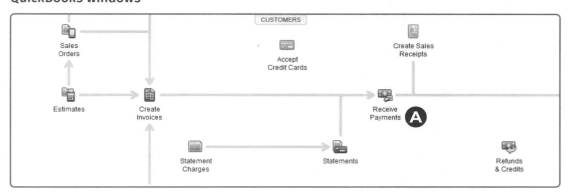

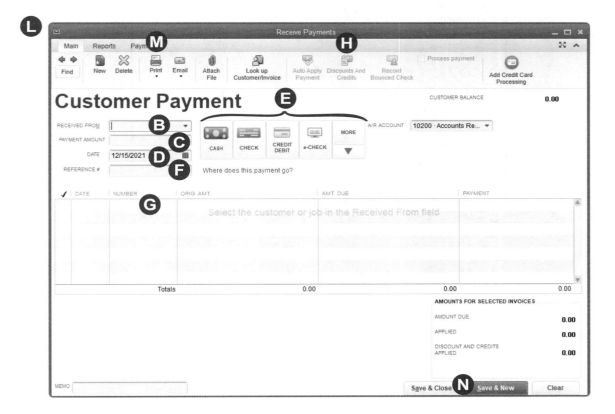

(windows continued on the following page)

Write Off an Uncollectible Account Receivable

***QuickBooks* windows** *(continued)*

(K)

Discount and Credits		✕

INVOICE

Customer:Job	McCarthy's Bed & Breakfast			
Number	2	Amount Due		3,333.75
Date	02/07/2021	Discount Used		**0.00**
Original Amt.	3,333.75	Credits Used		**0.00**
		Balance Due		3,333.75

Discount	Credits

Discount Date	02/17/2021
Terms	2% 10 Net 30
Suggested Discount	0.00
Amount of Discount	**(I)** 0.00
Discount Account	**(J)** ▼
Discount Class	▼

(K) [Done]   [Cancel]   [Help]

This page is intentionally blank.

Receive a Miscellaneous Cash Receipt

The Make Deposits window is used to process and record miscellaneous cash receipts. After the credit account is selected and the information completed, the following has occurred:

Transactions	DR	CR	Subsidiary Records Updated	General Ledger Updated
Undeposited Cash	$			✓
Applicable accounts*		$		✓*

*Examples include Notes Payable (new loans), Property Plant and Equipment (sales for cash), Marketable Securities (sales), Interest Income, and Miscellaneous Income.

QuickBooks keeps track of money received in the Undeposited Funds Account. Money is kept in the fund until it is deposited into the bank.

Quick Reference Table

Step	Box or Other Location	Procedure
A	Home Page	Click the Record Deposits icon under Banking. If the Payments to Deposit window opens (not shown), click Cancel. A Make Deposits window opens next.
B	Date	Accept the default date or edit.
C	Received From	Select an existing customer or vendor from the drop-down list or add new.**
D	From Account	Select the account to be credited from the drop-down list.
E	Memo	Enter descriptive information about the receipt.
F	Chk No.	If payment method was a check, enter the check number. Skip this box for electronic (ACH) payments received.
G	Pmt Meth.	Select the payment method from the drop-down list. For electronic (ACH) payments received, select E-Check
H	Amount	Enter the amount of the receipt.
I	Various	Repeat steps C–H on the next line if more than one account is to be credited.
J	Make Deposits window	Review the information to verify that it is correct.
K	Print button	Select the Print button at the top of the window if deposit is to be printed.
L	Save & Close / Save & New buttons	Click the Save & Close or Save & New button.

**For a new "Received From" source, Click <Add New> at the top of the drop-down list to open the Select Name Type window. Click the appropriate type and then OK to open the relevant maintenance window. Complete the maintenance window and save the information to proceed with the remaining steps to Receive a Miscellaneous Cash Receipt.

Receive a Miscellaneous Cash Receipt

QuickBooks windows

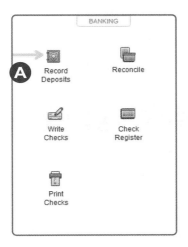

A Record Deposits

Reconcile

Write Checks

Check Register

Print Checks

BANKING

J **K** Make Deposits

◀ Previous ➡ Next 🖫 Save 🖶 Print ▾ | 🖳 Payments 🖳 History 🖳 Journal | 🔗 Attach

Deposit To 10100 · Cash-General Account ▾ Date 12/15/202**B** Memo Deposit

Click Payments to select customer payments that you have received. List any other amounts to deposit below.

RECEIVED FROM	FROM ACCOUNT	MEMO	CHK NO.	PMT METH.	CLASS	AMOUNT
C	**D**	**E**	**F**	**G**		**H**

I

Deposit Subtotal

To get cash back from this deposit, enter the amount below. Indicate the account where you want this money to go, such as your Petty Cash account.

Cash back goes to ▾   Cash back memo   Cash back amount

Deposit Total

Save & Close   **L** Save & New   Clear

Prepare a Statement for Accounts Receivable

The Create Statements window is used to create various account statements, including an Accounts Receivable Statement, which can then be sent to a customer. No accounting entries occur.

Quick Reference Table

Step	Box or Other Location	Procedure
A	Home Page	Click the Statements icon under Customers.
B	Statement Date	Accept the end of period default date or edit.
C	Statement Period From and To –or– All open transactions as of Statement Date	Accept the default radio button setting or select the next option.
D	Statement Period From and To (If another radio button is selected, skip this step.)	Accept the default dates to create a monthly statement or change dates.
E	Select Customers	Accept the default All Customers setting or select the desired radio button. **For Multiple Customers,** click the Multiple Customers radio button, click the Choose button, and select the desired customers in the Print Statements window, then click OK *(not shown)*. **For One Customer,** click the One Customer radio button, then select the customer from the drop-down list *(not shown)*.
F	Select Additional Options	Complete this section by adding and/or removing check marks to be consistent with the information that is to be included in the customer statement(s).
G	Preview button	Click the Preview button to verify that the information displayed is correct. Then click the Close button to return to the Create Statements window.
H	Print / Close buttons	Click the Print button if a printout is desired, or click the Close button.

Prepare a Statement for Accounts Receivable

QuickBooks windows

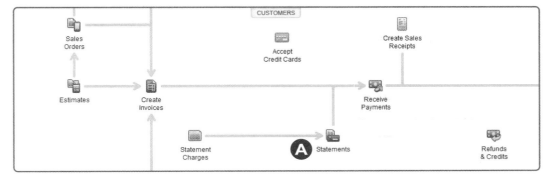

(windows continued on the following page)

Prepare a Statement for Accounts Receivable
QuickBooks windows *(continued)*

Statement

Jackson Supply Company

Date
12/31/2021

To:
McCarthy's B&B 511 Mansion Columbus, OH 43216

Amount Due	Amount Enc.
$6,465.11	

U/M	Date	Transaction	Amount	Balance
	11/30/2021	Balance forward		6,465.11

CURRENT	1-30 DAYS PAST DUE	31-60 DAYS PAST DUE	61-90 DAYS PAST DUE	OVER 90 DAYS PAST DUE	Amount Due
0.00	0.00	0.00	0.00	6,465.11	$6,465.11

This page is intentionally blank.

Pay Employees

The Review and Create Paychecks window is used to record payroll checks to employees. After entering information and creating employee paychecks, the following has occurred:

Transactions	DR	CR	Subsidiary Records Updated	General Ledger Updated
Salary and Wages Expense	$		✓	✓
Payroll Tax Expense (Employer Portion)	$			✓
Payroll Tax Withholdings and Other Employee Reductions		$	✓	✓
Payroll Tax Liabilities (Employer Portion)		$		✓
Cash		$		✓

Quick Reference Table

Step	Box or Other Location	Procedure
A	Home Page	Click the Pay Employees icon under Employees.
B	Start Unscheduled Payroll button	Select the Payroll tab and click Start Unscheduled Payroll to open the Enter Payroll Information window.
C	Pay Period Ends	Verify the date entered or change.
D	Check Date	Verify check date or change.
E	Handwrite & Assign check numbers radio button	Click the radio button if it is not already selected. Note that you will not be printing checks in this project, so you need to select the manual check option. *QuickBooks* will record the effects of the paychecks, but you will not have to print them.
F	First Check # box	Accept the default check number or change.
G	Check All button	Click the Check All button to select all employees. *Note:* If you are only paying one employee, click only on that employee's line, which will place a check mark next to the employee's name.
H	Regular Pay and Overtime hours boxes	Enter the regular pay hours and overtime hours for each hourly employee in the window.
I	Continue button	Click the Continue button to open the Review and Create Paychecks window.
J	Open Paycheck Detail button	Click the Open Paycheck Detail button to open the Preview Paycheck window for the first employee.
K	Preview Paycheck window	Review the information entered under Earnings and other payroll items. Accept the default information or edit the rate, hours, etc. Click Save & Next.

(table continued on the following page)

Quick Reference Table *(continued)*

Step	Box or Other Location	Procedure
L	Preview Paycheck window	Repeat step K for all remaining employees. When you have reviewed the last employee's paycheck, click Save & Close instead of Save & Next. This reopens the Review and Create Paychecks window.
M	Review and Create Paychecks window	Verify that all entered information is correct. If correct, click the Create Paychecks button. If there are errors, correct them in this window or use the Open Paycheck Detail button to open the Preview Paycheck Detail window and correct the information.
N	Confirmation and Next Steps window	Click Close. Note that in this project you will not be printing paychecks, so there is no need to select the Print Paychecks button.

Pay Employees

QuickBooks windows

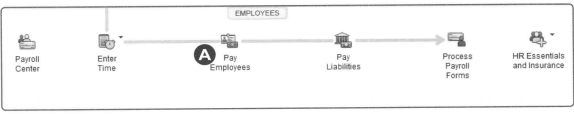

(windows continued on the following page)

Pay Employees

QuickBooks **windows** *(continued)*

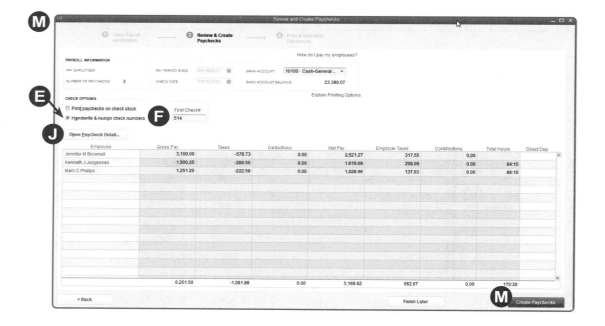

(windows continued on the following page)

Pay Employees
***QuickBooks* windows** *(continued)*

(K)
(L)

Preview Paycheck

Jennifer M Brownell PAY PERIOD 02/01/2021 - 02/15/2021

☐ Use Direct Deposit CLASS

Earnings

ITEM NAME	RATE	HOURS	WC CODE	CUSTOMER:JOB
Salary	3,100.00			

SICK AVAILABLE	64:00
VACATION AVAIL	80:00
SICK ACCRUED	
VAC. ACCRUED	0:00

☐ Do not accrue sick/vac

TOTALS 3,100.00 0:00 hrs

Other Payroll Items

ITEM NAME	RATE	QUANTITY

Employee Summary How are these items calculated?

ITEM NAME	AMOUNT	YTD
Salary	3,100.00	9,300.00
Medicare Employee Addl Tax	0.00	0.00
OH - School District	0.00	0.00
Federal Withholding	-253.00	-759.00
Social Security Employee	-192.20	-576.60
Medicare Employee	-44.95	-134.85
OH - Withholding	-88.58	-265.74

Company Summary How are these items calculated?

ITEM NAME	AMOUNT	YTD
Social Security Company	192.20	576.60
Medicare Company	44.95	134.85
Federal Unemployment	4.80	42.00
OH - Unemployment	75.60	243.00

Check Amount: 2,521.27

Save & Previous **(K) Save & Next** **(L) Save & Close** Cancel Help ☐ Enter net/Calculate gross

---

Confirmation and Next Steps

1. Enter Payroll Information → 2. Review & Create Paychecks → **3. Print & Distribute Paychecks**

✓ **You have successfully created 3 paychecks:**

3 handwritten checks **0** for direct deposit Learn more

Next step:

Print your paychecks/stubs, and distribute to employees.

Print Paychecks **Print Pay Stubs**

(N) Close

Prepare a General Journal Entry

The General Journal Entry window is used to prepare general journal entries that are not entered during the normal course of business. The accounts in the general ledger are updates with a debit, and a credit is also made from the journal entry.

Transactions	DR	CR	Subsidiary Records Updated	General Ledger Updated
Appropriate Account or Accounts	$		✓	✓
Appropriate Account or Accounts		$	✓	✓

Quick Reference Table

Step	Box or Other Location	Procedure
A	Home Page	Click the Company menu and select Make General Journal Entries. **Note:** If a window opens with information about automatic journal entry numbering, click OK.
B	Date	Accept default date or change.
C	Entry No.	Accept default journal entry number or change.
D	Account	Select an account to be debited from the drop-down list.
E	Debit	Enter the amount to be debited.
F	Memo	Briefly type a description of the journal entry.
G	Name	Select the appropriate customer, vendor, or employee, if applicable.
H	Debit	Repeat steps E – G for additional debits.
I	Account	Select an account to be credited from the drop-down list.
J	Credit	Enter the amount to be credited to the account selected in step I.
K	Name	Select the appropriate customer, vendor, or employee, if applicable.
L	Credit	Repeat steps I through K for additional credits.
M	Make General Journal Entries window	Review the information to verify that it is correct.
N	Save & Close / Save & New buttons	Click the Save & Close or Save & New button.

Prepare a General Journal Entry
QuickBooks windows

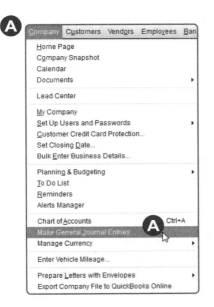

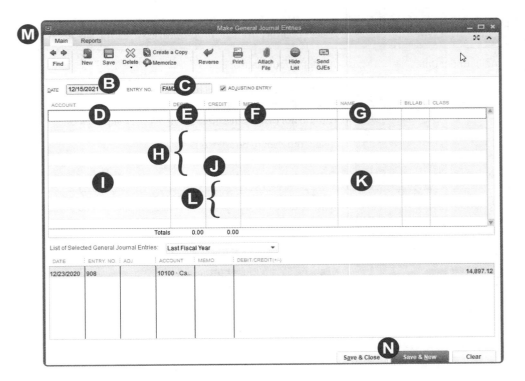

Adjust Perpetual Inventory Records

The Adjust Quantity / Value on Hand window allows users to adjust their inventory records.

Transactions	DR		CR	Subsidiary Records Updated	General Ledger Updated
Cost of Goods Sold	$	or	$		✓
Inventory	$	or	$	✓	✓

Quick Reference Table

Step	Box or Other Location	Procedure
A	Home Page	Click the drop-down arrow next to the Inventory Activities icon under Company.
B	Inventory Activities drop-down list *(not shown)*	Select Adjust Quantity/Value On Hand.
C	Adjustment Type	Select Quantity from the drop-down list if it is not already selected.
D	Adjustment Date	Accept default date or edit.
E	Adjustment Account	Select the account that will be adjusted from the drop-down list *(not shown)*. If a message appears titled Income or Expense expected, click the "Do not display this message again" box and click OK.
F	Item	Select the item to be adjusted.
G	New Quantity	Enter the correct quantity.
H	Various	Repeat steps F and G for each inventory item being adjusted.
I	Adjust Quantity / Value on Hand window	Verify the information entered.
J	Save & Close	Click the Save & Close button.

Adjust Perpetual Inventory Records
QuickBooks windows

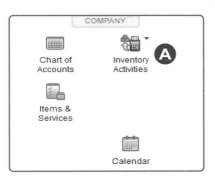

Prepare a Bank Reconciliation

The Reconciliation Window allows the user to prepare periodic bank reconciliations.

Transactions	DR		CR	Subsidiary Records Updated	General Ledger Updated
Appropriate Bank Account	$	or	$		✓
Other Appropriate Accounts	$	or	$		✓
Bank Service Charge	$				✓
Interest Income			$		✓

Quick Reference Table

Step	Box or Other Location	Procedure
A	Home Page	Click the Reconcile icon under Banking.
B	Account	Select an account from the drop-down list to be reconciled.
C	Statement Date	Accept the default date or edit.
D	Ending Balance	Enter the correct ending balance.
E	Service Charge	Enter the amount charged.
F	Date	Accept the default date or edit.
G	Account	Select the appropriate general ledger account for the service charge from the drop-down list.
H	Interest Earned	Enter the correct amount of interest earned.
I	Date	Accept the default date or edit.
J	Account	Select the appropriate general ledger account for the interest revenue from the drop-down list.
K	Continue	Select the Continue button to proceed to the Reconcile window.
L	Hide transactions checkbox	Click the "Hide transactions after the statement's end date" checkbox so that only transactions through the bank statement ending date are shown in the window.
M	Various	For each item cleared with the bank statement, click anywhere on that item's line to indicate the item is no longer outstanding.
N	Reconcile window	Review the information to verify that it is correct.
O	Reconcile Now	Click the Reconcile Now button.
P	Select Reconciliation Report window (not shown)	Click the Display button to preview the bank reconciliation. If you want to print a copy after previewing it, use the Print button.

Prepare a Bank Reconciliation
QuickBooks windows

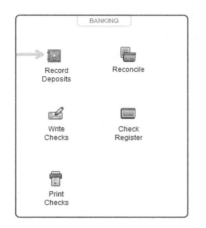

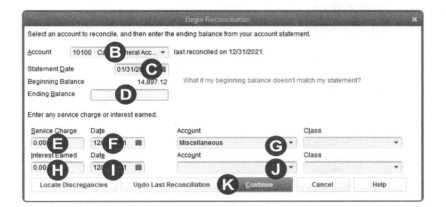

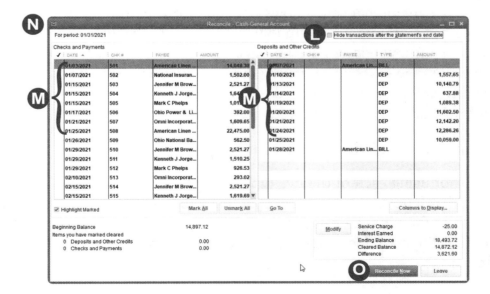

Perform Maintenance Activities

There are five types of maintenance in this project. The purposes of maintenance for each type are to (1) add, (2) change, or (3) delete default information for the five maintenance windows. Information that is changed through maintenance can be categorized into two types:

1. Information that makes it easier to record transactions. An example is information in a drop-down list to identify customers.

2. Information that directly affects the amounts recorded in subsequent transactions. Examples include a change in the unit selling price of a product and a pay rate increase for an employee.

In addition to the maintenance tasks described above, other areas of *QuickBooks* involve maintenance. For example, setting up a new company in *QuickBooks* requires knowledge of most maintenance windows and tasks. Chapter 10 provides instructions and practice for setting up a new company.

Accessing a Maintenance Window

The second column in the table on page 59 shows the sequence of steps necessary to access each maintenance window. Notice that the first step in accessing each maintenance window is to select an icon from the Home Page.

Additional Windows Within Each Maintenance Window

Three of the five maintenance windows have additional windows (sub-windows) that are accessed from the main window by the use of tabs. Inventory and General Ledger maintenance windows have no tabs. The main tab is shown for these three maintenance windows when the main window is first opened. The sub-windows contain additional information related to the main maintenance window. Only certain sub-windows are used in the project.

Instructions for Each Type of Maintenance Window

Instructions for using each of the five types of maintenance windows is explained in a section that follows. Each section contains window illustrations, along with reference tables for adding, changing, and deleting a record. The Quick Reference Table on the facing page identifies the Reference book page numbers for each type of maintenance.

Perform Maintenance Activities

Quick Reference Table

Maintenance Window Name	Steps Necessary to Access Maintenance Window	Functions Performed by Maintenance Window
Customer Maintenance (pages 60–63)	**Add a new record:** *Click the Customers icon → Customers & Jobs tab → New Customer & Job button → New Customer.* **Change a record or delete a record:** *Click the Customers icon → Customers & Jobs tab → right-click on any customer → Edit Customer: Job or Delete Customer: Job.*	Used to add a new customer, view and/or change data for an existing customer, or delete a former customer.
Vendor Maintenance (pages 64–67)	**Add a new record:** *Click the Vendors icon → Vendors Tab → New Vendor button → New Vendor* **Change a record or delete a record:** *Click the Vendors icon → Vendors tab → right-click on any vendor → select Edit Vendor or Delete Vendor.*	Used to add a new vendor, view and/or change data for a vendor on file, or delete a former vendor.
Inventory Item Maintenance (pages 68–72)	*Click the Items & Services icon → right-click on any item → select New, Edit Item, or Delete Item.*	Used to add a new inventory item, view and/or change existing information, or delete an item no longer being purchased or sold.
Employee Maintenance (pages 74–80)	**Add a new record:** *Click the Employees icon → Employees Tab → New Employee button.* **Change a record or delete a record:** *Click the Employees icon → Employees tab → right-click on any employee → select Edit Employee or Delete Employee.*	Used to add a new employee, view and/or change existing employee information, or delete a former employee.
General Ledger Account Maintenance (pages 82–85)	*Click the Chart of Accounts icon → right-click on any account → select New, Edit Account, or Delete Account.*	Used to add a new general ledger account, view and/or change data for an account on file, or delete an account no longer being used.

Customer Maintenance

The table below and the two tables on the following page include instructions to add a customer record, change information for an existing customer, and delete a former customer's record. The *QuickBooks* windows for these maintenance activities are shown on pages 62 and 63.

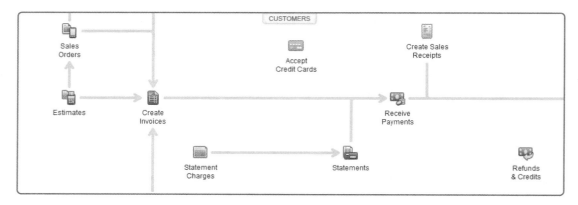

Add a Customer Record
Quick Reference Table

Box or Other Location	Procedure
Home Page	Click the Customers icon to display the Customer Center.
Customers & Jobs Tab	Click the Customers & Jobs tab if it is not already open.
New Customer & Job button	Click the New Customer & Job button. Select New Customer to open the New Customer window.
Customer Name	Enter the name of the customer.
Opening Balance	Do not enter. Will be done later if there is a balance.
As of	Enter date the customer is added.
Remainder of Address Info tab	Complete the remaining boxes to the extent that the information is available. Some boxes may not be applicable for the customer. For the Address Details section, you can use the Copy button if the Ship To address is the same as the Invoice/Bill To address.
Payment Settings tab	Select the Payment Settings tab. Complete the boxes to the extent that the information is available. Some boxes may not be applicable for the customer.
Sales Tax Settings tab	Select the Sales Tax Settings tab. Complete the boxes to the extent that the information is available. Some boxes may not be applicable for the customer.
OK button	Click the OK button to save the new customer information and close the window.

Change Information in An Existing Customer's Record
Quick Reference Table

Box or Other Location	Procedure
Home Page	Click the Customers icon to display the Customer Center.
Customer Center	Click the Customers & Jobs tab to display the customer list.
Customer List	Right-click on the customer name that is to be changed and select Edit Customer: Job to open the Edit Customer window.
Edit Customer window	Change appropriate information in the windows for the Address Info, Payment Settings, and Sales Tax Settings tabs.
OK button	Click the OK button to save the edited customer information and close the window.

Delete a Former Customer's Record
Quick Reference Table

Box or Other Location	Procedure
Home Page	Click the Customers icon to display the Customer Center.
Customer Center	Click the Customers & Jobs tab to display the customer list.
Customer List	Right-click on the customer name that is to be deleted and select Delete Customer: Job. (*Note:* Be sure you want to delete the customer record before you do so. If you want that customer included later, you will need to find and reenter the information as you would for a new customer following the guidance in Add a Customer Record – Quick Reference Table.) Click OK to delete the customer, or click Cancel if you choose not to delete the customer.
QuickBooks message	If the account is associated with at least one transaction in the current year or has a prior balance, a warning message will appear. Either click Cancel to cancel the attempted deletion or click the Make Inactive button. If you choose to inactivate the customer, click Yes if you receive a message saying that the customer has an outstanding balance. Making a customer inactive only eliminates that customer from view when Active Customers are shown in QuickBooks. It does not delete the customer entirely.

Customer Maintenance

QuickBooks windows

Customer Center → Customers & Jobs Tab →
New Customer & Job → New Customer

New Customer Window—Address Info Tab

(windows continued on the following page)

Customer Maintenance

QuickBooks windows *(continued)*

New Customer Window—Payment Settings Tab

New Customer Window—Sales Tax Settings Tab

Vendor Maintenance

The table below and the two tables on the following page include instructions to add a vendor record, change information for an existing vendor, and delete a former vendor's record. The *QuickBooks* windows for these maintenance activities are shown on pages 66 and 67.

Add a Vendor Record
Quick Reference Table

Box or Other Location	Procedure
Home Page	Click the Vendors icon to display the Vendor Center.
Vendors Tab	Click the Vendors tab if it is not already open.
New Vendor button	Click the New Vendor button. Select New Vendor to open the New Vendor window.
Vendor Name	Enter the name of the vendor.
Opening Balance	Do not enter. Will be done later if there is a balance.
As of	Enter date the vendor is added.
Remainder of Address Info tab	Complete the remaining boxes to the extent that the information is available. Some boxes may not be applicable for the vendor.
Payment Settings tab	Select the Payment Settings tab. Complete the boxes to the extent that the information is available. Some boxes may not be applicable for the vendor.
Account Settings tab	Select the Account Settings tab. Enter the general ledger account(s) that purchases from this vendor are likely to be charged to.
OK button	Click the OK button to save the new vendor information and close the window.

Change Information in An Existing Vendor's Record
Quick Reference Table

Box or Other Location	Procedure
Home Page	Click the Vendors icon to display the Vendor Center.
Vendor Center	Click the Vendors tab to display the vendor list.
Vendor List	Right-click on the name of the vendor whose record you wish to change and select Edit Vendor to open the Edit Vendor window.
Edit Vendor window	Change appropriate information in the windows for the Address Info, Payment Settings, and/or Account Settings tabs.
OK button	Click the OK button to save the edited vendor information and close the window.

Delete a Former Vendor's Record
Quick Reference Table

Box or Other Location	Procedure
Home Page	Click the Vendors tab to display the Vendor Center.
Vendor Center	Click the Vendors tab to display the vendor list.
Vendor List	Right-click on the vendor name that is to be deleted and select Delete Vendor. (*Note:* Be sure you want to delete the vendor record before you do so. If you want that vendor included later, you will need to find and reenter the information as you would for a new vendor following the guidance in Add a Vendor Record–Quick Reference Table.)
QuickBooks message	If the account is associated with at least one transaction in the current year or has a prior balance, a warning message will appear. For this project, click cancel and do not delete the account.

Vendor Maintenance
QuickBooks windows

Vendor Center → Vendors Tab → New Vendor button → New Vendor

New Vendor Window—Address Info Tab

(windows continued on the following page)

Vendor Maintenance

QuickBooks windows *(continued)*

New Vendor Window—Payment Settings Tab

New Vendor	_ □ ×

VENDOR NAME

OPENING BALANCE ___ AS OF **12/15/2021** 📅 How do I determine the opening balance?

- Address Info
- **Payment Settings**
- Tax Settings
- Account Settings
- Additional Info

ACCOUNT NO.

PAYMENT TERMS

PRINT NAME ON CHECK AS

CREDIT LIMIT

BILLING RATE LEVEL

☐ Vendor is inactive   **OK**   Cancel   Help

New Vendor Window—Account Settings Tab

New Vendor	_ □ ×

VENDOR NAME

OPENING BALANCE ___ AS OF **12/15/2021** 📅 How do I determine the opening balance?

- Address Info
- Payment Settings
- Tax Settings
- **Account Settings**
- Additional Info

Tell us which expense accounts to prefill when you enter bills for this vendor.

Spending a little time here can save you time later on.

Accounts you select here show up automatically in the accounts field when you enter a bill for this vendor.
Example: Bills from the phone company would be assigned to the Telephone Utilities expense account.

Clear All

How do Account Prefills work with Bank Feeds?

☐ Vendor is inactive   **OK**   Cancel   Help

Inventory Item Maintenance

The table below and the two tables on the following page include instructions to add an inventory item, change information for an existing inventory item, and delete a former inventory item. The *QuickBooks* windows for these maintenance activities are shown on pages 70 through 72.

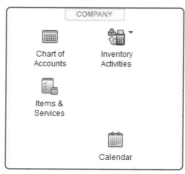

Add an Inventory Item Record
Quick Reference Table

Box or Other Location	Procedure
Home Page	Click the Items & Services icon on the right under Company to open the Item List window *(not shown)*.
Item List window	Right-click on any inventory item on the list and click New to open the New Item window.
New Item window	Select Inventory Part from the drop-down list under Type.
Item Name/Number	Enter the item name and/or number.
Purchase Information	Complete the boxes in the Purchase Information section to the extent that the information is available. Some boxes may not be applicable for the inventory item.
Sales Information	Complete the boxes in the Sales Information section to the extent that the information is available. Some boxes may not be applicable for the inventory item.
Inventory Information	Complete the boxes in the Inventory Information section to the extent that the information is available. Some boxes may not be applicable for the inventory item.
OK button	Click the OK button to save the new item information and close the window.

Change Information in An Existing Inventory Item's Record
Quick Reference Table

Box or Other Location	Procedure
Home Page	Click the Items & Services icon.
Item List window	Right-click on the inventory item that is to be changed and select Edit Item to open the Edit Item window.
Edit Item window	Change the appropriate information in the window.
OK button	Click the OK button to save the edited inventory information and close the window.

Delete an Inventory Item No Longer Being Purchased or Sold
Quick Reference Table

Box or Other Location	Procedure
Home Page	Click the Items & Services icon.
Item List	Right-click on the item that is to be deleted and select Delete Item. (*Note:* Be sure you want to delete the inventory item before you do so. If you want that inventory item included later, you will need to find and reenter the information as you would for a new inventory item following the guidance in Add an Inventory Item Record – Quick Reference Table.)
QuickBooks message	If the inventory item is associated with at least one transaction in the current year or has quantities in the inventory item, a warning message will appear. The message will inform you that the item cannot be deleted. For this project, click cancel and do not delete the item.

Inventory Item Maintenance
QuickBooks windows

New Item Window—Type

New Item Window—Type → Inventory Part

(windows continued on the following page)

Inventory Item Maintenance

QuickBooks windows *(continued)*

New Item Window — Item Name / Number

New Item Window — Purchase Information

(windows continued on the following page)

Inventory Item Maintenance

QuickBooks windows *(continued)*

New Item Window—Sales Information

New Item Window—Inventory Information

This page is intentionally blank.

Employee Maintenance

The table below and the two tables on the following page include instructions to add an employee, change information for an existing employee, and delete a former employee. The *QuickBooks* windows for these maintenance activities are shown on pages 76 through 80.

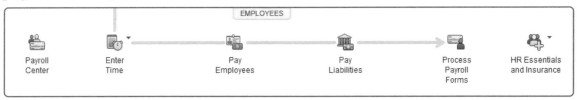

Add an Employee Record
Quick Reference Table

Box or Other Location	Procedure
Home Page	Click the Employees icon to display the Employee Center.
Employees Tab	Click the Employees tab if it is not already open.
New Employee button	Click the New Employee button to open the New Employee window.
Personal tab	Complete the boxes to the extent that the information is available. Some boxes may not be applicable for the employee.
Address & Contact tab	Select the Address & Contact tab. Complete the boxes to the extent that the information is available. Some boxes may not be applicable for the employee.
Additional Info tab	Select the Additional Info tab. Enter the employee account number, if applicable.
Employment Info tab	Select the Employment Info tab. Enter the hire date.
Payroll Info tab	Select the Payroll Info tab. Enter the pay frequency, then enter the salary, hourly, and/or overtime amounts/rates into the Earnings section of the window. Click the Taxes button.
Federal tab	Complete the boxes to the extent that information is available, including dependents.
State tab	Select the State Worked and the State Subject to Withholding from the drop-down menu. Enter the number of allowances.
Other tab	Use this tab to Add new payroll item such as surcharges, contributions, or other User-Defined taxes.
OK button	Click the OK button to save the entered employee information and close the window.

Change Information in An Existing Employee's Record
Quick Reference Table

Box or Other Location	Procedure
Home Page	Click the Employees icon to display the Employee Center.
Employee Center	Click the Employees tab to display the employee list.
Employee List	Right-click on the employee name that is to be changed and select Edit Employee to open the Edit Employee window.
Edit Employee window	Choose the relevant tab(s). Change appropriate information in the windows.
OK button	Click the OK button to save the edited employee information and close the window.

Delete a Former Employee's Record
Quick Reference Table

Box or Other Location	Procedure
Home Page	Click the Employees icon to display the Employee Center.
Employee Center	Click the Employees tab to display the employee list.
Name column	Right-click on the employee name that is to be deleted and select Delete Employee. (*Note:* Be sure you want to delete the employee record before you do so. If you want that employee included later, you will need to find and reenter the information as you would for a new employee following the guidance in Add an Employee Record – Quick Reference Table.)
QuickBooks message	If the employee is associated with at least one transaction in the current year or has a prior balance, a warning message will appear. For this project, click cancel and do not delete the employee.

Employee Maintenance
QuickBooks windows

Employee Center → Employees Tab → New Employee

New Employee Window—Personal Tab

(windows continued on the following page)

Employee Maintenance
QuickBooks windows *(continued)*

New Employee Window—Address & Contact Tab

New Employee Window—Additional Info Tab

(windows continued on the following page)

Employee Maintenance

QuickBooks **windows** *(continued)*

New Employee Window—Employment Info Tab

New Employee Window—Payroll Info Tab

(windows continued on the following page)

Employee Maintenance
QuickBooks **windows** *(continued)*

Taxes Window — Federal Tab

Taxes Window — State Tab

(windows continued on the following page)

Employee Maintenance

QuickBooks **windows** *(continued)*

Taxes Window — Other Tab

This page is intentionally blank.

General Ledger Account Maintenance

The table below and the two tables on the following page include instructions to add a general ledger account, change information for an existing general ledger account, and delete a former general ledger account. The *QuickBooks* windows for these maintenance activities are shown on pages 84 and 85.

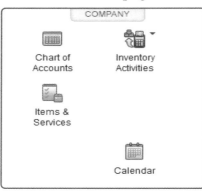

Add a General Ledger Account Record
Quick Reference Table

Box or Other Location	Procedure
Home Page	Click the Chart of Accounts icon to open the Chart of Accounts window.
Chart of Accounts window	Right-click on any chart of accounts name and select New.
Add New Account: Choose Account Type window	Select the type of account being created and click the Continue button.
Number	Enter the account number.
Account Name	Enter account name.
Description	Enter a description of the new account, if appropriate.
Tax-Line Mapping	Accept default entry or change based on information given for the new account.
Save & Close / Save & New buttons	Click the Save & Close or Save & New button to save the account created.

Change Information in An Existing General Ledger Account's Record Quick Reference Table

Box or Other Location	Procedure
Home Page	Click the Chart of Accounts icon to open the Chart of Accounts window.
List of Accounts	Right-click on the account name that is to be changed and select Edit Account to open the Edit Account window.
Edit Account window	Change appropriate information in the window.
Save & Close button	Click the Save & Close button to save the edited account information and close the window.

Delete a General Ledger Account Record No Longer Being Used Quick Reference Table

Box or Other Location	Procedure
Home Page	Click the Chart of Accounts icon to open the Chart of Accounts window.
List of Accounts	Right-click on the account name that is to be deleted and select Delete Account. (*Note:* Be sure you want to delete the account before you do so. If you want that account included later, you will need to find and reenter the information as you would for a new account following the guidance in Add a General Ledger Account Record – Quick Reference Table.)
QuickBooks message	If the account is associated with at least one transaction in the current year or has a prior balance, a warning message will appear. For this project, click cancel and do not delete the account.

General Ledger Account Maintenance

QuickBooks windows

Chart of Accounts Window → New

Add New Account—Choose Account Type Window

(windows continued on the following page)

General Ledger Account Maintenance

QuickBooks **windows** *(continued)*

Add New Account Window